THE CHALLENGE OF C

)

1

Also available from Cassell:

P. Ainley: *Class and Skill: Changing Divisions of Knowledge and Labour*
P. Ainley and M. Corney: *Training for the Future*
P. Ainley: *Vocational Education and Training*
D. Coffey: *Schools and Work: Developments in Vocational Learning*

The Challenge of Competence:

Professionalism through Vocational Education and Training

Edited by

Phil Hodkinson and Mary Issitt

CASSELL

Cassell
Villiers House
41/47 Strand
London WC2N 5JE

387 Park Avenue South
New York
NY 10016–8810

British Library Cataloguing-in-Publication Data
A catalogue record for this book is available from the British Library.

ISBN: 0-304-32999-1 (hardback)
    0-304-32987-8 (paperback)

Typeset by Colset Private Limited, Singapore
Printed and bound in Great Britain by Redwood Books, Trowbridge, Wiltshire

Contents

The contributors

Elaine Barnes is Principal Lecturer in Primary Education at the Crewe and Alsager Faculty of Manchester Metropolitan University.

Richard Dunne is Lecturer in Education at the School of Education, University of Exeter.

Mary Durkin has worked in formal and informal education for many years and is now a member of the publications team at the National Youth Agency.

John Field is Professor of Continuing Education at the University of Ulster.

Andy Green is Lecturer in Education at the Post-16 Centre of the London Institute of Education.

Gareth Harvard is Lecturer in Education at the School of Education, University of Exeter.

Phil Hodkinson is Principal Lecturer in Education at the Crewe and Alsager Faculty of Manchester Metropolitan University.

Terry Hyland is Lecturer in Adult and Continuing Education at the University of Warwick.

Mary Issitt is Senior Lecturer in Youth and Community Work at the Crewe and Alsager Faculty of Manchester Metropolitan University.

Jocelyn Jones is the Course Director of the post-qualifying Child Protection Studies programme at Leicester University.

Carol Maynard is Head of Curriculum at West Cheshire College.

Chapter 1

The Challenge of Competence for the Caring Professions: an Overview

Phil Hodkinson and Mary Issitt

For many of those who would define themselves as professionals working in the public sector in Britain, the 1990s mark a threshold as market forces are applied to their occupational areas with the avowed intention of making them 'leaner', 'fitter' and 'more efficient'. The new managerialism in the public sector (Stewart, 1992) requires that the quality of service can be demonstrably measured as can the competence of those employed as service providers, whether they are working within education or welfare. Indeed, 'on the job' competence – 'the ability to perform work activities to the standard required in the workplace' (NCVQ, 1988) – is increasingly being used to assess fitness to practice in any occupation.

In this book we are concerned to understand the breadth and depth of the term 'competence', its roots in vocational education and training, and the ideology and methodology that has grown up around the concept. Through the National Council for Vocational Qualifications (NCVQ) the emphasis on qualification has moved away from the notion that preparation for effective practice involves the right kind of training 'inputs' on or off the job. The shift to competence-based assessment has been towards 'outputs' or the 'standards that need to be achieved at the end of a learning programme' (Jessup, 1990, p. 2). Jessup contrasts the new standards which would be more detailed and specific and would be set out in a statement of competence with what he sees as the 'generalised and loose concept of standards which has prevailed in educational circles in the past' (ibid.).

We are therefore concerned to address the challenge for professionals working in education and welfare that this shift involves, for the implication is that competence-based assessment offers the promise of enabling practitioners to be more detailed and specific about their work, the assumption being that these attributes have been lacking in previous forms of professional practice. The deceptively simple concept of 'competence' cannot, however, be understood alone. It is necessary to delve into the baggage of which it is a part and with which it is inextricably linked. This involves us in the examination of the context in which competence is being introduced as industrial methods and models are being imposed. Though slightly over-simplified, it is easiest to present these changes as the difference between two contrasting ideal-type views of professionalism, quality and management. Let us examine each of these ideal-types in turn.

PATERNALISM AND PROFESSIONALISM UNDER THE WELFARE STATE

Between World War II and about 1979, there was a broad consensus in Britain about the organization of state-funded professional support, whether in teaching, medicine or social work. Such services were to be provided free to all who needed them, admittedly with a parallel private sector for those with the wealth and inclination to choose it. The free services were provided by the state, and were controlled, in slightly different ways for each service, through broad national legislation, public planning and strategic management. Within this ideal-type, quality of provision was to be ensured in the following ways.

1. There was a general belief in practitioner professionalism, backed up in most cases by independent study in higher education to degree level or beyond. Recruiting and educating a 'good' teacher or social worker was seen as integral to the guarantee of high-quality provision. The reward for this professionalism within public service included job security and, especially in teaching, clear ladders of promotion through a job-specific status hierarchy.
2. This professionalism operated in the context of public policy-making, strategic planning and resource allocation, with service delivery at the local level. Essentially bureaucratic structures provided support for professional activity and controlled and limited its development and direction. Public sector professionals did not have the same autonomy as lawyers or doctors. Furthermore, this sometimes paternalistic planning and control was underpinned by local democracy, in that local authorities had been elected by local constituents.
3. All this activity took place within a framework of national legislation, which set broad objectives, national pay scales and conditions of service and state funding, although there would be considerable variation from one local authority to another in terms of available resources, forms of provision and policy priorities.

It is perhaps inevitable that when a system has been in existence for thirty or more years its inadequacies appear more obvious than its strengths, and this bureaucratic and paternalistic model of provision has been increasingly under attack. Local authorities sometimes seemed to interfere with the most trivial details of practice, and at worst this system denied professional autonomy to senior practitioners and individual choice to clients. Thus parents were told which school their children would attend. There were occasional scandals, such as the William Tyndale affair in education, or 'pin down' in social work, which seemed to call into question the efficacy of the system and the professionalism of practitioners. Furthermore, expanding demand for services under a Government constantly hoping to cut expenditure caused questions to be asked about 'value for money'. Vocal individuals complained when the system did not give them exactly what they wanted and, inevitably, problems received more press coverage than successes.

Criticism of the professional role in education, social work, and youth and community work increasingly gathered momentum through the 1970s and 1980s. Fitness to practice of those people who were the products of higher education was first questioned in youth and community work and social work, and more recently in teaching. Professional expertise in education, social work, and youth and community work has increasingly been challenged by radical practitioners and educators themselves as well as by consumers on the receiving end of services (Bailey and Brake, 1977; Dominelli and McLeod, 1989; Knowles, 1990).

During the 1980s, this model of social provision was also challenged by radical thinking from what was often called the 'new right'. Based on a version of classical economics, this thinking rejected the 'nanny state', suggesting that the country needed to free up individual responsibility and choice (Johnson, 1991). This was supplemented by a belief in competition and the market as the best way to allocate scarce resources (Davies, 1992). During this period, industrial and manufacturing metaphors for educational and social provision proliferated. All this thinking gave rise to a new ideal-type for social provision, that of the market, or 'quasi-market' (Le Grand and Bartlett, 1993).

THE MARKET MODEL

The central tenet of this approach was to 'free up' provision from local state control giving more power and choice, at least in theory, to separate institutions such as schools or colleges, and also to individual clients who were increasingly being called 'customers'. Within this ideal-type, quality was to be achieved in very different ways.

1. Individual institutions and service providers compete with each other so that, in theory, they have to improve quality and value for money in order to stay 'in business', as customers choose their services.
2. To facilitate this 'market', funding has been focused increasingly on individual institutions as cost centres, rather than local authorities. In some cases, such as further education colleges, institutions have been completely removed from authority control. In the delivery of 'Care in the Community', local authorities are expected to develop 'care packages' drawing upon the voluntary and private sectors and are financially penalized for direct provision of old people's homes (DHSS, 1989).

    Furthermore, funding increasingly comes either from competitive tendering for contracts, or through performance-related formulae. In education, for example, the key criterion is the ability of an institution to recruit pupils or students, which in turn is supposed to reflect customer choice in a market-place.
3. Such performance-related funding requires the setting of measurable performance indicators, such as examination results and truancy rates in schools. Such indicators are intended to give an objective measure of quality, which enables the customer to make informed choices and quality improvements to be logged.
4. To ensure that this market functions, Government has become increasingly prescriptive about service outcomes and processes and is creating new funding structures. A local authority's role in all services is shifting towards that of an 'enabler' which purchases services through contracts with other bodies, rather than acting as direct 'service provider' (Le Grand and Bartlett, 1993). Alongside this

process is the devolution of funding to semi-independent, but not democratically elected 'quangos' and 'qualgos' such as the Training and Enterprise Councils, the NCVQ and the Further Education Funding Council.

5.   Finally, quality is to be ensured by a series of regular external inspections, which for schools are run by yet another quango – the Office of Standards in Education (OFSTED).

We shall, in a moment, explore the significance of the industrial metaphor in this second ideal-type, but before we do, it is important to highlight the changing nature of professional practice between these two models. As we have seen, a possibly naïve belief in the efficacy of professionalism to ensure high-quality provision was central to the local authority ideal-type, despite the practical restrictions on true professionalism that bureaucracy sometimes produced. However, in the market forces ideal-type, practitioners are seen more as technicians, playing their part in the production and sale of quality services, as part of a team. If the old professional was legitimated through academic education and the status of his/her position, the new technician needs better-quality training, to help ensure better achievement against the measured performance indicators. A key part of this market ideal-type has become the notion of competence, as the term is used by the NCVQ, although other conceptions of this term are available and may be more relevant in the caring professions.

POST-FORDISM AND INDUSTRIAL QUALITY

It has become part of contemporary received wisdom about industrial organization that most 'leading edge' manufacturers are now operating very differently than in the past. Murray (1991) suggests this can be summarized as a move away from old 'Fordist' (after Henry Ford) mass production, to what he calls 'post-Fordist' approaches. Central to post-Fordism are notions of flexible specialization. In modern global markets, manufacturing industry has to compete with international competitors. In many areas, markets change very rapidly, and the days when the Model T could be run off the production line for several years are long gone. Furthermore, in this highly competitive environment, there are two ways to survive (Finegold and Soskice, 1991). There is the 'low skills' route, which focuses on mass production of low-quality goods as cheaply as possible. It is very difficult for Britain to compete at this low skills end, because labour costs are too high in relation to newly emerging developing countries. The alternative is the 'high skills' route, which is successfully followed by many of our more successful rivals, such as Germany, Japan and other Pacific Rim countries.

Within this 'high skills' route, quality of output is the key to market success. Increasingly, major manufacturers are striving to focus all their activity on raising quality. Sometimes this is described by the term 'total quality management', and sometimes by the Japanese word 'Kaisen'.

This post-Fordist scenario assumes that quality can be discovered by measuring the products, or outputs, thus enabling the firm to decide which changes make sense and which do not. Firms committed to these approaches argue cogently that under Kaisen, quality improvement and cost cutting can go on simultaneously.

In striving for the post-Fordist future, there has been an emphasis in Britain on the need to improve the training and skills of the British workforce. Study after study shows British workers and school-leavers to be relatively poorly educated and qualified when compared to their counterparts in almost every other developed capitalist country (for example, see Green, 1991; Bynner and Roberts, 1991; CBI, 1993; Smithers, 1993, and Chapter 2 in this book). One of many strategies proposed to address this problem was the development of a system of National Vocational Qualifications (NVQs).

The NVQ project is huge, beginning in 1986 with the objective of designing and implementing the same framework for assessing and defining standards for all occupations. NCVQ was to streamline and rationalize the 'qualification jungle' which led to 'numerous awarding bodies competing in the same or overlapping occupation areas, with qualifications with different objectives, style and structure, often with no procedures for recognising each other's qualification' (Jessup, 1990, p. 17). NCVQ is currently engaged on the mapping out of standards required in all occupations at all levels. It also aims to identify standards which are common to and transferable between occupational areas.

NCVQ operates through a system of Industrial Lead Bodies (ILBs), each of which covers a particular occupational area and includes representation of employers and employees (see Chapter 3 for a critique of employer representation on ILBs). Each ILB is charged with the task of developing nationally applicable standards for their occupational area. The standards development process involves the identification of all the occupations that come within the remit of the ILB, and through a process called 'functional analysis' the establishment of what each of these occupations entails. A 'statement of competence' is arrived at after consultation with members of each occupation. This 'statement of competence' is further subdivided into 'units' and 'elements' of competence. The 'elements' of competence contain the 'performance' and 'range' criteria for assessment. The standards identified for an occupational area can be allocated within a general framework of levels of occupational performance. These levels are shown in Figure 1.1, overleaf.

Even within an industrial setting, this view of competence has been heavily criticized and challenged (Smithers, 1993). It is claimed that it is based on narrow behaviourist conceptions of learning, and on a functional analysis of current jobs, which risks atomizing the job, so that the whole becomes less than the sum of its parts, and which is, in any event, backward looking. These and other such criticisms are taken up in some of the chapters which follow. However, what we are centrally concerned with here is the relevance of this view of competence and the wider industrial view of quality from which it derives to caring professions such as education, social or youth and community work.

TECHNICAL RATIONALITY AND PROFESSIONALISM

By seeing youth work or education through an industrial metaphor, this mode of quality and competence is an example of what is sometimes called instrumental or technical rationality. The notion of technical rationality derives from what Habermas (1971, 1972) calls technical interests. Gibson (1986, p. 7) defines it thus: 'Instrumental rationality . . . is concerned with *method* and efficiency rather than with *purposes*. . . . It is the divorce of fact from value, and the preference, in that divorce, for fact.'

Figure 1.1   *The NVQ framework. Based on NCVQ (1991).*

Level 1
Performance of a range of varied work activities, most of which may be routine and predictable.

Level 2
Competence in a significant range of varied work activities, performed in a variety of contexts. Some of the activities are complex or non-routine, and there is some individual responsibility or autonomy. Collaboration with others, perhaps through membership of a work group or team, may often be a requirement.

Level 3
Competence in a broad range of varied work activities performed in a wide variety of contexts and most of which are complex and non-routine. There is considerable responsibility and autonomy, and control or guidance of others is often required.

Level 4
Competence in a broad range of complex, technical or professional work activities performed in a wide range of contexts and with a substantial degree of personal responsibility for the work of others and for the allocation of resources is often present.

Level 5
Competence which involves the appplication of a significant range of fundamental principles and complex techniques across a wide and often unpredictable variety of contexts. Very substantial personal autonomy and often significant responsibility for the work of others and for the allocation of substantial resources feature strongly, as do personal accountabilities for analysis, design, planning, execution and evaluation.

In effect, this industrial model treats education, youth work or caring for others as if it were an engineering problem. Clients become customers who 'buy' a technical product. That product can be 'improved' by measuring the efficiency of the production line and working to increase it. However, if such approaches are relevant to manufacturing, it is questionable whether they can be applied to professional services focused on interactions with people. There are several reasons for this.

To begin with, quality in the caring professions is not value free, but about values. Skilbeck (1976) and others have shown that there are different ideological views of education which colour and underpin our understanding of what education is about. Such value positions determine what we look for in education. They also affect how we see and judge any education we come into contact with. Indeed, the view that education can be likened to a production line, with important outputs that can be measured, is an ideological value judgement in itself. Such measurement may be central to much industrial production, but need not be for education (Friere, 1972; Stenhouse, 1975). The same is true of other caring professions. For example, to claim that there are measurable outputs from youth work is a value-laden position.

Furthermore, outputs in the caring professions, even where they can be identified and agreed, are notoriously difficult to measure. We almost always fall back on *performance indicators*, which are believed to give a partial view of quality. The term is important. Truancy rates may be a performance indicator of the success of a school in relating to its pupils. High truancy rates may indicate a problem that needs further investigation, but are not themselves a measure of school/pupil relationships. They do not tell us whether school relations are actually as good as they could reasonably be expected to be in the context in which teachers are working, nor do they tell us what should be done, if anything, to improve relationships.

Then again, in a production line, changes are one way. We change the system and that changes the output. Yet interaction between people is a dialectical process, involving professionals working through the medium of their relationships with pupils or clients. While it may be possible to see school pupils as customers, they can also be seen as the raw material, a key part of the educational process or 'production line', and indeed as the very output they are supposed to be buying. It is difficult to see how industrial approaches to quality would work if the product was also the production process, the raw material and the customer.

Technically rational approaches to quality presuppose that it is possible to stand outside and measure objectively what is being produced. The post-Fordist industrial model of quality, of which the NVQ conception of competence is a part, assumes that quality can be accurately and independently measured. It is the precise measures of quality that justify changes, resource allocation or spending. If quality cannot be measured, then a hard-pressed manager will simply cut costs and resources. They can be measured, and if quality cannot be demonstrated to be threatened, there is no technically rational reason not to cut.

This creates a central dilemma when such a technically rational model is introduced into the caring professions. Quality cannot be accurately defined, let alone measured. Performance indicators are adopted, and the institution develops ways of doing better against those indicators. They may, for example, improve truancy rates by: (i) authorizing more absences, (ii) excluding pupils on a semi-permanent basis, or (iii) trying not to recruit from those social groups where there is a greater tendency to absence from school. None of these strategies, of course, changes in itself the quality truancy rates were supposed to indicate. Because improvements in measures are taken as improvements in quality, efforts which will not bring about changes to performance indicators quickly are discouraged. It is not inconceivable that this results, in some cases, in actual loss of quality in some respects, while achieving a rising performance against the indicators. Finally, because quality cannot be precisely measured, managers cut costs without any clear view as to whether the cuts are harmful or not.

COMPETENCE AS TECHNICALLY RATIONAL PRACTICE

The NVQ version of competence, which is coming increasingly to dominate the British debate, is part of this industrial, technically rational approach, is governed by the same principles, and is subject to the same advantages and weaknesses. The output is worker performance, which is measured primarily in the workplace. The model of working towards specified measured outputs sees the learning process itself as a production line. It is then up to each 'team' of learners and teachers/trainers to work on their own production processes in order to improve the quality of their output. Quite apart from the numerous ways in which such a model distorts learning, it is also significantly different in one respect from the industrial parallel it is based on. In industry, the measured output changes. The whole point of Kaisen is to alter the output by improving its quality. In the NVQ system, the outputs are defined and given. The teams cannot change their specifications, but merely strive to achieve them more efficiently. This puts real pressure on some providers to cut resources, in order to achieve minimum NVQ standards as quickly and cheaply as possible.

Enough has already been said to show how such a technical model differs from more traditional views of professionalism, a theme which forms the focus for this book, and will be further explored in the chapters which follow. The NVQ system, as we have shown, is intended to reach postgraduate training standards, which the NCVQ label as Level 5. If the model of learning and assessment they advocate is problematic at lower levels, it reaches its greatest challenge when applied to such advanced professional work. Yet attempts are being made to extend it into just these areas. There is already a lead body – the Care Sector Consortium – working on NVQ qualifications in Social Care. The Training and Development Lead Body (TDLB) is establishing NVQ standards and competencies for training, which may increasingly affect all person-centred occupations including teaching and youth work. Even though the NVQ process is only now about to be applied at the professional levels, which have traditionally been validated by higher education, the competence approach has been adopted at least in part within teaching, social work and youth and community work (Issitt and Woodward, 1992). As we write (autumn 1993) there are moves to adopt TDLB standards for teaching qualifications in the post-16, further education sector. All teachers working on the new General National Vocational Qualifications (GNVQs) are already required to achieve two TDLB units on competence in assessment.

It would be easy to be dismissive, and to hanker after the good old days of professionalism under local authority control, described at the beginning of this chapter. But that model was flawed too, and the growth of the NVQ system has highlighted several key weaknesses in the old model. This challenge of competence cannot be ignored.

THE CHALLENGE OF COMPETENCE: WEAKNESSES IN THE OLD PROFESSIONAL MODEL

In areas such as teaching, youth and community work and nursing, the idea of professionalism has always been problematic. None of these groups is seen as being made up of 'true professionals'. They do not have their own elected governing bodies, like the British Medical Association, which control access, set standards of professional performance and behaviour, and have the ultimate power to strike off a member whose performance breaches professional codes. Whether or not such systems are an adequate guarantor of professional quality anyway is a topic for debate. Of more importance here is the fact that this crucial part of the quality mechanism is missing in the professions which are the focus of this book.

Local authority control in effect fulfilled this role. The authority provided policy guidelines, codes of practice and often bureaucratic procedures for getting approval for activity. At best, with a sensitive and supportive authority, this could work quite well. But there are two all too common types of situation where it failed. Sometimes the support and guidance was too lax, permitting the occasional excesses that have been so well publicized, and which gradually undermined the notion of professionalism. On other occasions, bureaucratic control was so tight that professionals were prevented from thinking for themselves, bound up in reams of red tape.

There were serious questions about the training as well. It was often front loaded, so that a trainee teacher did either a BEd degree or a PGCE course and then, having qualified, started the job. There was very little further training once in post, and the impact of this initial training on the ways in which teachers worked was often less influential than either the way they had themselves been taught at school, or the ways other teachers worked in the school where they finally got a job.

Even the best Initial Teacher Education schemes have struggled to blend theory and practice successfully and the poor schemes, especially in the past, may not even have tried very hard. At worst, therefore, initial education was seen as 'irrelevant' theory, and could be more of a rite of passage permitting entry to the profession than real training for the job. When it was introduced by NCVQ, the term 'competence' was supposed to bridge this divide between theory and practice, by making the former subservient to the latter. It was supposed to incorporate knowledge, understanding and skills in a holistic view of performance.

> The requirements for knowledge and understanding which underpin competence in NVQs should be derived afresh from the statement of competence . . . whatever [knowledge] is required will be directly relevant to performance in an occupational or professional area
> (Jessup, 1991, p. 28)

In addition, the fragmentation of qualifications into elements of competence, described through performance criteria and range statements, supposedly made this holism accessible to the workers and learners themselves, provided the difficult problem of language was overcome. In later chapters it will be suggested that this model is over-simplified and ultimately fails, but this does not absolve us from continuing to address the problem and a different conception of competence from that used by NCVQ may be one way forward.

The other well-known problem with academic entry and training into the professions is that it is exclusive. Training was not primarily about performance but about membership. From this perspective, older models of professionalism failed to address issues of quality improvement in a changing environment, however the term 'quality' is defined. Furthermore, the full-time academic professional entry makes access to the professions more difficult for those groups in society who do less well in the British education system, including the working class and some ethnic minorities. The NVQ competence system attempts to address this problem by giving equivalent credit to learning on and learning off the job, and by encouraging the accreditation of prior experience and learning towards the achievement of a qualification.

These issues form the focus for the various contributions to this book. We argue that if the caring professions are to continue to improve the quality of their services, neither of the ideal-type models for quality, management and training described in this chapter will do. To meet the challenge of the new model of quality and competence, both competence and professionalism themselves have to be rethought. Contributors do that in several ways.

Green (Chapter 2) and Field (Chapter 3) provide a general underpinning to our understanding of the place of competence-based assessment and training and the role of the NCVQ. Drawing lessons from post-compulsory education and training across Europe, Green argues that education and training have unprecedented importance in the new economic order, which requires a workforce with analytical and creative abilities that are transferable from one occupational setting to another. He shows that the output model being developed through NCVQ is out of step with trends in the rest of Europe which continue to emphasize the importance of general educational content in vocational courses.

Chapter 3 is Field's examination of whether NVQs are 'employment-led' as it is claimed they are. His research shows that employers are in the most part unaware of NVQs, and that employment interests on ILBs, which determine the standards for each occupation, are a 'highly selective coalition'. He argues that the penetration of NVQs has been uneven across occupational areas, and is focused, in the main, at the lower levels. He suggests that the NVQ system has been kept alive by central government funding through the quasi-market of state agencies. This serves as a tool for policy management, particularly in relation to unemployment, rather than meeting the needs for a skilled workforce as defined by employers.

In Chapter 4, Hyland addresses the behaviourist and reductionist underpinnings of competence. He characterizes the NCVQ competence model as atomistic and individualistic, and 'a most unlikely vehicle' for the upskilling of the workforce. He urges us to distinguish between the NCVQ approach to competence which 'is concerned first and foremost with the collection of evidence', and the professional approach which requires the primary focus to be on learning *per se* in order to develop reflective practice. Hyland refers to competence models developed in social and care work which seek to expose weaknesses in the orthodox NCVQ format and develop a framework more conducive to the assessment of reflective practice.

The remainder of the book focuses in detail on professional practice in social work, youth and community work and teaching. In Chapter 5, Hodkinson explores key issues for professionals in these work areas and calls into question the applicability of a 'technically rational' competence-based approach for the development of practice that is empowering both for professional workers and their clients. He argues that professionals have to operate in an interactive way with clients and colleagues in a world in which rapid change is endemic and clear-cut judgements are rare.

Issitt (Chapter 6) highlights the need for professionals to be able to deal with and understand controversial issues. Drawing upon material from social, youth and community work, she examines the link between equal opportunities values and competence, and raises questions as to whether values at the centre of the professional task become distorted through the process of the development of standards using NCVQ procedures.

One of the most controversial areas in which professionals from the health, care and educational sectors can be involved is that of child abuse. This area of work demands the highest levels of skill and judgement among practitioners. In Chapter 7, Jones explores the 'professional artistry' that is required at post-qualifying level by social workers engaged in this work. She highlights the problem of reducing the emotional element that professional judgement demands to a list of competences. She shows that the complex decision-making involved requires a holistic approach that may sometimes be in conflict with the managerialist orientation of the agency.

The next four chapters describe and evaluate the practical application of competence in youth and community work and teaching. Durkin (Chapter 8) and Barnes (Chapter 9) each deal with projects that were part of national programmes funded by the Department for Education, while the following two chapters consider local case studies in teacher education. Maynard (Chapter 10) describes a scheme developed in the further education (FE) context, while Harvard and Dunne (Chapter 11) discuss work on an Initial Teacher Education course based in higher education.

Durkin focuses on employer-led 'apprenticeship schemes' in youth and community work, involving 24 different local authorities in England and Wales over a period of four years. She compares the education and training delivered through two schemes that were competence-based with one that carried the hallmarks of a more 'traditional' approach to professional qualification. She identifies the commonalities and differences in terms of process, methodology and outcome in both approaches.

Barnes analyses work developed under the 'articled teacher' scheme, whereby mature entrants to the teaching profession could train while working in schools, rather than having to complete a teaching course first. Barnes examines the ways in which competence-based approaches were used on one such scheme, and stresses the importance of tutor support and reflection as part of the learning process.

Maynard describes a very different type of competence approach, but in a similar context. FE in Britain has a tradition of recruiting lecturers who do not possess teaching qualifications, and the certificate scheme she describes provided training for such teachers whilst in post. In this context, Maynard stresses the need to see competence as only part of what is required, and the importance of taking a holistic rather than atomized perspective to assessment and the accreditation of prior learning.

Harvard and Dunne describe another different model of competence, which they argue allows them to address 'state of the art' practice as part of the training programme. They also see competence as merely part of a wider whole, and argue that the underlying structure and principles of a competence-based scheme are of vital importance if it is to facilitate high-quality professional development rather than low level technicianship.

Finally, in Chapter 12, we draw together the main issues that have been identified by the book's contributors and seek to find a way forward for professionals to synthesize 'the competence approach' into a holistic reflective practice relevant to the challenges and complexities of the twenty-first century. We also question whether the status division between professionals and other workers should be as sharp as it has been in the past. Some of the weaknesses of the NVQ approach for caring professions transfer across to other occupations and levels. In this way, the clash between competence and professionalism has implications for the whole of vocational education and training.

We recognize the complexity of professional practice, and give pointers to future development, rather than yet another over-simplistic, all-embracing panacea to all problems. Development, we argue, must be based on existing good practice, existing expertise and existing structures and systems. While all these can and should be challenged and, if necessary, changed, we must avoid the sorts of externally designed, technically rational solutions which seem to have increasing appeal to hard-pressed politicians looking for a quick fix.

REFERENCES

Bailey, R. and Brake, M. (eds) (1977) *Radical Social Work*. London: Edward Arnold.

Bynner, J. and Roberts, K. (eds) (1991) *Youth and Work: Transition to Employment in England and Germany*. London: Anglo-German Foundation.

CBI (1993) *Routes for Success – Careership: A Strategy for All 16–19 year old Learning*. London: CBI.

Davies, H. (1992) *Fighting Leviathan: Building Social Markets that Work*. London: The Social Market Foundation.

DHSS (1989) *Community Care: The Next Decade and Beyond*, CM 849. London: HMSO.

Dominelli, L. and McLeod, E. (1989) *Feminist Social Work*. London: Macmillan.

Finegold, D. and Soskice, D. (1991) 'The failure of training in Britain: analysis and prescription.' In G. Esland (ed.) *Education, Training and Employment. Volume 1: Educated Labour – the Changing Basis of Industrial Demand*. Wokingham: Addison-Wesley.

Freire, P. (1972) *Pedagogy of the Oppressed*. Harmondsworth: Penguin.

Gibson, R. (1966) *Critical Theory and Education*. London: Hodder and Stoughton.

Green, A. (1991) *The Reform of Post-16 Education and Training and the Lessons from Europe*, Working Paper No. 11. London: Post-16 Centre, Institute of Education, University of London.

Habermas, J. (1971) *Towards a Rational Society*. London: Heinemann.

Habermas, J. (1972) *Knowledge and Human Interests*, 2nd edn. London: Heinemann.

Issitt, M. and Woodward, M. (1992) 'Competence and contradiction.' In P. Carter, T. Jeffs and M. K. Smith (eds) *Changing Social Work and Welfare*. Buckingham: Open University Press.

Jessup, G. (1990) 'National vocational qualifications: implications for further education.' In M. Bees and M. Swords (eds) *National Vocational Qualifications and Further Education*. London: Kogan Page.

Jessup, G. (1991) *Outcomes: NVQs and the Emerging Model of Education and Training*. London: Falmer.

Johnson, R. (1991) 'My New Right Education.' In Education Group II *Education Limited: Schooling and Training and the New Right Since 1979*. London: Unwin Hyman.

Knowles, M. (1990) *The adult learner a forgotten species*, 4th edn. Houston, Texas: Gulf Publishing Co. ·

Le Grand, J. and Bartlett, W. (1993) (eds) *Quasi-Markets and Social Policy*. Basingstoke: Macmillan.

Murray, R. (1991) 'Fordism and post-Fordism.' In G. Esland (ed.) *Education, Training and Employment. Volume 1: Educated Labour – the Changing Basis of Industrial Demand*. Wokingham: Addison-Wesley.

NCVQ (1988) *The NCVQ Criteria and Related Guidance*. London: NCVQ.

NCVQ (1991) *Guide to National Vocational Qualifications*. London: NCVQ.

Skilbeck, M. (1976) 'Three educational ideologies.' In The Open University *E203 Curriculum Design and Development, Unit 3: Ideologies and Values*. Milton Keynes: Open University Press.

Smithers, A. (1993) *All Our Futures: Britain's Education Revolution*. London: Channel 4 Television.

Stenhouse, L. (1975) *An Introduction to Curriculum Research and Development*. London: Heinemann.

Stewart, J. (1992) 'Guidelines for public service management: some lessons not to be learnt from the private sector.' In P. Carter, T. Jeffs and M. K. Smith (eds) *Changing Social Work and Welfare*. Buckingham: Open University Press.

Chapter 2

The European Challenge to British Vocational Education and Training

Andy Green

As part of the drive towards upgrading the skills of the UK workforce, major efforts are being made to spread competence-based approaches to vocational education and training (VET) into professional areas such as teaching and social work. The extension of NVQs up to Level 5 is a central part of this initiative (see Chapter 1). This work is being undertaken on the assumption of the efficacy of the approach as it has been first applied to the lower levels of VET for 16- to 19-year-olds. However, this new and radical British development, which has been taken much further than elsewhere in Europe, is still relatively untested and issues arising from a European perspective raise questions about the assumed validity of these processes in foundation (16- to 19-year-olds) VET, and therefore their relevance to more advanced professional education and training. This chapter looks at the broad canvass of changes in European VET and seeks to understand developments in British VET in relation to these as part of a complex process of convergence and divergence.

THE CHALLENGE TO EUROPEAN VET

Western European states, like all economically advanced democracies around the world, place a high value on the quality of their vocational education and training. VET has become a key policy issue as its importance to national economic performance has become generally recognized (Porter, 1990). In the face of rapid technological advance, economic globalization and the intensification of competition both within Europe and from the rapidly advancing economies of the Pacific Basin, it is now clear that human resources are the key to continuing prosperity in the advanced economies. It is also clear to most governments, although to some perhaps more than others, that a maximum diffusion of education and training are necessary prerequisites for a healthy democracy and for maintaining a level of social cohesion and solidarity in fast-changing and increasingly pluralistic societies (Ruberti, 1993). European VET systems thus face unprecedented challenges from a wide range of economic, demographic and political developments.

Education and training have assumed unprecedented importance in the new international economic order. Advances in computer technology have transformed the labour process to a point where knowledge and analytical skills are fast becoming the key productive force; the globalization of capital, goods and labour, which allows international corporations to shift parts of their operations around the world with increasing ease, means that human resources are now the primary capital assets of national economies (Reich, 1991). Against the competition of newly industrialized nations with immensely efficient systems of mass production and relatively low labour costs, European nations have little choice but to maximize their knowledge and skills advantages through pursuing strategies of knowledge-intensive production and service provision in the high value-added, high quality end of the market. Leading enterprises are typically reorganizing, adopting new 'post-Fordist' forms of flexible specialization, with flatter organizational hierarchies, 'just-in-time' production systems and new forms of total quality control (Piore and Sabel, 1984; Brown and Lauder, 1992).

The effects of these changes on human capital requirements will be considerable. Fewer jobs will depend on manual and routine administrative skills, while more will require high-level analytical and creative abilities: the skills of system thinking, abstraction, experimentation and collaboration which Robert Reich calls the skills of the 'symbolic analyst' (Reich, 1991). The multi-skilled or 'polyvalent' worker will require aptitudes that range from the communicative skills of working with people and in teams and the manipulative skills of working with things, to the analytical or 'intellective' skills of working in symbolic languages (Zuboff, 1988). Increasingly the demand is not for people trained with particular occupational skills but with the general 'over-arching' capabilities that will allow them to cope with continual change in their working environment. Adaptability, flexibility and the aptitude for continual re-learning will be the chief characteristics of the workers of the future.

While European VET systems face up to these new demands for skills, they also have to cope with the changing aspirations of young people. As the youth labour market has progressively declined in most countries, due to recession and the elimination of many unskilled jobs traditionally taken by young people, so has the incentive increased for young people to remain longer in education, particularly if they want to gain the qualifications that are increasingly necessary to gain access to a wide range of jobs (OECD, 1990).

Mass participation in post-compulsory education and training (PCET) is thus now a reality in most countries in western Europe (OECD, 1992). This means that PCET systems have to cope with a larger and increasingly diverse population of students, some of whom are preparing for entry into higher education and others who are preparing for direct entry to employment (OECD, 1990). Changing labour-market conditions and other social factors have made more problematic young people's transitions both to work and to adult life and it is the education systems of European countries that have been called upon to mediate these changes.

European VET systems are also subject to a host of political forces and particularly to those emanating from the European Commission which takes an increasing interest in them. While European law recognizes the autonomy of individual states in relation to education policy, the Commission has been increasingly active in promoting innovations in VET across Europe to improve economic competitiveness of member states, to enhance equal opportunities and social cohesion and to promote European integration through increased emphasis on the European dimension in educational provision. Among its chief priorities at present are: to improve labour mobility by facilitating greater transparency among national qualifications and by promoting improved language and European awareness training; to encourage cultural and technology transfer through exchange programmes; and to promote lifelong learning in national systems of VET by encouraging greater continuity between schooling, foundation training, higher education and adult continuing training. Underpinning all its substantive initiatives are the principles of subsidiarity and social partnership, whereby decisions are devolved to the lowest effective level and involve the maximum participation of employers, unions, educationalists, and other relevant parties (Ruberti, 1993).

European systems of PCET are responding to these challenges in a variety of ways and the patterns across Europe are far too complex and diverse to identify a single model of change. Each country has its own distinctive traditions in education and training which have been shaped by its history and by a host of nationally specific social, economic, cultural and political characteristics. There continue to be important distinctions, for instance, between countries which have national systems, like France and Sweden, and those which have federal systems, where the region has autonomy in education, as in Spain and Germany. There is an important distinction between those countries where foundation VET is mainly employment-based, as in Germany, Austria and parts of Switzerland, and those countries where it is primarily school- or college-based, as is the case in most of the remaining European countries (OECD, 1985). Continuing adult training tends to be largely employment-based in most countries. There are also long-standing and significant differences between countries with traditions of centralization in educational administration, like France, Sweden and Germany (at the Länder, or regional, level), and those with traditions of greater decentralization, like the Netherlands and, until recently, the UK. However, some common patterns are emerging, particularly among the continental and Scandinavian states of western Europe, which are related to the common challenges mentioned above.

Most western European states have, or are moving towards, high-participation systems of PCET where the majority of young people stay in education and training for two or three years after the end of compulsory schooling, and then progress either to HE or to employment with training (OECD, 1992). In France, (western) Germany and Sweden, for instance, over 75 per cent of 18-year-olds are still in education and training and over 50 per cent of young people gain qualifications at the technician or HE entry level (Green and Steedman, 1993). Lower-participation systems like those in Spain and the UK are gradually beginning to follow this trend.

These mass systems of PCET are having to respond both to the changing demands of work and to the aspirations and aptitudes of their enlarged student bodies. Typically they have done this in two ways: they have attempted to increase the diversity and flexibility of provision to cater for the greater plurality of student needs and they have tended to broaden the base of courses, both in their general and vocational content, to meet the demands of employers for more flexible and multi-skilled employees (OECD, 1990).

As European PCET systems have evolved during the last thirty years from elite to mass systems they have increasingly diversified their provision, usually by adding to the traditional academic courses a new range of general and vocational courses.

What has emerged from this in most European states has been a division of PCET into three tracks which can be broadly designated as the academic, the technical and the vocational. The academic tracks include the traditional general subjects and generally lead towards qualifications which give access to HE (Abitur, 'A' level, Highers, Baccalauréat, Maturita); the technical tracks tend to include general education and more theoretical vocational studies and lead towards qualifications, like the Baccalauréat Téchnologique in France, which could lead to HE or employment entry at technician level; and the vocational courses tend to concentrate more on practical skills and are aimed at direct labour-market entry at skilled and semi-skilled levels. Continuing training after entry into work is thereafter seen as a lifelong process. In most countries these tracks in foundation PCET were initially fairly clearly separated, not only in countries like Germany where they have differing institutional locations, but even in countries like Sweden where they are combined within a single institution (OECD, 1990).

The boundaries of these tracks have become somewhat blurred in recent years as attempts have been made to upgrade and broaden the vocational tracks as part of the effort to increase flexibility and choice within systems (OECD, 1990). There has been a general tendency towards reforms that attempt to enhance the vocational tracks, giving them increased social prestige and bringing them more into line with the perceived economic demands for flexible and transferable skills. This has often involved upgrading the general education content of vocational courses; increasing the breadth of vocational studies; and realigning the qualifications with those in the other tracks to enhance prestige and allow greater possibilities for progression.

In Sweden the vocational lines have been lengthened from two to three years, their general education content has been upgraded, and provisions have been made for increased access to HE for those following these lines. In France the occupationally specific, craft level, CAP (Certificat d'Aptitude Professionnel) courses (some 250 types) are rapidly being superseded by the BEP (Brevit d'Enseignement Professionnel) courses (30) which have higher general education requirements and broader vocational studies based around families of occupations (Tanguy, 1991). The creation of the 26 new Baccalauréat Professionnel courses alongside the existing Baccalauréat Téchnologique, now provides a progression route for students on this new broad vocational track and this is taken by over half of the students who register on the BEP courses (Tanguy, 1991). Like the Maturita Professionale in Italy (OECD, 1990), the Baccalauréat Professionnel is a higher-level vocational qualification whose prestige may be enhanced by its common title with the traditional academic qualification and by its concomitant entitlements to HE entry, although it is seen primarily as a passport for direct entry to technician-level employment. Even in countries where VET is organized on an apprentice model of occupational training, there have been attempts to broaden the vocational programmes. In Germany, dual system training now normally involves two days per week (or its equivalent) in the study of general and theoretical subjects in the Berufsschulen, and the number of classified apprenticeships were reduced from 465 in 1980 to 332 in 1988, with a concomitant broadening of content within each (Casey, 1990). In Switzerland the number of apprenticeships has also been reduced (OECD, 1990).

Although the structure of PCET which is emerging in many European countries is thus still quite clearly tracked, there is a general attempt to make systems more flexible and fluid, allowing more choice for young people so that they can more easily transfer between tracks (Raffe, 1993). Greater flexibility is achieved by changes both in the institutional structures and in the organization of curricula and qualification systems.

The main institutional structures of European PCET systems have not changed markedly in as much as institutions are still for the most part differentiated by type, except in Sweden where there is a comprehensive or multilateral upper secondary school. However, the boundaries between institutions have often become more fluid as the search for greater flexibility and relatedness has led to increasing institutional collaboration. There has been some limited but significant combination of institutional types as in the English tertiary college, which combines school sixth-forms with further education colleges, and the French lycée polyvalent, which combines general and technical lycées. However, perhaps most significantly there have been numerous attempts in different countries to bridge the divide between schools and the workplace and education and training. France, Sweden and England, among other countries, have been prominent in introducing structured work experience as a required component of vocational, and sometimes academic, school- and college-based courses and other forms of 'alternance' training are increasingly common, particularly for adults; employers are increasingly drawn into the process of standard setting for vocational programmes, as through the industry lead bodies in England, the CPCs (Commissions Professionnelles Consultatives) in France, and the BIBB (Federal Institute of Vocational Training) in Germany; EC programmes such as COMETT and PETRA have encouraged collaboration between enterprises and educational institutions in R & D and curriculum development; and other forms of collaboration, such as industrial 'mentorship' schemes and 'compacts' between schools and local firms, are increasingly common. The line between employment-based training and school-based vocational education is being progressively eroded as more forms of provision are based on mixed modes of delivery based on employer–education collaboration. This tendency towards collaborative networks can be seen as part and parcel of the EC policy of promoting social partnership as the guiding principle in the delivery of education and training.

At the level of curriculum organization there have also been attempts to increase flexibility by allowing more choice for students in the selection of subject combinations and in the pace and mode of study. This is most evident in the development of modular systems in England and Scotland and to a lesser degree in vocational areas in Sweden and the Netherlands. Modular systems are generally thought to offer the greatest flexibility, since the breaking down of areas of learning into small, free-standing and separately-assessed units, with qualification based on the accumulation of unit credits, can allow the greatest variety in subject combination and pace and mode of study. However, even in the linear systems which predominate in continental Europe, scope has been found for increasing flexibility. Lines of study are normally defined by an elective specialist subject, attached to which is a large prescribed core of other subjects which must be taken in a predetermined sequence. Apart from the choice of specialism, the system thus traditionally allows little choice in combination, sequence, pace or mode. However, attempts have been made, in France and elsewhere, to design the systems in such a way as to facilitate transfer between lines. This generally involves achieving a higher level of system integration with close horizontal and vertical articulation between lines and along progression routes (Green and Steedman, 1993). The different lines are brought closer together by increasing the commonalty between the curricula cores, their forms of assessment and their value systems. This allows students to transfer horizontally between tracks while still progressing vertically. In other words, each track has a variety of progression routes at each stage thus leaving options open as to final qualifications and destinations.

The emergence of the flexible multi-track system (Raffe, 1993) as a model of the future for European PCET, and the increasing integration of tracks it implies, is by no means inevitable and is not without its critics. Lucy Tanguy (1991) has warned that the upgrading of vocational tracks in France, and their increasing integration into an education-led framework, have had a number of unintended and undesirable consequences to set against the beneficial effects on participation and progression. The academicization of the vocational tracks has reduced enrolments on the traditional craft courses, undermined the value of their CAP qualification on the labour market, and has probably acted to marginalize some of those young people who relate better to practical craft training than to academic study. The upgrading of vocational courses has also been associated with a secular tendency in the system towards academic drift and credential inflation. Enrolments on general and technical baccalauréat courses have expanded faster than those on vocational courses during the last decade, accounting for 76 per cent of the increase in enrolments in the terminale between 1986 and 1990, and the prevalence of young people with baccalauréat qualifications has led employers to demand this for jobs which formerly required only lower-level qualifications (Tanguy, 1991). A similar tendency towards academic drift can be observed in Germany, where the proportion going to the Gymnasium has now increased to over 30 per cent, putting additional strains on higher education and the graduate labour market. Not only are enrolments on academic courses increasing proportionally to those on vocational courses but the vocational courses themselves are increasingly sliding towards a vocationally oriented form of general education.

These patterns have led Raffe (1993) and Squires (OECD, 1990) to argue that the status of vocational courses may well be undermined precisely by the attempt to bring them closer in form and content to the academic courses, since the closer they are, the harder it is to differentiate them except in hierarchical terms, and the more likely the vocational are to be judged (adversely) in terms of the criteria for the academic. However, this may not always be the outcome.

Although it may be the case that the traditional occupational/practical conception of the vocational is devalorized by the enhancement through generalization of the vocational tracks, the latter process is at the same time constructing a new definition of the vocational as general and transferable competencies. This is more in tune with vocational requirements of modern economies and thus more likely to be valued. Whether or not the new vocational tracks acquire status will probably depend as much on the external context and on the value that societies place on new forms of knowledge and skill than on the internal logics of the education system.

On past experience of PCET systems in different countries, there is no invariable relation between the proximity of vocational and academic tracks and the nature of status hierarchies. In countries such as France, Italy and the UK, apprenticeship systems have become increasingly marginal and have seen whatever prestige they once had eroded. Youth Training, the most recent British attempt to create an employment-based training system, did not generally acquire a high status despite its separation from the education system. On the other hand, employment-based training systems in Germany, Denmark and Austria have enjoyed a relatively higher status. This may be partly because they are based in the world of work and not in education which confers on them a certain occupational legitimacy, but it is no doubt also due to the broader cultural context in which vocational qualifications are highly valued both for historical reasons and because they are currently required by law for entry into many jobs.

While European systems of PCET have retained diverse characteristics, there appear to be some common trends which can be summed up as follows. Most countries are moving towards high-participation systems which aim to produce rising proportions of young people with qualifications at technician and higher-education entry level. This is accompanied by the extension of adult continuing training into a process of lifelong learning. In order to meet the changing needs of employers and universities, and to cater for the enlarged numbers staying on after compulsory schooling, PCET systems are having to become increasingly diverse and flexible in their provision. This is achieved partly by creating more flexible curriculum pathways and partly through institutional collaboration, which may have the added benefit of bringing the worlds of education and work closer together. While this process is not without its potential hazards, there are already clear signs that it is capable of yielding benefits in terms of the numbers of young people who achieve a level and breadth of knowledge and skill that will equip them for work in the economies of the future.

THE EUROPEAN CHALLENGE TO EDUCATION AND TRAINING IN THE UK

Post-compulsory education and training in the UK is having to respond to many of the same pressures as PCET systems in other European states. International economic forces create similar pressures for highly skilled workforces in all advanced national economies wishing to compete successfully, and British policy-makers are clearly well aware of this (DES/DOE, 1991). The UK, like other European states, has seen a dramatic decline in its youth labour market and a consequent rise in young people's participation in PCET. This is still lower than the EU (European Union) average, particularly at 18, but it is rising fast. In England in 1992/93 an estimated 81 per cent of 16-year-olds and 46 per cent of 18-year-olds enrolled in full- or part-time education or training (DFE, 1993a), and similar levels of participation have been achieved in Scotland. This new level of demand for PCET is no doubt partly due to the tightness of the youth labour market during the recent recession but is likely to continue. Many young people's jobs have disappeared permanently and aspirations are rising among a generation of youth who have benefited from the GCSE reforms (in England and Wales) and who are increasingly conscious of the need for qualifications and more confident of their ability to achieve them (Raffe, 1992). Schools and colleges are thus experiencing for the first time mass participation in PCET and are having to adapt their provision accordingly.

In many respects recent trends in PCET in the UK broadly coincide with those identified above in other European PCET systems. Having traditionally been a 'mixed system', split between work-based and school-based modes (OECD, 1985), English and Welsh PCET is rapidly moving towards a predominately school/college-based model like Scotland and the majority of other European countries. In both Scotland and

England and Wales new vocational tracks have been added to the existing academic tracks in upper secondary education through the work of SCOTVEC and NCVQ and in both cases attempts have been made to link these more flexibly with the academic tracks. In England and Wales a three-track system has emerged including the academic 'A' level track, the occupational NVQ track and the broad vocational General NVQ track. Attempts have been made to align the levels of each qualification in a five-level system and to allow students to incorporate NVQ and GNVQ units with single GCSEs and 'A' levels. The Scottish system of Highers and SCOTVEC National Certificates seems likely to fall into a similar pattern with the new Scottish Vocational Qualifications (SVQs) and General SVQs likely to become the two types of vocational qualifications (thus replacing the existing system and the proposals in the Howie report). Although distinct in various ways, these systems are both gradually coming to acquire some of the characteristics of the flexible multi-track systems emerging as the typical form in continental Europe. NVQs are also stimulating the growth of work-based training for adults but there is still a long way to go before the UK attains the levels of some other European countries and reaches its target of 50 per cent of employees working towards NVQs.

In some other respects reforms in the UK have been considerably more radical than reforms in other parts of Europe since they have challenged traditional forms of curriculum design and assessment (Gordon and Parkes, 1992). NCVQ and SCOTVEC qualifications are based on forms of curriculum modularization whereas most continental European countries have persisted with lines of study, only introducing modular frameworks on the margins. Furthermore, unlike in North America where the traditional module is defined in terms of credit hours (i.e. hours of teaching corresponding to a certain credit value), the NCVQ modules are units which are defined solely in terms of learning outcomes (competence criteria for NVQs and attainment criteria for GNVQs), involving none of the traditional prescriptions as to syllabus content and ways of learning. Although functional skills analysis is widely used on the continent, as in CEDEFOP's work on transparency and equivalence in European qualifications, and although several countries, like the Netherlands, are beginning to express learning outcomes in terms of competence criteria, most countries have held on to the traditional forms of syllabus specification for courses. The référentiel used to describe the Baccalauréat Professionnel courses, for instance, uses some competence statements to describe desired skill outcomes but also retains the traditional means of specifying learning content in terms of a syllabus.

The modes of assessment adopted in the NCVQ qualifications are equally radical in European terms. NVQs and GNVQs are assessed purely on the basis of a candidate's demonstrated performance against specified competence or attainment criteria. There are no requirements as to mode or length of study at all. Assessment for NVQs is largely based on the observation of candidate performance in tasks, preferably in real work situations, where judgements are made as to whether a candidate passes or fails on each element of competence. Written examination only has to be used where the candidate's underpinning knowledge cannot be inferred from the evidence produced in the normal performance of tasks (NCVQ, 1994). Assessment for GNVQs involves a combination of written tests, performance observation and coursework assessment, but a similar pass/fail principle is applied on each criteria. This form of assessment departs somewhat from typical practices on the continent where most countries still rely to a considerable extent on written examinations on all courses to ensure understanding of the theory underlying vocational skills and to ensure reliability in assessment (Prais, 1989). It is also unique in the extent to which it stresses outcomes rather than processes. Although some continental countries, such as France, have begun to look at accrediting the prior learning of their mature students, this principle is not generally applied at the earlier stages where candidates for assessment are still required to have undergone specific courses of stated duration and content. The English VET system is uniquely assessment-led. With fewer controls over process, and with content, quality control and increasingly funding being driven by the assessment of outcomes, enormous responsibility is placed on the assessment system. It has become a matter of great controversy as to whether the assessment methodology is sufficiently precise and reliable to carry this burden (Smithers, 1993; NCVQ, 1994).

In policy areas concerning the finance and control of the education system, the UK is both converging with and diverging from the general patterns in continental Europe, so far as these form a clear pattern. The introduction of a national curriculum in 1988 brought England and Wales into line with what has been the norm in most European countries for many years and remains so despite recent moves in countries such as Sweden towards allowing schools limited discretion over subjects taught. The use of national testing of pupils to monitor and make accountable school performance is also common practice in many European countries, although Britain is alone in the use of comprehensive as against sample testing and in the publication of school league tables of results at all ages to promote market competition between schools (OECD, 1993). While several EU countries have partially decentralized their systems by devolving more control to the regional level, Britain has reduced control at the level of the local education authority (LEA) and gone much further than other countries in passing control to individual schools and colleges through local management and financial delegation systems. Parental power of 'voice' and 'choice' in education has been increased in Britain and other European states through the increased involvement of parents in school management and through increased scope for parental choice of schools, although few countries, excepting perhaps the Netherlands, have gone as far as the UK in promoting 'open enrolment'. British education has become at once both the most market-oriented of systems and one of the most centralized.

How has this complex pattern of convergence and divergence in policy reforms affected the outcomes of UK PCET relative to other European nations? This question is extremely difficult to answer both because it is difficult to compare outcomes in different national systems and because it is hard to assess how different policy changes have impacted on British outcomes in recent years. However, a number of points can be made with reasonable certainty. The first is that although participation in British PCET has risen considerably in recent years (from 32.5 per cent of 18-year-olds in full- and part-time education in England in 1988 to 46 per cent in 1993) (DFE, 1993a), the rate is still low by comparison with a number of European countries such as France, western Germany and Sweden where over 75 per cent are still enrolled at 18 years old. The second point is that the proportion of the cohort gaining Level 3 qualifications is considerably lower than the proportion in some other countries, such as France and Germany, who gain qualifications at a similar level. In England in 1991/92, some 22 per cent of 19-year-olds had gained two or more passes at 'A' level (or their A/S level equivalent); 8 per cent gained a BTEC National Diploma; and 6 per cent a BTEC

National Certificate (BTEC, 1992, 1993). Altogether around 36 per cent qualified at Level 3 (excluding the very small proportions gaining other Level 3 qualifications). In France in 1991, 51 per cent of a typical year cohort gained a baccalauréat qualification. In western Germany in 1991, 32 per cent of 20-year-olds had gained the Abitur or the Faschhoschulreife and over 60 per cent this or an apprentice qualification (Green and Steedman, 1993).

A variety of explanations has been given for the fact that rates of participation and attainment in PCET in the UK are not higher than they are and not as high as the best in Europe, and while it is difficult to demonstrate any of these conclusively it is important for policy-making that the issues are discussed and analysed as far as is possible. Most frequently these explanations focus on three areas of concern: the nature of the labour market and its articulation with education and training; the culture of young people and their expectations and aspirations; and the nature of the PCET system itself. Only a brief review of the arguments under each of these headings will be possible here (for a fuller discussion see Raffe, 1992; Green and Steedman, 1993; Gray *et al.*, 1993; National Commission on Education, 1993; Green, 1994).

The labour market is often said to have an adverse effect on PCET in the UK. A number of reasons are given for this. Until recently when recession and structural changes wiped out many young people's jobs, the labour market exercised a strong pull on young people to leave education and training at the first opportunity. Young people's earnings relative to adult earnings have traditionally been relatively high by European standards and many training opportunities in firms have an age ceiling which creates an additional incentive to enter work early. Employers in the UK often expect less in terms of qualifications among new recruits than is the case in more credentialist countries like France and Germany which have traditionally had a closer articulation between the job market and the qualification systems and where many sectors operate national agreements linking job entry and pay levels to particular qualifications (Green and Steedman, 1993). It has also been argued that UK firms have tended to organize their work processes on the basis of low skill levels. Finegold and Soskice have described a 'low-skills equilibrium' in the UK whereby poorly trained managers employ low-skill workforces to produce low-cost, low-quality goods and services (Finegold and Soskice, 1988). The net effect of these labour market characteristics, it has been argued, is to alter the balance of advantage for young people between staying on in education and training to gain further qualifications and entering work early to earn a wage.

Many young people have not had high aspirations as regards gaining qualifications (Ball, 1991). In the past this attitude was perpetuated by an elitism in the system which encouraged excellence among the few but gave relatively little incentive to the majority of young people. Secondary modern schools, when they were first set up, were not allowed to enter students for the school certificate and when the GCE 'O' and 'A' level examinations were introduced they were designed only for the top 25 per cent of attainers. Other qualifications available generally had little status (Green and Steedman, 1993). The introduction of the GCSE exam has arguably improved incentives for the majority of young people and this may be one of the factors that has increased staying on in recent years (Raffe, 1992). However, the PCET system still fails to provide sufficient incentives for the majority who are not academic high-fliers.

Currently only 41 per cent of young people gain the four higher-grade GCSEs that are normally required for direct entry onto the prestigious Level 3 courses ('A' level, BTEC National Diplomas and GNVQ 3s). Most of these (the 36 per cent of the cohort in 1993) will join 'A' level courses where they have a reasonable (70 per cent) chance of coming out with a usable batch of two or three 'A' levels (Audit Commission, 1993): for the remainder there is the alternative of direct entry onto BTEC National Diploma and Level 3 GNVQ courses on which they have a good chance of attaining a qualification valued by employers. However, for the 60 per cent of young people who do not attain four higher-grade GCSEs at Key Stage 4 the options are more limited and the incentives to further study are not strong. The courses for which they are immediately qualified – Level 2 NVQs or GNVQs – often do not carry much clout on the labour market; the progression routes up to Level 3 qualifications, through Level 2s and GCSE re-sits, are long and relatively uncertain. In a society which still has relatively low expectations for most of its young people, and where, unlike in continental countries, it is still not the norm to stay on until 18 years old, motivation is understandably low among lower attainers to persist on uncertain progression routes through PCET.

Much has been written about failings on the supply side of PCET in Britain and various explanations have been given for the relatively low rates of progression within the system. The Audit Commission/OFSTED (1993) report, *Unfinished Business*, found rates of drop-out of up to 30 per cent on many FE courses and questioned the suitability of courses for many of those following them and the inadequacies of advice and counselling which allowed young people to go onto inappropriate courses. Numerous commentators have criticized the 'A' levels for their narrow specialization and lack of vocational relevance (DES, 1988; Finegold *et al.*, 1991; Ball, 1991; National Commission on Education, 1993) which is said to make them unsuitable for many of the students who take them, while recent criticism of the NVQs and GNVQs has also focused on their supposed lack of depth and rigour as regards general education (Smithers, 1993). Others (CBI, 1993; Finegold *et al.*, 1991; Young, 1991) have seen weaknesses not only in each individual track but also in the relationship between the tracks and the division that exists between the vocational and academic courses. While it is extremely difficult to disentangle the various factors which affect attainment in education systems and thus to judge how far characteristics like the above are responsible for impeding progression, useful insights can be gained from comparative analysis. There would seem to be at least three areas where the organization of PCET in England and Wales differs markedly from that in higher-achieving European systems.

Many analysts of British PCET have noted the high degree of fragmentation and division within the system and the negative effects this may have on student progression and attainment due to the lack of flexibility in choice of subjects and the poor opportunities for transfer this imposes on students (Finegold *et al.*, 1991; Green and Steedman, 1993; Green, 1994). It would certainly seem to be the case that the system has achieved less integration than some other European systems and particularly those that are school-based, as in France and Sweden. This is true both in terms of the structure of administration and control, and in terms of delivery and curriculum organization.

The finance and control of PCET in England and Wales is multiply fragmented with several different bodies responsible for financing colleges and school sixth-forms

(LEAs, School Funding Authority, Further Education Funding Council, Training and Enterprise Councils) and different bodies responsible for overseeing academic qualifications (SCAA) and vocational qualifications (NCVQ). In addition to this there are over 180 lead bodies responsible for standard setting and hundreds of awarding bodies. Such diversity in policy-making and control has made it exceptionally difficult to achieve coherent long-term planning and implementation and this remains a notable lack compared with many European systems (Gordon and Parkes, 1992).

Related to the above is the fragmented nature of the provision itself. English PCET has now three main tracks and some efforts have been made to link these as in the flexible multi-track systems elsewhere in Europe. However, as yet there is still a very low level of integration between the academic, general vocational and occupational tracks. Each track has a different way of expressing its objectives (syllabus in 'A' levels; attainment criteria in GNVQs; and competence criteria in NVQs); there is no common core of subjects or skills that is shared between the courses on different tracks; methods of teaching and forms of assessment differ radically (terminal written exams for 'A' levels; task-based assessment for NVQs; a mixture of written tests and coursework for GNVQs); and qualifications are organized into different parallel systems, rather than forming one subdivided but integrated framework as with the baccalauréats in France. One result of this level of division is that it remains difficult to combine units from the different tracks or indeed to change tracks without losing ground.

Courses in England and Wales and, to a lesser extent, Scotland are generally narrower, in terms of the range of subjects and skill areas covered, than their equivalents in other European countries. 'A' level courses, often involving only two subjects, are much more specialized than their equivalents elsewhere in Europe. The Abitur requires four examined subjects and coursework assessment in other subjects while the baccalauréats generally entail more than six compulsory subjects, all of which are assessed. The general education component on vocational courses in countries such as France, Sweden, the Netherlands and Japan is also generally much broader than in British NVQs and GNVQs. While all vocational courses in France (CAP, BEP and BP) involve a minimum of 15 hours per week study of general subjects, in England NVQs and GNVQs generally include general educational subjects as optional units (Wolf and Rapiau, 1993).

A final striking peculiarity in England and Wales lies in the nature of core skills teaching on vocational courses. The NCVQ has adopted a policy of 'embedding' core skills in the vocational units in NVQ and GNVQ qualifications. In NVQs, core skills are only a compulsory part of the learning and assessment in as much as they are necessary for the performance of competencies. In GNVQs, core skills (communications, numeracy and Information Technology) are represented in separate units for the purposes of assessment but the advice from the NCVQ is that their learning should be embedded in the teaching of the vocational attainments. In most European countries general educational is normally provided in discrete subjects taught by specialist teachers. Whether or not this leads to higher levels of attainment in core skill areas such as language and maths, thus providing a better foundation for progression, remains a controversial question (Wolf and Rapiau, 1993; Green, 1994).

CONCLUSIONS

The above analysis of different European approaches to foundation VET would suggest that a number of issues need to be carefully examined before we can be confident about extending the competence-based approach from foundation to professional levels of VET. First, it seems clear that there is a variety of factors influencing progression and attainment in VET which extend far beyond the specific issues about how learning outcomes should be expressed and assessed. These relate both to the education and training provision itself and to the context in which it is set. Successful VET systems need to ensure not only an adequate supply of skills training but also an adequate demand for it from individuals and employers. Different European states have adopted a variety of labour market policies to ensure the latter and these cannot be discussed here, but the point to note is that while competence-based approaches may enhance demand to some extent through their greater transparency, this in itself is unlikely to be sufficient to make a major impact on the demand for qualifications without other labour market measures. As regards the supply side of the equation, the European experience would also seem to suggest that a competence-based approach which focuses exclusively on outcomes will also have serious limitations. Structures and processes are also crucial variables in successful VET. A system driven by the assessment of outcomes is not necessarily going to develop adequate structures and processes simply because the outcomes have been well specified.

The second general conclusion relates to specification and assessment methodology itself. While there is considerable interest across Europe in the use of functional analysis to specify the skills involved in different jobs, there has been a clear resistance in most continental countries to adopting the competence-based model wholesale in VET systems. The reason for this would seem to be that there is still considerable scepticism about some aspects of the approach. There are doubts about whether skills and related knowledge can be clearly and adequately specified in competence terms, particularly at the higher levels, where performance involves complex combinations of skills, knowledge and judgement. There are doubts about the reliability and viability of assessment methods based primarily on the observation of task performance in real work contexts since such methods can rarely cover a wide range of contexts without excessive cost and since they tend to ignore the underlying theoretical knowledge and understanding which is often crucial to the flexible application of skills. There is also a tendency in many countries to resist any approach which reduces the theoretical and general educational components of VET since these are considered essential not only for skills transfer but also for the potential of individuals both as citizens and as learners and employees seeking to progress to higher levels. These considerations apply as much at higher as at lower levels and they must be given careful consideration before the competence-based approach is more widely adopted.

REFERENCES

Audit Commission/OFSTED (1993) *Unfinished Business: Full-Time Education Courses for 16–19 Year Olds*. London: HMSO.

Ball, C. (1991) *Learning Pays*. London: RSA.

Brown, P. and Lauder, H. (1992) 'Education, economy and society: an introduction to a new agenda.' In P. Brown and H. Lauder (eds) *Education for Economic Survival.* London: Routledge.

BTEC (1992) *Annual Report.* London: BTEC.

BTEC (1993) *Staying the Course.* London: BTEC.

Casey, B. (1990) *Recent Developments in West Germany's Apprentice Training System.* London: Policy Studies Institute.

CBI (1993) *Routes for Success, Careership a Strategy for all 16–19 Year Old Learning.* London: CBI.

DES (1988) *Advancing A Levels.* London: HMSO.

DES/DOE (1991) *Education and Training for the 21st Century.* London: HMSO.

DFE (1993) *Statistical Bulletin*, 16–93. London: HMSO.

Finegold, D. and Soskice, D. (1988) 'The failure of training in Britain: analysis and prescription.' *Oxford Review of Economic Policy*, 4(3), 21–53.

Finegold, D., Keep, E., Millibond, D., Raffe, D., Spours, K. and Young, M. (1991) *A British Baccalaureate.* London: Institute for Public Policy Research.

Gordon, J. and Parkes, D. (1992) *Strategies for Vocational Education and Training in Europe.* AVCI/IFCVE.

Gray, J., Jesson, D. and Tranmer, M. (1993) *Boosting Post-16 Participation in Full-Time Education. A Study of Some Key Factors.* Education Youth Cohort Report, No. 20.

Green, A. (1994) 'Core skills, participation and progression in post-compulsory education and training in England and France.' *Comparative Education* (forthcoming).

Green, A. and Steedman, H. (1993) *Educational Provision, Educational Attainment and the Needs of Industry: A Review of the Research for Germany, France, Japan, the USA and Britain*, Report no. 5. London: National Institute of Economic and Social Research.

National Commission on Education (1993) *Learning to Succeed: A Radical Look at Education Today and a Strategy for the Future.* London: Paul Hamlyn.

NCVQ (1994) *A Statement by the National Council for Vocational Qualifications on 'All Our Futures – Britain's Educational Revolution'.* London: NCVQ.

OECD (1985) *Education and Training Beyond Basic Schooling.* Paris: OECD.

OECD (1990) *Pathways to Learning.* Paris: OECD.

OECD (1992) *Education at a Glance.* Paris: OECD.

OECD (1993) *Curriculum Reform: Assessment in Question.* Paris: OECD.

Piore, M. and Sabel, C. (1984) *The Second Industrial Divide: Possibilities for Prosperity.* New York: Basic Books.

Porter, M. (1990) *The Competitive Advantage of Nations.* London: Macmillan.

Prais, S. J. (1989) 'How Europe would see the new British initiative for standardising vocational qualifications.' *National Institute Economic Review*, August 1989.

Raffe, D. (1992) *Participation of 16–18 Year Olds in Education and Training*, Briefing No. 3, National Commission on Education.

Raffe, D. (1993) *Ready for Adult Life: Reforming the Post-16 Curriculum. Some Lessons from the 'Howie' Debate in Scotland.* Paper for the BAAS Annual Meeting, Keele University, August 1993.

Reich, R. (1991) *The Work of Nations.* London: Simon and Schuster.

Royal Society (1991) *Beyond GCSE.* London: Royal Society.

Ruberti (1993) *'Guidelines for Community Action in the Field of Education and Training.'* European Commission working paper, unpublished.

Smithers, A. (1993) *All Our Futures: A Dispatches Report on Education.* London: Channel Four Television.

Smithers, A. and Robinson. P. (1989) *Increasing Participation in Higher Education.* British Petroleum.

Smithers, A. and Robinson, P. (1991) *Beyond Compulsory Schooling: A Numerical Picture.* CIHE.

Spours, K. (1992) *Recent Developments in Qualifications at 14+.* PSEC Working Paper No. 12. London: London Institute of Education.

Tanguy, L. (1991) *Quelle Formation Pour les Ouvriers et les Employés de France.* Paris: La Documentation Française.

Wolf, A. (1992) *Mathematics for Vocational Students in France and England: Contrasting Provision and Consequences*, Discussion paper no. 23. London: National Institute of Economic and Social Research.

Wolf, A. and M.-T. Rapiau (1993). 'The academic achievement of craft apprentices in France and England: contrasting systems and common dilemmas.' *Comparative Education*, 29(1).

Young, M. (1991) *The Post-16 Core*. PSEC Working Paper No. 6. London: London Institute of Education.

Zuboff, S. (1988) *In the Age of the Smart Machine*. New York: Basic Books.

Chapter 3

Reality Testing in the Workplace: are NVQs 'Employment-led'?

John Field

Work and the workplace play a central role in the new system of National Vocational Qualifications. For individual employers, trainees and workers, like all occupational qualifications, an NVQ only pays off when its owner is working at their job. Indeed, the design of NVQs makes the workplace the primary site of learning and assessment of the skills that the owner of an NVQ is deemed to possess. Those whose job it is to develop, promote and sell NVQs have consistently claimed that, unlike previous qualifications, the new system is 'employment-led'. The underpinning ideology of the NVQ system places great emphasis upon the workplace as a guarantor of relevance, reliability and demand. At the level of rhetoric, a contrast is frequently drawn both implicitly and explicitly between the kinds of skills and knowledge taught and examined within educational institutions (characterized as academic, abstract, imprac- tical and knowledge-based), and those learned and observed within the workplace (characterized as useful, applied, practical and skills-based). The goal of the reform has been from the outset to shift the emphasis irrevocably from the former to the latter.

NVQs are, then, defined in all essentials as reflecting more reliably and accurately than in the past the demands of the workplace. This chapter takes that claim as its starting point. It deals with the concept of NVQs as driven by the requirements of the workplace, and more particularly as reflecting the needs of employers. The analysis is presented in four stages:

1. a brief description of the new system as it is now settling into shape;
2. analysis of conditions in the labour market, in order to judge how far they mirror the kinds of assumptions upon which NVQs are predicated;
3. an outline of the ways in which NVQs appear to be being received within the workplace; and
4. an indication of some possible explanations of the social determination of the NVQ system, and vocational qualifications systems more generally.

Underlying this critique is the belief that, whatever the merits or faults of NVQs in themselves, what counts is how they are received in actually existing workplaces, each of which has its own social relations and organizational cultures.

Much of the empirical research associated with the debate over NVQs has been frankly technical, and concerned chiefly with identifying, clarifying and resolving the practical problems of implementation. This is not meant to be a dismissive comment, but rather to indicate the limits of much of the empirical work undertaken to date. Typically, it has been concerned with such questions as the identification of task-related skills, the assessment of broadly applicable skills, and the best balance of competence with 'underpinning knowledge' in higher-level qualifications. Other interventions have been of three kinds. There has been some discussion of the psychology of learning which informs the NVQ system; a number of critics have suggested that NVQs are based upon a simplistic and out-moded behaviourism which has no place either for individual cognitive differences nor for the context-specific nature of some human learning (Marshall, 1991, pp. 61–2). From a philosophical standpoint, it has been suggested that NVQs are narrowly utilitarian (Hyland, 1991), although this of course begs the question of what wider human qualities British vocational qualifications measured before 1986. Associated with the philosophical analysis of NVQs is a concern for terminology, with a number of attempts – not least by NCVQ – to define more precisely what is meant by 'competence' (Short, 1984; Ashworth and Saxton, 1990; Hodkinson, 1992).

By comparison, the social and economic analysis of NVQs remains in its infancy. As a result no serious challenge has been offered to the view that NVQs are 'employment-led'. This phrase, used both by NVQs' proponents and supporters and their critics, is understood by the system's enthusiasts to mean that it reflects the 'needs of the workplace', and by its neo-Marxist critics as confirming that it reflects capital's latest, post-Fordist mode of subordination of labour (Edwards, 1993). As a consequence, the relationship between NVQs and employment has been taken for granted by all sides. In particular, there has been relatively little study of the operation of NVQs in the labour market. This is understandable; much of the social and economic research into NVQs has concerned their impact upon training institutions, and chronologically it is at this end that the new system has been most noticeable. However, it is the labour market that forms the primary context of vocational qualifications. Yet, with the significant exception of Lorna Unwin's case study of NVQs in Courtaulds' Coventry fibre plant, this context has been largely taken as given (Unwin, 1991). I now propose to look underneath this particular stone.

In part, this chapter is research-based, drawing on evidence from a mixture of published material and original research collected during the course of a study of NVQs and the organization of work in contemporary Britain (Field, 1991; Field and Weller, 1992; Field, 1993). Material is taken from interviews conducted during autumn 1993 with managers responsible for personnel and training issues in large and medium-sized enterprises; these followed on an earlier study of trade union officers' perceptions of the new system (Field and Weller, 1992). Published statistics are drawn on, in order to quantify the availability and take-up of NVQs. Other supporting evidence is drawn from analysis of published material, which can be used to shed light on both the real level and nature of the market demand for NVQs, and on the processes by which a particular definition of 'employment interests' has been constructed and inserted into the NVQ system. This arises from a long-standing interest in what I think of as 'the pedagogy of labour'. As I see it, the concept and practice of using work in itself as a didactic instrument has a history which has in modern times assumed a new character (Field, 1992). What is significant about the NVQ system is that it represents an attempt to construct at national level a rational, coherent and transparent system of qualifications, based on national standards which are drawn from social scientific methods of occupational analysis. Furthermore, its founding principles are designed in such a way as to uncouple the traditional association between qualifications and courses of training; rather, in principle at least, the link between qualifications and occupations is direct and potentially unmediated, so that an individual may work towards a qualification simply through the assessment of her performance in her job. This development has been tied in some critical accounts to the predominance of an allegedly 'post-Fordist' organization of work in the contemporary economy (Edwards, 1993). However, the evidence presented here suggests that NVQs have arisen less because of demand from those involved in managing labour than from the ideas and aspirations of a small coalition of modernizing civil servants and highly-placed training professionals. In essence, the market for NVQs is largely confined to different arms of the Government.

NATIONAL VOCATIONAL QUALIFICATIONS: THE IMPLEMENTATION

Responsibility for the introduction of NVQs is usually accorded to the 1986 *Review of Vocational Qualifications* chaired by Oscar de Ville (MSC/DES, 1986). However, this is to foreshorten a more sustained reform effort. Quite aside from the election of the Thatcher Government in 1979, with its vigorous interest in youth training as an instrument for managing unemployment, the decline of the apprenticeship system throughout much of industry can be dated back to the later 1960s, with consequences in turn for the qualifications system which it had nurtured. One of the major concerns expressed by the Donovan Commission on industrial relations in its 1968 report was the apprenticeship system's 'failure to develop objective standards' (Aldcroft, 1992, pp. 57-8). Hints of reform in the vocational qualifications system came in 1982, with the publication of the *New Training Initiative* (MSC, 1981). As well as identifying priorities in youth and adult training, the report called for the establishment of clear occupational standards to guide the training system. These were introduced in the Youth Training Scheme as 'standard tasks' then grouped in 1984 into 'modules of accreditation'. *Training for Jobs* in early 1984 foreshadowed the creation of 'a coherent system of training standards and certificates of competence' (HMSO, 1984). In 1985, unit-based schemes were tried out in the catering and horse management industries (Marshall, 1991, p. 56).

Some years of criticism and experiment, then, predated de Ville's review committee, with its call for 'an effective national system for vocational qualifications' which 'recognises competence and capability in the application of knowledge and skills' (MSC/DES, 1986, pp. 16, 30). The *Review* criticized existing arrangements for identifying occupational standards; however, it was agnostic about precisely how these should be drawn up, and how individual attainment against them should be assessed, calling for a National Council for Vocational Qualifications to be created which should have oversight of these matters. The NCVQ was created almost immediately, and was set the ambitious target of putting NVQs in place covering 80 per cent of the workforce by the end of 1992. In the event, that broad target was apparently achieved, in that according to government estimates, those occupations engaged in by some 76 per cent of the workforce were covered potentially by NVQs up to Level 4 by the end of October 1992 (*Times Higher Education Supplement*, 30 October 1992).

Why did NVQs emerge when they did and in the shape that they now assume? There seems little doubt that they were conceived and promoted as part of a wider strategy designed to encourage the creation of a more flexible, skilled and mobile workforce. Put at its crudest, the early designs for what later became NVQs were being drafted at a time when Government was expressing growing concern about the lack of flexibility of the British workforce. The resulting rigidities in the labour market could in part be corrected by forms of training which encouraged the acquisition of new skills, and by the development of a qualifications system which was both transparent and focused upon the demands of the workplace. A series of official reports published in the early 1980s linked Britain's 'training deficit' with her economic performance (Aldcroft, 1992), claiming that it was not only the possession of skills which counted but the capacity to carry skills between jobs. Flexibility and skill transfer therefore became important goals within wider fields of government policy on training and the labour market.

Much critical comment so far has tended to share the assumptions behind the official diagnosis, even if they do not endorse the prescriptions. If we start to question the underlying assumptions, though, two sets of questions arise. The first set concerns flexibility: is it true that there is a marked rise in the demand for greater flexibility in the workforce, and to what extent is this linked to the possession of portable qualifications as opposed to other factors such as physical and geographical mobility? The second set concerns the nature of the 'training deficit': what kinds of skills bottlenecks can be identified, and to what extent might they be alleviated by interventions in the qualifications system?

VOCATIONAL QUALIFICATIONS AND THE LABOUR MARKET

Occupational flexibility has been the subject of intense debate in recent years. On the one hand are those who argue that capitalism has surpassed its 'Fordist' phase, which was characterized by the aggregation of un- and semi-skilled labour in large units undertaking the mass production of standardized goods (Murray, 1989; Allen, 1992). In the place of the Fordist 'mass worker', contemporary capital is held to require an increasingly adaptable labour force, which can adjust (or be adjusted) to dramatic changes in increasingly global product markets. While the range of those who detect the presence of occupational flexibility range from the NCVQ and, of course, the Government through to neo-Marxists such as Robin Murray, there is considerable doubt whether they are right to detect a major, generalizable shift across the labour market as a whole, rather than a series of situationally specific transitions in particular segments of the labour market (Kern and Schumann, 1990, pp. 300–18). Thus together with change and transformation we can also detect major continuities, such as the secular change in the economy and workforce which has led to the numerical dominance of white-collar occupations (Pollert, 1991). It is clear that some of the phenomena which were taken in the late 1980s as signs of enhanced flexibility were in fact relatively short-lived; thus the growth of the small-firm sector can be explained primarily through the job-shedding policies of large firms throughout the 1980s, rather than their collective impulse to subcontract parts of their operation to peripheral organizations (Johnson, 1991, p. 255). Similarly with the growth of part-time work, much of which can be explained through increased participation in the labour market among women; or multi-skilling, whose extent remains extremely small scale. Empirically, it is hard to determine the scale of flexibilization with any accuracy. Nor is it clear how far flexibilization is simply another way of describing ongoing managerial responses to uncertainty and competition in the product market. To the extent that product markets are increasingly subject to worldwide competitive pressures, flexibilization may indeed represent more of a return to the highly com-petitive capitalism of Victorian and Edwardian Britain – what might be called 'pre-Fordism' – rather than an absolute break with the past. As Hyman (1991, p. 282) has argued,

> the multiple sources of instability in national and international economic relations offer the prospect of a sustained phase of disturbance and disruption. Flexibilisation is therefore not simply a one-off process of removing a set of entrenched rigidities, but also a means of adapting institutions and expectations to the certainty of uncertainty.

How particular managements respond to these uncertainties, Hyman (1991, p. 283) reminds us, is another matter; and each response selected carries with it the risk of introducing new rigidities, or of destabilizing those rigidities that were not on the agenda of management-led change. The point is, then, to emphasize that there is no single, abstract labour market in general; but rather a series of overlapping markets for labour, both internal and external, which are subject to a range of pressures for change, some long-term and some short-term. It is by no means clear that greater flexibility has as yet become a powerful requirement within these specific labour markets on any scale.

It is reasonable to suppose, then, that flexibility is more talked about than experienced. None the less, intensified competitive pressures have fostered at least a search for flexibility; to what extent can changes in the qualifications system support that search? Many of the features of NVQs – their unit-based structure, their trans-parency, and their transferability – make them at least potentially a highly portable qualifications system. On the surface, then, they seem to display many of the design features which meet the requirements of occupational flexibilization. However, this is to overplay the significance which qualifications of any kind are likely to possess in the labour market.

A number of separate issues arise here. First is the question of whether or not vocational qualifications routinely play a significant role in employers' recruitment decisions. Empirically, there is abundant evidence that they do not; in general, formal qualifications are one of a number of variables involved in obtaining and advancing in a particular job (Dale and Pires, 1984). In the external labour markets for un- and semi-skilled occupations, for both workers and employers it costs more to seek to match each individual's formal qualifications with a job specification than the search yields in rewards; the more specialized the occupation, the more economical the search. Other than in more specialized occupations, only where there are other rewards – or sanctions – will both parties submit to this search. An example would be an enterprise that has adopted a policy towards equal opportunities which then requires both employer and job-seeker to scrutinize job specifications in the light of the applicant's proven capabilities. In internal labour markets, it remains the case that experience of a job is often deemed to be the strongest basis for career advancement; the internal information system, formal and informal, largely displaces the need for any formal certification. Hence the preference is for recruiting labour and then, if at all, developing a training plan, rather than rigorously seeking to recruit those with the best formal qualifications. Any attempt, for example by trade unions, to enhance the role of formal qualifications is likely, in my own findings, to be resisted by personnel managers as a contract upon flexibilization.

Second, there is the question of whether the information required in labour markets is supplied by the vocational qualifications system. This is particularly at issue if the flexibilization thesis does hold water, as many of the capabilities which employers are likely to seek are not likely to be categorized reliably by the qualifications system. Blackburn and Mann found in the 1970s that managers stressed such affective qualities as 'responsibility, stability, trustworthiness' in making their recruitment and promotions decisions (Blackburn and Mann, 1979, p. 280). More recently, a Dutch study found personnel managers identifying such 'social-normative' attitudinal requirements as 'responsibility, reliability, accuracy', communication skills and obedience to company norms (Onstenk, *et al.* 1991, p. 5). My own findings repeat those of Blackburn and Mann in the 1970s: 'From the employer's point of view, the internal labour market allows workers to demonstrate these qualities (if they have them) over a number of years before they reach jobs where mistakes would matter' (Blackburn and Mann, 1979, p. 280). Occupational qualifications which are necessarily silent on social-normative qualities will tend to be largely disregarded in the labour market.

NVQs AND THE LABOUR MARKET

Conceptually, changes in qualifications systems need to be distinguished from changes in skills outputs. What are the skills shortage areas in Britain, and how do changes in qualifications systems affect them? Considerable effort has been spent in recent years on the identification of skills shortage areas in Britain, especially in comparison with our major competitor nations, and the results appear to be reasonably consistent. A number of researchers have concluded that although there are question marks over Britain's performance in basic numeracy and communicating training, as well as over the economic relevance of the higher education system, it is at the intermediate skills level (i.e. those above routine skills but below professional ones) that there is a marked discrepancy between the British labour force and those of its major competitors (the research is summarized in Ryan, 1991; and Aldcroft, 1992). Yet despite this identifiable deficit at the intermediate level, there is strong evidence to suggest that the market for NVQs is confined mainly to rudimentary entry qualifications to low-skill-level occupations.

Stated bluntly, the NVQ system has failed to tackle this key skills problem. By the end of 1993, some 1346 NVQs were in place, compared with 392 twelve months previously (see Tables 3.1 and 3.2). The 1993 list of NVQs in place was published approximately one year after the Government judged that some 76 per cent of the workforce was covered by the new system. Of these qualifications, nearly three-fifths

Table 3.1.   *The scope of national vocational qualifications in place by autumn 1992*

	Total NVQs in place	Certificates awarded
Level 1	23.9%	18.6%
Level 2	43.9%	62.2%
Level 3	18.1%	3.7%
Level 4	13.3%	15.4%
Level 5	0.8%	0.1%
Total	(392)	(92,905)

Source: *The NVQ Monitor*, September 1992, December 1992.

Table 3.2.   *The scope of national vocational qualifications in place by autumn 1993*

	Total NVQs in place December 1993	Certificates awarded, September 1993
Level 1	16.1%	34.3%
Level 2	42.6%	57.6%
Level 3	28.0%	2.8%
Level 4	12.4%	5.2%
Level 5	0.8%	0.1%
Total	(1,346)	(341,812)

Source: *The NVQ Monitor*, Winter 1993/1994.

were at the lowest two levels. Indeed, 16 per cent of all NVQs listed in late 1993 were at Level 1; nothing corresponds to such an elementary skills level in either the German or French vocational qualifications systems. The intermediate skills level overlaps the upper part of Level 3, with just 28 per cent of the NVQs in place, and Level 4, with a further 12 per cent. However, the Level 3 NVQs, and to a lesser extent Level 4, are predominantly in the areas of goods and services, construction and health care, rather than engineering and other manufacturing occupations. At this stage, the important fact to note is that the vast majority of NVQs in existence were at an elementary level.

Similarly with the NVQ certificates so far awarded. By the end of September 1993, a grand total of 341,812 NVQ certificates had been awarded (*NVQ Monitor*, Winter 1993/1994). While this represents a substantial rise on the total of 92,905 certificates awarded under the NVQ system by September 1992, the proportion of certificates at the lowest skills levels, far from changing since September 1992, had in fact increased over the intervening twelve months: whereas four-fifths were at Level 1 or 2 in September 1992, by the autumn of 1993 the proportion at these levels had risen to 92 per cent! Meanwhile, while a mere 3.7 per cent were awarded at Level 3 in autumn 1992, twelve months later the figure had shrunk to 2.8 per cent. By far the largest single numbers of NVQs were at Level 2; almost one-third of the Level 2 certificates were issued in business administration and a further one-quarter were in hairdressing. At Level 1, one-half of the certificates awarded were in business administration and a further quarter were in 'public service (armed service)'.

Thus in the early years at least, the qualifications being awarded were almost entirely at the lowest levels of skill and competence envisaged. Furthermore, across the board they reflected skill areas with little or no connection with the manufacturing sector.

If it would be wrong to make too much of these figures, they suggest that NVQs' contribution towards the identified shortages of intermediate skills, especially in technician and manufacturing occupations, is negligible.

Further evidence of the bias inherent in the system can be seen in the higher level of qualification. At the professional level, the impact of NVQs has mostly been indirect rather than direct. Few qualifications exist at Levels 4 and 5, and fewer still have been awarded. Indeed, the take-up at higher levels has grown much more slowly than at Levels 1 and 2, where the purchasing power of TECs and the Further Education Funding Council have made themselves felt. Almost all of the Level 4 certificates were in accountancy, involving chiefly such awards as those of the Association of Accounting Technicians. From 1993 on, demand for higher-level NVQs started to grow, albeit slowly. Demand is mostly from Government agencies and departments such as Royal Mail and the Benefits Agency where the influence and support of the Cabinet Office has encouraged human resources managers to switch their purchasing to higher-level NVQs and away from more traditional forms of management development. In addition, the autumn 1993 Budget introduced tax exemptions for individuals' expenses incurred while working towards an NVQ, in an attempt to stimulate the market among higher band tax-payers. While it was notable that demand for higher-level NVQs was, outside accountancy, minimal in late 1993, the momentum for higher-level NVQs in the public sector had started to rise by early 1994. In turn, providers had started to position themselves to compete in this new market, for example with the creation of the Management Verification Consortium by the Association of Business Schools. Once more, though, the main purchasing forces were Government-led.

It remains the case, though, that demand for professional-level qualifications is low. In the field of training and development, for example, 22 qualifications existed by the end of 1993, but a mere 49 had apparently been awarded (*NVQ Monitor*, Winter 1993/1994, p. 34). While it is true that much larger numbers are registered for NVQs, or are being assessed for single units within NVQs, the overall numbers completing are remarkably low. The largest single number of qualifications awarded at Level 4 is in Management, where 1621 certificates had been issued at Level 5. This, however, reflected the peculiarities of a niche market within the wider management development market; in addition, the lead body for management (the Management Charter Initiative) is also an awarding body and a private company, and has managed to exert some independence within the broad NVQ framework. However, it was not to reform professional-level qualifications that NVQs were introduced, but to address the much broader challenges of upgrading the skills, flexibility and qualifications of the labour force as a whole, especially in those areas regarded as vital to national prosperity. The system that has emerged, however, has been heavily biased towards the lowest end of the range.

It is relatively simple to explain why this pattern has emerged. Typically, intermediate skills are costly to develop, and are likely to fall victim to market failure; they are at least potentially highly transferable across employers, thus providing an incentive to employers to poach rather than train wherever possible. This is therefore a field where state action is likely to prove both effective as an investment and to possess legitimacy amongst most major players. However, changes in the qualifications system are probably the least effective means of dealing with skills shortages at this level. For example, poaching has hardly been hindered by the absence of transparent, coherent, nationally-determined occupational standards! On the other hand, the NVQ system has found a ready market among public purchasers of qualifications. In fact, the single largest market has been among colleges offering full-time training to young people; these are financed through the Further Education Funding Council, whose funding priorities – largely set by Government – favour the purchase of NVQs. The second major market has been among providers of training programmes for unemployed people; these are mainly financed through Training and Enterprise Councils and Local Enterprise Companies, whose Government-set funding priorities also favour the purchase of NVQs. There is thus a powerful bias in the market towards the mass purchase of low-skill, entry-level qualifications.

Changes in the qualifications system are therefore unlikely to make much of a contribution towards the identified shortages in the labour market. When it comes to considering the actual role of NVQs within the workplace, it is also important to recall that they are, by international standards, relatively narrowly focused and have been developed chiefly at the most basic skills level. This skewed pattern suggests that the determining factors may lie at least in part on the supply rather than the demand side. This can be confirmed by such evidence as currently exists of the existing impact of NVQs within the workplace.

NVQs IN THE WORKPLACE

In November 1992, the Employment Secretary announced the launch of a campaign in the spring 'to put NVQs on the map' (*Times Educational Supplement*, 13 November 1992). A month later, a survey of 70 companies in the leisure industries with 260,000 employees concluded that employers were 'mainly unaware' of NVQs (*Times Educational Supplement*, 11 December 1992). Similar conclusions have come from HM Inspectors in their reports on NVQs in further education colleges, as well as from other surveys of industrial responses to NVQs including those carried out by employers' organizations (Maguire *et al.* 1993, p. 23). These messages alone should cause some scepticism over the claim that the NVQ system is 'employment-led'. That claim will now be put under closer scrutiny.

The claim that NVQs are 'employment-led' relies largely upon the role of the industry lead bodies in determining the national standards frameworks for their respective industries. This is an area which deserves far closer study. Constitutionally, the lead bodies are dominated by employers' representatives. Superficially, then, employment interests do indeed lead the system. However, there are two intervening factors which shape the way in which that representation of the employment interest operates in practice. First, there is the question of which types of 'employer' actually sit on the lead bodies; although no comprehensive study of their membership has yet been carried out, my own preliminary investigations have led me to question how far we can describe the lead body membership as representing employers at all. Rather, they consist of a mix of particular types of managerial profession, the majority of whom have senior personnel responsibilities (usually in the larger companies) or who work in training administration (for example, in TECs, training boards, or the training departments of the larger firms). They also include a wide sprinkling of 'consultants', some of whom have a long history of involvement in the Employment Department and its quangos (the most visible of this group is Canon George Tolley, but he is far from the only example). These highly specialized professionals are far from the generalized 'employers' who are represented in the rhetoric as driving the system; rather, they bring their own organizational expertise and interests into the NVQ system. Second, there is the question of how the lead bodies have gone about the process of identifying the national occupational standards. In practice, most lead bodies have contracted the task out to consultants, and scrutinized the results through a series of small working groups, supported by advisers from the Employment Department. These working groups have commissioned consultants to produce the standards around which particular NVQs are organized; it is reportedly rare for the lead bodies to discuss the standards in any detail once they have been agreed by the working groups. This process casts further doubt upon the claim that the lead bodies are employer-led, at least in any straightforward sense of the term. Rather, as with many of the training innovations of the past decade (Shackleton, 1992), the initiative has lain very substantially with the professional training lobby, working through the MSC and its successor bodies.

Indeed, there is evidence that many general managers are suspicious of the new system. Their chief concern focuses around costs. Implementation costs are clearly high, largely because of the labour-intensive nature of the assessment process in NVQs. Most personnel managers complained that the NVQ process was 'bureaucratic' or 'time-consuming'. Such complaints emerge even in enterprises who are at an extremely early stage of development. A personnel development officer in an urban NHS trust, for example, stated that: 'it is time-consuming . . . It takes time to get NVQs into the organization, and time is money, and there is the release of the assessor to be trained, that also takes time.' Almost all personnel managers interviewed also made critical comments over the volume of paperwork generated by the NVQ system once it was in place.

Particular criticism was levelled at the assessment procedure. Assessors tend to be drawn from the supervisory ranks, and their labour costs are therefore higher than the average; the assessment process rests upon repeated observation over time within the workplace, often requiring extreme detail. One training manager, working in a large public agency and otherwise highly enthusiastic about NVQs, said that 'we do have a responsibility to get the work done so we have to be careful that the tail isn't wagging the dog, and that our staff are actually working in the workplace.'

In another workplace (a Midlands pig station), it was clear that assessment by supervisors was functioning in quite a different way from that intended; so long as the supervisor was satisfied with trainees' performance at the level of overall output (in this instance, weaning piglets), they were simply ticking all the relevant boxes in the trainees' log books, with little concern for whether or not each particular unit of competence was being demonstrated in performance.

Flexibility of employment has been a hallmark of Government policy towards training for those in work. However, personnel managers saw things rather differently. One pointed out that although the new system was unit-based, thus allowing consumer choice in principle, in practice qualifications were only available for those who followed centrally prescribed routes:

> NVQs are supposed to be flexible but I find them quite rigid. For example, the way that they group their awards, like in Care – if you can't get one of the units you cannot get an award, so you have got to be able to prove yourself in a certain area, even if you are not involved in it. . . . In Mental Health Care, for example, one of the units is maintaining and control of stock and equipment – how they decide upon that as a unit for a Mental Health Care award I do not know! . . . In order for someone to pass that unit we are going to have to place them in a situation that they will never be in again in their job.

Another training manager was running simulation exercises in order to cover the range of competences required for the award. The phrase 'red tape' was constantly used to describe what most of our sample – admittedly very restricted – saw as needless rigidity in the system.

Finally, and ironically, personnel managers were concerned that the transparency of the NVQ system might encourage more labour flexibility than they deemed desirable. Underlying such views were two practical concerns. First, several interviewees said that the possession of NVQs might encourage employees actively to seek work elsewhere, contributing to a rise in labour turnover to damaging levels, particularly among the more motivated and highly qualified staff. Second, a number of interviewees feared that the NVQ system might foster 'unrealistic' expectations of promotion and career development among staff. One training manager argued that the nature of NVQs could be taken as encouraging stability rather than flexibility in the internal labour market, but he was alone in our sample in doing so. He expressed this view as follows:

> When people first came onto the scheme they thought they could aspire to a higher level and this isn't possible. The competence programmes are designed to enable people to demonstrate the competences in the job they are currently in, not for somebody to look higher because it just isn't possible if you haven't got the job role to demonstrate the competences.

More typical was the view that the possession of a transparent qualification encouraged staff to seek greater mobility; this was held to be undesirable, potentially creating conflicts over such issues as gradings of staff whose vocational qualification showed them to be working at a higher level than that at which they were paid.

As against the criticisms, there was of course also a number of perceived benefits. Those identified in the interviews included the fact that NVQs are workplace-based (and therefore subject to direct managerial control, as well as potentially facilitating cost-cutting); the quality assurance gains of training against defined national standards; the coherence of the new system; and NVQs' compatibility with modern strategies of human resource management (one public agency manager claimed that NVQs were a strand in the wider process of 'empowerment of field staff and the inversion of the pyramid', for instance). At the same time, no one had as yet been able to think of a way of quantifying the benefits; indeed, one manager – himself keen on NVQs – described his investment in the new system as representing 'a massive act of faith'. Thus the benefits remain to some extent uncertain and unproven; for most managers in our sample, NVQs are a 'motherhood' concept at the general level but this is hardly surprising given that the system was allegedly designed to meet their needs. What is more significant is the evidence that, even among this group who are actively involved in the NVQ system, the practical drawbacks are as salient as they are.

Given the nature of the NVQ system, it is reasonable to suppose that managers who express doubts are generally rational in their approach. Compared with time-based exams NVQs are indeed an expensive process; moreover, the charge is made visible and is direct to the employer (or sometimes the candidate), rather than being absorbed by the public education system (which anyway relies on the availability of the examiners willing to work for pin money). Costs can be avoided by short-circuiting the assessment procedures (like the pig station supervisor who assessed a trainee weaning every day for a week), but this then tends to devalue the currency. A study of companies in the leisure industry suggested that two-fifths of firms did not intend even to test the NVQ system because of the costs (*Times Educational Supplement*, 11 December 1992). Given the intensive nature of assessment and verification, there are substantial economies of scale in principle (Hawes, 1990); but these can only be triggered where a substantial group of candidates are submitting simultaneously. Where NVQs have a role in firms, it is frequently as a screen for initial recruitment; the expectation that the new recruit will pick up the job as they go along is apparently as strong as ever. While there is some evidence that trade unions are keen to use NVQs as a bargaining lever, training still tends to be seen as a supplementary item which can be 'traded off' during negotiations (Field and Weller, 1992).

It appears that NVQs have a limited market among companies, then. In so far as there has been sufficient demand to keep the system alive, it has been almost entirely created by the state. Central Government has focused its purchasing power in the training market in order to create a viable demand for NVQs; for example, limits on the use of youth credits, TEC funding for Youth and Adult Training and public funding for further education colleges have all been focused in this way. This has had the effect of creating an enormous demand for entry-level NVQs for younger people and the long-term unemployed; naturally, these are at levels and in sectors where there is a demand for new, usually young entrants. The Employment Department has also sought to encourage other government departments to use NVQs in personnel policies, but with more limited success; the Department of Health was among those who withdrew from the pilot scheme, allegedly as a cost-cutting measure. Demand for NVQs consists, then, largely of what might be called 'quasi-markets', created largely by the focused purchasing power of the state. Like other quasi-market systems, the costs of introduction and maintenance can be high; in the case of the TECs there have been persistent complaints of the detailed administration required in order to achieve performance-related funding (see also Hudson, 1992). The consequences can also be seen in the existing shape of the NVQ system: a handful of higher intermediate level NVQs in areas where a particular lobby has made itself felt (such as management development), and a mass of lower-level NVQs for newcomers and re-entrants to the labour market.

Of course, there are employers who are positive about NVQs and see them as contributing greatly towards their human resource strategies. Unwin's case study of Courtaulds Grafil is a case in point: the switch to a company-based system, which cost some £500,000 as part of a shift in the reward system for process operators (Unwin, 1991, pp. 174–80). However, this requires a longer-term view of human resource investments than is common in the UK – a point made by the company's chief executive. It also rests upon a desire to separate out a relatively homogeneous operative-level workforce, a specific context which will only apply in similar circumstances. Against this must be set the far more frequent complaints of employers that NVQs are too expensive and too complex.

VOCATIONAL QUALIFICATIONS AS A TOOL FOR POLITICAL MANAGEMENT

NVQs have developed then through a heavily sponsored quasi-market, and have been shaped in large part by the nature of that market. They are indeed driven by 'employment interests', but that broad term needs to be further defined. It is no easy matter to reconcile the abstract phrase 'employment interests' with the human reality of the industry lead bodies and the NCVQ. In practice, those who have led the system have been a very loose and broad coalition of enlightened civil servants, chiefly from within the Employment Department, together with professional training specialists, often with close commercial connections with the Employment Department, and with personnel managers in some of our larger companies. What this amounts to is a highly selective coalition which has sought to present itself as plausibly representing the interests of 'employment'. The system itself was created in a context of considerable concern over skills shortages, combined with politically driven attempts to erode Welfare State systems and increase the role of the market in the provision of services. Finally, it was created during the high point of the Manpower Services Commission's influence – an influence which has now itself been substantially, though far from fatally, weakened. It is against this background that the creation of the NVQ system must, I would argue, be understood, and its prospects for the future assessed.

In itself, the NVQ system represents an abstract design for a national standards-based qualifications system. Its design stage was undertaken in the relatively rarified atmosphere of the hotel and seminar circuit, involving a number of highly specialized studies of particular occupational groupings which were then translated into a series of behavioural objectives. Once the design stage was over, the products had to be brought to market. This process was dominated, and continues to be dominated, by the purchasing power of the State; the consequence is that the actual demand for NVQs continues to be dominated by particular policy imperatives. The most significant of these is the need to manage unemployment; thus the main market for NVQs has been among those Government agencies such as TECs and the Further Education Funding Council who provide full-time training for young people who are, or who would otherwise become, unemployed. Visibly, the consequence has been to skew demand towards those types of NVQ which are most in demand in that part of the market: essentially, lower-level NVQs in areas where the prospects of a successful outcome are highest. Demand among employers is higher in the public than in the private sector, and this too can be traced to government policy. Thus major government departments and agencies have been stimulated by advice and support from the development division of the Cabinet Office in elaborating their own proposals for introducing NVQs. Here there is more scope for widening the market for NVQs above Level 2, although it is notable that even in the public sector the largest market by far has been for Level 1 qualifications in the armed services. This downward drift may be helpful in political management in a number of ways, but it has little to do with generating a genuine demand for the product.

Rather, it seems that the market among employers for NVQs is limited because qualifications in themselves are the answer to a set of problems which employers neither recognize nor accept ownership over. This may well be inevitable: from the point of view of any individual employer, reform of the qualifications system may be a good thing in general, but in practical terms it has little to do with them in particular. Restructuring of the qualifications system may, by generating increased labour flexibility, even run counter to the wishes and aims of the individual employer; it is therefore only defensible as a public good, undertaken by the State as a counter-balance to the allegedly destructive consequences of an otherwise untrammelled market. The difficulty with NVQs is that they are presented as an employment-led qualifications system, which it is then claimed are offered on a market basis. In fact they are entirely a creation of the State. When implemented in actually existing work-places, they therefore appear to function in very different ways from those intended in the abstract by their designers.

Where does all this leave professional trainers and educators? First, from a purely pragmatic perspective, it seems reasonable to expect that involvement in NVQs represents a worthwhile investment of time and energy, at least so long as Government continues to back the NVQ bandwagon. In particular, the purchasing power of TECs, Government departments and the Further Education Funding Council is sufficient to ensure a market for NVQs of very substantial size. Second, it then follows that the market will be a skewed one. Demand will continue to be buoyant in areas where Government bodies make the purchasing decisions. Government will seek to influence the markets of individuals and private employers, for example by linking tax breaks for training expenditure to the purchase of NVQs; it remains to be seen whether these sweeteners will overcome the undoubted reluctance of these markets to purchase the product. Third, it also follows that the likely impact of NVQs upon the labour market will be to place limits on labour mobility and flexibility. In large parts of the labour market, and particularly the growth areas where polyvalency and multi-skilling are at a premium, NVQs play a very limited role. NVQs will continue to be widespread among those who have been on unemployed training programmes, studied full-time in further education, or work for Government departments and agencies, thus contributing further to labour market segmentation. Fourth, trainers and educators should be hard-headed about acquiring NVQs for themselves; while they may make for greater employability in certain labour markets at the present time, NVQs' association with low-level entry qualifications and training for the unemployed must ultimately affect their perceived status. Finally, it makes sense for educators and trainers to try to influence the content of NVQs, particularly where they impinge closely upon the fields of professional practice where trainers and educators are most directly involved. Given the dominance of professional trainers and modernizing civil servants in the construction of NVQs, it is not surprising that the system has proven itself open to influence from related groups such as academics or the management development industry to whom the NVQ movement sees itself as closely related. It is therefore reasonable to press for a more holistic and integrated concept of competence which would mark a further step away from the atomized, behaviourist and bureaucratic conception which so dominated the early thinking of the competence movement in Britain.

As things stand, current policy and practice in fact seem to have very little relationship with 'employment interests'. Rather, it seems that the main function of the NVQ initiative is to serve as a tool for policy management. Much as the training revolution of the 1980s was in fact concerned primarily with the political management of high unemployment levels, so the NVQ initiative appears to be chiefly an attempt to provide a visible response to poor economic performance and the associated public criticisms of the British training system. It is therefore not surprising that in the early stages, NVQs found so few purchasers outside the quasi-markets created by the State.

REFERENCES

Aldcroft, D. (1992) *Education, Training and Economic Performance, 1944 to 1990*. Manchester: Manchester University Press.

Allen, J. (1992) 'Fordism and modern industry'. In J. Allen, P. Braham and P. Lewis (eds) *Political and Economic Reforms of Modernity*. Cambridge: Polity.

Ashworth, P. D. and Saxton, J. (1990) 'On Competence'. *Journal of Further and Higher Education*, 14(2), 1-25.

Blackburn, R. M. and Mann, M. (1979) *The Working Class in the Labour Market*. London: Macmillan.

Dale, R. and Pires, E. (1984) 'Linking people and jobs: the indeterminate place of educational credentials'. In P. Broadfoot (ed.) *Selection, Certification and Control: Social Issues in Educational Assessment*. Lewes: Falmer.

Edwards, R. (1993) 'The inevitable future? Post-Fordism in work and learning'. In R. Edwards, S. Sieminksi and D. Zeldin (eds) *Adult Learners, Education and Training*. London: Routledge.

Field, J. (1991) 'Competency and the pedagogy of labour'. *Studies in the Education of Adults*, 23(1), 41-52.

Field, J. (1992) *Learning through Labour: Unemployment, Training and the State 1890-1939*. Leeds: Leeds University Press.

Field, J. (1993) 'Developments in vocational qualifications: emerging implications for industrial relations'. *The Industrial Tutor*, 5(7), 5-14.

Field, J. and Weller, P. (1992) 'Trade unions and human resource development'. *The Industrial Tutor*, 5(6), 41-8.

Hawes, B. W. V. (1990) *Verification of Work-place Assessment: Cost Indicators and Organisational Implications*. Sheffield: Employment Department.

HMSO (1984) *Training for Jobs*. London: HMSO.

Hodkinson, P. (1992) 'Alternative models of competence in vocational education and training'. *Journal of Further and Higher Education*, 16(2), 30-9.

Hudson, P. (1992) 'Quasi-markets in health and social care in Britain: can the public sector respond?' *Policy and Politics*, 20(2), 131-42.

Hyland, T. (1991) Taking care of business: vocationalism, competence and the enterprise culture. *Educational Studies*, 17(1), 77-87.

Hyman, R. (1991) 'Plus can change. The theory of production and the production of theory'. In A. Pollert (ed.) *Farewell to Flexibility*? Oxford: Blackwell.

Johnson, S. (1991) 'The small firm and the UK labour market in the 1980s'. In A. Pollert (ed.) *Farewell to Flexibility*? Oxford: Blackwell.

Kern, H. and Schumann, M. (1990) *Das Ende der Arbeitsteilung? Rationalisierung in der industriellen Produktion*. Munich: CH Beck.

Maguire, M., Maguire, S. and Felstead, A. (1993) *Factors Influencing Individual Commitment to Lifetime Learning*. Sheffield Employment Department.

MSC (1981) *A New Training Initiative*. Sheffield: MSC.

MSC/DFS (1985) *Review of Vocational Qualifications*. London: HMSO.

Marshall, K. (1991) 'NVQs: an assessment of the "outcomes" approach to education and training. *Journal of Further and Higher Education*, 15(3), 56-64.

Murray, R. (1989) 'Fordism and post-Fordism'. In S. Hall and M. Jacques (eds) *New Times: The Changing Face of Politics in the 1990s*. London: Lawrence and Wishart.

Ostenk, H. J., Moerkamp, T. and Dronkers, J. (1991) 'Broadly applicable occupational qualifications: a challenge for vocational education.' Conference on Learning Across the Life Span, University of Groningen.

Pollert, A. (ed.) (1991) *Farewell to Flexibility*? Oxford: Blackwell.

Ryan, P. (ed.) (1991) *International Comparisons of Vocational Education and Training for Intermediate Skills*. London: Falmer.

Shackleton, J. R. (1992) *Training too Much? A Sceptical Look at the Economics of Skill Provision in the UK*. London: Institute of Economic Affairs.

Short, E. (1984) 'Competence re-examined'. *Education Theory*, **34**(3), 201–7.

Unwin, L. (1991) 'NVQs and the Man-made Fibres Industry: a case study'. In P. Raggatt and L. Unwin (eds) *Change and Intervention: Vocational Education and Training*. London: Falmer.

Chapter 4

Behaviourism and the Meaning of Competence

Terry Hyland

INTRODUCTION

Although National Vocational Qualifications (NVQs) and the competence-based education and training (CBET) strategy which underpins them were introduced with the establishment of the National Council for Vocational Qualifications (NCVQ) in 1986 principally as a means of accrediting work-based vocational education and training (VET), the influence of the NCVQ approach has expanded exponentially with the growth of NVQs to the extent that CBET now has an influence on just about every sphere of education and training. It is argued that this strategy is seriously flawed and dangerously misguided, and should be challenged critically and forcefully by all educators and trainers committed to experiential learning and the rational development of knowledge, skills and understanding. Criticisms of the NCVQ model of CBET will be developed and illustrated through an examination of the impact of this approach on the work of professionals in post-school education, although I suggest that the main points are equally applicable to all forms of VET and professional education and training. Similarly, the alternative models suggested in the form of programmes based on expertise and reflective practice are intended as recommendations for professional education and development programmes in general.

THE EXPANDING INFLUENCE OF THE NCVQ

Since the idea of competence-based assessment seems to have originated in performance-based teacher education in America in the 1960s (Tuxworth, 1989), I suppose it was only a matter of time before its unremitting spread throughout the whole sphere of VET in Britain via the work of the NCVQ would extend to the professional preparation of teachers and lecturers. Although CBET strategies for school teacher education were reported to have been ruled out initially by the former DES (Jackson, 1991), the consultation document on the reform of initial teacher education issued in early 1992 contained ominous references to criteria which would 'place more emphasis on the achievement of professional competence' (DES, 1992, p. 3). More recently the DFE has been reported to be considering the sponsoring of research on competences and teacher training (*Times Educational Supplement*, 1992, p. 18) in the wake of circular 9/92 which required 'schools and students to focus on the competences of teaching' (DFE, 1992, p. 1).

In further and adult education, CBET strategies are now well established. The City and Guilds 730 Further and Adult Education Certificate course, the nationally recognized introductory route into further and adult education teaching, has been experimenting with competence-based modifications, not always successfully (Hyland, 1992a), since 1991, and similar strategies for the Certificate in Education for Further Education (FE) lecturers are now in operation in a number of regions (McAleavey and McAleer, 1991; and see Maynard, Chapter 10). In this latter area, the establishment of CBET approaches as an acceptable and legitimate foundation for the education, training and development of FE staff has been considerably aided by the Further Education Unit (FEU) which piloted and publicized widely its work with standards developed by the Training and Development Lead Body (TDLB). The results of the FEU field trials outline a range of competences to cover the assessing, lecturing, staff development and management roles undertaken by staff in the FE sector, with the suggestion that competences in the various areas will be accredited at Levels 3 and 4 (assessor/lecturer) of the NCVQ framework with a Level 5 category to cover staff development and management functions (FEU, 1992).

As Chown (1992, p. 56) rightly points out, the 'TDLB standards are about instruction and the supervision of training; they are not about teaching and education', and the fact that such significant and far-reaching changes in the professional preparation and development programmes for post-school staff can be so arbitrarily imposed in such a top-down manner with minimum consultation and negotiation is symptomatic of the underlying 'political' nature (Chown, 1992) of much of the so-called NVQ reforms. This is a process of educational change that has become only too familiar in the last decade or so. Gipps characterizes the approach as an 'impoverished process in which the think tanks (for example, Centre for Policy Studies, Adam Smith Institute) promote policy through strong value assertions and then proceed directly to detailed prescriptions. Argumentation is intuitive; there is an appeal at most to anecdotal evidence but not to research' (Gipps, 1993, p. 36). Although this description was written primarily with the various recent Government reforms of schooling in mind (a process described less kindly by Wragg [1993, p. 80] as 'Stalinist') it is nevertheless remarkably appropriate as an account of recent NVQ developments.

As mentioned above, it is worth remembering that NVQs were introduced principally as a way of accrediting work-based VET (Hyland, 1992b). They were originally intended to apply only to vocational areas and be 'independent of the mode of learning' (Jessup, 1991, p. 19) and assessed 'in the workplace' (NCVQ, 1988, p. v). Indeed, Fletcher (1991, p. 26) insists that 'NVQs have nothing whatsoever to do with training or learning programmes'. Increasingly, however, presumably so that they could be more easily sold to colleges, employers and other VET providers, NVQs came to be linked with specific BTEC or City and Guilds courses taught in colleges and assessed in simulated work environments.

Along with the growth of NVQs there has been an increasing tendency for CBET strategies to stray beyond the original sphere of VET which was their original and natural home. In addition to the forays into teacher education under discussion, NVQs have extended their remit downwards into schools through the BTEC First Diploma (Hyland, 1991) and upwards into higher education through the research on learning outcomes (Otter, 1992) and the various projects funded by the Employment Department to determine how National Standards (i.e. TDLB standards!) may be introduced into Master's courses (Glasgow University, 1992). Moreover, in response to the development of higher-level NVQs, we are told that a 'fundamental review of university provision is about to begin as the NCVQ spreads its influence into higher education' (Tysome, 1993, p. 3).

Since the CBET approach which underpins the NCVQ model is, as I will argue, not even remotely appropriate to the sort of teaching, learning and educational activity generally associated with all this work (Hyland, 1993a), the sudden and apparently effortless success of NCVQ interventionism is indeed remarkable. It becomes less so, however, in the light of the political processes already referred to. Central Government is now firmly and unequivocally behind the extension of the NVQ competence-based framework throughout all levels of the system. The NVQ framework was officially endorsed in the 1991 White Paper *Education and Training for the 21st Century* (DES, 1991), and since then the commitment has been extended and reinforced (Field, 1993). The position is made abundantly clear in recent DFE correspondence with the Further Education Funding Council in which it is stated that the 'Government is committed to implementing a framework of NVQs covering all employment sectors and at all levels. The Education Departments [*sic*] and the Department of Employment will continue to encourage the development and implementation of competence-based approaches' (DFE, 1993, p. 1). Moreover, there is every indication that this position is to be maintained in the face of all contrary research evidence (Nash, 1993).

THE POVERTY OF CBET

The unremitting spread of CBET practices is worrying and fully justifies the call by Collins (1991, p. 45) for concerted and vigorous 'resistance to this destructive approach to education and training'. Collins describes all CBET strategies as instances of a 'narrow technicist approach to education which defines knowledge in the light of bureaucratic and corporate needs'; such strategies, resulting in 'technocratic formulations and reductionistic competence-statements', have served to de-skill the educator's role and marginalize the vocational commitment of professionals (ibid.).

I want to argue that such criticisms can be applied equally to the TDLB standards currently being introduced throughout the post-school sector. Chown is broadly correct in describing these standards as the embodiment of a 'crude, political, five-level, perception of people, power, roles and functions (Chown, 1992, p. 56), and it is important to explain just why this is so in making a case against the use of the NCVQ-inspired framework in further education. My principal target will be the behaviourist foundation of the NCVQ model of CBET but, before examining this, it would be useful to summarize briefly some of the other key weaknesses and shortcomings of this model of education and training.

The NCVQ version of CBET is conceptually confused, epistemologically ambiguous and riddled with logical inconsistencies. In spite of its pivotal position in the system, there is considerable confusion and equivocation about what competence actually is. McAleavey and McAleer (1991, p. 20) are quite correct when they state that there 'is no agreed definition of competence'. Indeed, this is something of an understatement since definitions of competence 'abound in the literature' (UDACE, 1989, p. 15) and the term 'competence has different meanings to different people' (Debling and Hallmark, 1990, p. 9). All this was confirmed by the research of Haffenden and Brown (1989, p. 139) on the implementation of NVQs in FE colleges which reported a wide range of different conceptions in operation and a 'plethora of opinions about competence and its definition'. In a similar vein, the examination by Ashworth and Saxton of the concept of competence revealed serious ambiguities and inconsistencies. They concluded that competences were of 'unclear logical status' and that the meaning of competence had 'not yet been clearly defined'; in particular, 'it is not clear whether a competence is a personal attribute, an act, or an outcome of behaviour' (Ashworth and Saxton, 1990, pp. 3, 9).

There are clearly 'holistic' and 'minimalist' versions of competence (Hyland, 1993b) operating alongside each other in the theory and practice of NVQ assessment, and this might account for the fact that the terms 'competence' (competences) and 'competency' (competencies) are used interchangeably without explanation. However, there are good grounds for arguing that 'competence' is a broad capacity more properly applied to persons, whereas 'competency' refers to dispositions and is more applicable to tasks or activities (for the capacity/disposition distinction, see Carr, 1993).

Ashworth (1992) may be right to suggest that the NCVQ 'adopts an individualistic orientation by emphasising *personal* competences' (p. 8, original italics) but then goes on to talk about 'competencies' or 'elements of competence' (ibid, p. 9) as if there were no relevant distinctions to be made here. Since NVQs are based on occupational roles or functions, it might be thought that the broader capacity sense of the term was the more appropriate and, indeed, 'competent' is the favoured term in much of the discourse (although its use is unjustified). However, in view of the fact that the NCVQ model tends to fragment whole work functions into units and elements, it is more likely that it is 'competencies' or particular dispositions that are being picked out in much of the mainstream literature on NVQs (although the opacity and normal level of discourse discourages any serious search for precise meanings and distinctions!).

These questions of meaning and definition are neither trivial nor purely academic or pedantic. After all, how can a system which purports to be based on precise standards and explicit outcomes (Jessup, 1990, 1991) be allowed to get away with such confusion about the basic terms which are at the heart and foundation of the whole process? Moreover, the nature of particular concepts and categories is used to pick out concrete items and properties in the real world which educators and trainers wish to emphasize in relation to specific programmes of action. Questions of status and value are, thus, inextricably bound up with questions of meaning and application.

The equivocation over the meaning of competence in the NVQ assessment system is paralleled by fuzziness and ambiguity about the relationship between knowledge and competence. Wolf (1989, 1990) has criticized the incoherence of the NCVQ model in this respect and has attempted to outline an epistemological framework in which competence may be located. On this account, knowledge and understanding are said to be 'constructs which have to be inferred from observable behaviour, just as much as competence itself' (Wolf, 1989, p. 45). Certainly, there is a sense in which knowledge may be described as a 'construct', but we should avoid the tendency here to gloss over the fact that there is a world of difference between assessing the knowledge and understanding we hope to develop in, say, history or science, which needs to take account of a wide range of cognitive abilities, skills and values, and concentrating only on that knowledge which is thought to underpin competent performance.

Mansfield further defines the knowledge relevant to the assessment of competence in terms of 'outcome evidence', 'content evidence' and 'process evidence' (Mansfield, 1990, p. 19), and Bartram wants to distinguish between 'declarative knowledge' as a 'body of facts' and 'procedural knowledge', which 'can be inferred from one's actions' (Bartram, 1990, p. 55). However, if, as Wolf claims, both knowledge and competence are to be inferred from behaviour, how is it possible to distinguish between procedural and declarative knowledge on the grounds of inference from actions? For that matter, if both knowledge and competence are treated as behavioural constructs, how can it make sense to mark a division (as Wolf does in the 're-contextualized' version of NVQ assessment) between 'first order measures', which look at performance only, and 'second order measures' (Wolf, 1990, p. 34) which examine performance underpinned by knowledge and understanding?

All this confusion and equivocation seems to be the outcome of trying to capture and describe in behaviouristic terms something which is not altogether behaviourist, namely, the development of knowledge and understanding. In spite of the concessions made to knowledge and understanding in the newer 're-contextualized' accounts of competence assessment, the fundamental concern with performance and evidence is never far way. As Mansfield asserts, we begin to 'recognise and place knowledge in its rightful place' when we come to regard it 'as a source of evidence, along with performance evidence' (Mansfield, 1990, p. 20). Jessup might well admit that the 'relationship between knowledge, skills and competent performance are [sic] not well understood' (Jessup, 1991, p. 132). In order to maintain the desired contact with behaviour and observable performance, competence theorists have clearly been forced to manipulate knowledge so that it fits the desired framework. The upshot is a conception of knowledge, understanding and human agency which is not just viciously reductionist, but also utterly naïve and simplistic.

CBET, BEHAVIOURISM AND SOCIAL EFFICIENCY

Although, as noted earlier, the immediate origins of the NCVQ model can be found in the performance-based teacher education movement which was popular in the USA in the 1960s (although only briefly, thanks to the attacks of critics such as Smith, 1981 and Broudy, 1975; see also Hertzberg, 1976) its roots go back much further to the 'social efficiency' theorists who were dominant in American education at the beginning of the century. As Norris (1991, p. 338) notes in his wry comment on the origins of competence strategies, 'we have been here before and others have been here before us'. Among those 'others' must be included leading pioneers in the behavioural objectives field such as Tyler, Thorndike, Bloom and Popham. Tyler, in particular, has observed that his research in the 1920s on statistical techniques for evaluating teacher training curricula was inspired by the prevailing climate of opinion concerned with 'finding the competences of teachers and trying to focus on them' (ibid. p. 338). It is no accident that these ideas have been resurrected in this country in an educational climate characterized by greater control and accountability of teachers, market forces, consumer choice and overt policies of de-professionalization (Chitty and Simon, 1993).

The climate of opinion referred to by Tyler was established in the main by the theories of the 'social efficiency' school of educators such as Snedden and Prosser who criticized the educational practices of the early twentieth-century American public system and recommended instead a system of 'utilitarian training which looks to individual efficiency in the world of work'. The ultimate aim of such training was 'the greatest degree of efficiency' (Wirth, 1991, p. 57) and this was to be achieved by making schooling completely responsive to the needs of industry. These ideas were brought to full prominence by educators who, influenced by the Manual Training and Trade schools pioneered by Woodward in the nineteenth century (Lewis, 1991), sought to establish a no-nonsense vocationalism which tied schooling to the requirements of industry and commerce.

Taking the view that in the interests of 'social efficiency . . . it was the business of society to fit each individual to a station in life' (Lewis, 1991, p. 99), Snedden and Prosser (Snedden as Commissioner of Education in Massachusetts and Prosser as Secretary of the National Society for the Promotion of Industrial Education) propagated a view of 'real vocational education' based on 'training for useful employment' (Wirth, 1991, p. 58). The writings of these educators were 'marked by a conservative social philosophy, a methodology of specific training operations based on principles of S-R psychology, and a curriculum designed according to a job analysis of the needs of industry . . .' (ibid. p. 56).

The parallels between social efficiency philosophy and the more recent new vocationalism which surrounded the establishment of the NCVQ in 1986 are quite striking. All the essential ingredients of NVQs are present in the early American model: a conservative ideology, a foundation in behaviourist psychology and a determination to link vocational education to the specific requirements of industry. Little wonder that a movement which was constructed out of a 'fusion of behavioural objectives and accountability' (Fagan, 1984, p. 5) should come to provide the ideology for the neo-behaviourism of the NCVQ system which was to have such an irresistible appeal to those seeking control, accountability and input–output efficiency in the new economic realism of the 1980s.

COMPETENCE AND BEHAVIOURISM: A CRITIQUE

There is no denying or disputing the fact that the NCVQ model of CBET, both in terms of its design and implementation, is based on and informed by behaviourist learning theory. The connections have been explored by a number of writers (Ashworth and Saxton, 1990; Norris, 1991; Hodkinson, 1992) and it might be useful as a preliminary to cite some examples from the literature concerned with the learning foundations of the NCVQ system.

> Competency-based vocational education – just appearing in the UK from the US – is a good example of a system using behavioural objectives. In behaviourist ideology a Stimulus (S) is associated with a response (R) and a Stimulus–Response (S–R) bond formed. Competency-based vocational education involves students being trained to

associate SR so that, given the proper job cue (S), the appropriate occupational task will be performed (R).

(Bull, 1985, p. 74)

The [NCVQ] procedure is unashamedly behavioural. It is the outcome of the training which is to be assessed and the overt behaviour of the Trainee is the significant variable. The requirements of the performance criteria set out the parameters and performance is judged against those parameters. This procedure clearly draws upon the work of the classical behaviourist school of psychology. The work of Watson, Guthrie, Thorndike and Skinner is strongly represented.

(Marshall, 1991, p. 61)

The most prevalent construct of competence is behaviourist. It rests on a description of behaviour (sometimes called performance) and the situation(s) in which it is to take place (sometimes referred to as range statements) in a form that is capable of demonstration and observation.

(Norris, 1991, p. 332)

This behaviourist foundation of the NCVQ model accounts for at least some of its quite serious weaknesses in terms of the current requirements of the education and training system. A system which is characterized by a 'myopic perspective on needs' (Collins, 1991, p. 90), which is 'atomistic, individualistic and unable to cover all types of relevant behaviour or mental activity' (Ashworth and Saxton, 1990, p. 4) , and which 'even the most radical behavioural psychologist would not now subscribe to' (Marshall, 1991, p. 62) is a most unlikely vehicle for the upgrading of VET and the general upskilling of the workforce currently being called for by the alliance of educators and employers' organizations (Whiteside, *et al.* 1992). Such a system is also utterly inappropriate for programmes of preparation and development in teaching and other professional spheres, and it is important to state precisely just why this is so.

We can make a start with the standard criticisms of behaviourism found within general psychology which allude to its minimalist and impoverished conception of human thought and action, and its failure to account adequately for key aspects of human reasoning, understanding and learning (see, for example, Radford and Govier, 1980; Gross, 1987). In terms of its applications to education, there is a body of work within philosophy of education which points to the logical inconsistencies in behaviourist theory, the failure to distinguish fully between voluntary and involuntary action, and the generally mechanistic conception of human agency which informs much of behaviourist learning theory (Clark, 1979; Burwood and Brady, 1984).

Dearden (1984, p. 140) provides perhaps the clearest account of these criticisms and points to the 'absurd consequence of ignoring the understanding which accompanies and indeed importantly constitutes human behaviour'. Human behaviour is unintelligible without references to the context of learning and to the development of understanding, and this focuses attention on aspects of cognition and the nature of the learning process. Dearden goes on to argue that: 'what someone is doing and why he [sic] is doing it are unintelligible without reference to certain of his beliefs, desires, intentions, experiences, imaginings, attitudes, sentiments, or in general his understanding'. In so far as behaviourism is silent on these aspects of thinking and understanding, it is, therefore, inadequate as an educational theory and thus a 'theory of cognitive learning' is required (ibid. p. 142).

In terms of current research and knowledge about how students learn most effectively, particularly mature students, behaviourism simply does not match up to requirements. Examining work in the psychology of adult education, Tennant (1988, p. 117) notes that a 'reservation commonly expressed about behavioural objectives is that they fragment learning into narrowly conceived categories of behaviour'. Of particular interest is Tennant's discussion of behavioural objectives in terms of their suitability for the measurement of 'competence' (evidently interpreted in the broad capacity sense). In answer to the question 'Do behavioural objectives offer us the best method for measuring competence?', Tennant outlines four main reasons for believing that they do not (ibid. pp. 117–120):

(i)   the behavioural indicators of competence can rarely be determined in advance;
(ii) the emphasis on terminal outcomes undervalues the importance of the learning process;
(iii) not all learning outcomes are specifiable in behavioural terms;
(iv) learning may be occurring which is not being measured.

All these considerations lead Tennant to conclude that behaviourism is 'incompatible with the ethos of adult education' (ibid. p. 120).

I would go further than this and suggest that behaviourism is incompatible with *any* educational activity concerned with the development of knowledge, rationality and critical thinking.

COMPETENCE, NVQs AND LEARNING

A number of studies have indicated that the introduction of NVQs into certain vocational areas has led to a narrowing of focus, a loss of important theoretical knowledge and a de-skilling of occupational roles. Jarvis and Prais' study of training for retailing in France and Britain, for instance, concluded that the NCVQ's lower-level qualifications for these trades were too 'narrowly job-specific' and could lead to 'a section of the workforce inhibited in job-flexibility, and inhibited in the possibilities of progression' (Jarvis and Prais, 1989, p. 70). Similarly, Raggatt's study of NVQs in a number of vocational areas concluded that an 'inherent weakness' was that they were 'too occupationally specific' and 'provided no basis on which workers could transfer the competences that they develop to different occupational sectors' (Raggatt, 1991, p. 78). In the same vein, the study of NVQ implementation in the construction industry by Callender (1992) painted a picture of restrictive and mechanistic training, widespread de-skilling, a lack of co-ordination between courses and excessive narrowness of employer-defined competences. Too many NVQs in the area were found to be 'limited and too mechanistic'; often 'their educational content has been squeezed out along with pedagogic concerns' and the 'narrowness of employer-defined competence training highlights the conflict between the short-term needs of employers for very specific skills and the long-term interests and training needs of individual trainees, the industry and the economy' (Callender, 1992, p. 27).

These criticisms, also reflected in more recent studies by McHugh *et al.* (1993) and the widely publicized Smithers survey (Nash, 1993), must be a cause of grave concern for they indicate that NVQs are not even successfully delivering the goods in the area of work-based VET for which they were originally designed! The lack of educational and pedagogic content referred to by Callender becomes especially worrying as the NCVQ model extends its influence into adult, continuing and professional education. At these levels there is a clear mismatch between the behaviouristic foundation of CBET and the cognitive/experiential features of learning programmes concerned with the development of expert, committed and reflective practitioners in these spheres of work.

Experiential learning theory – an umbrella term bringing together a wide range of perspectives from humanistic psychology – has emerged as the preferred methodology within adult education (Mezirow, 1990) and, in a slightly more systematic and practical form, it is arguably the most influential model operating in the further education sector (Gibbs, 1988). Kolb (1993) offers a summary of the key features of the approach, noting distinctive emphases on learning as a continuous process grounded in experience, on the idea of holistic development through the resolution of conflicts and opposing viewpoints, and on the idea of learning as the creation of knowledge rather than the reinforcement of existing norms. All these ideas are brought together in the broad definition of experiential learning as the 'process whereby knowledge is created through the transformation of experience' (ibid. p. 155).

This conception of learning has striking similarities with the 'reflective practitioner' model (Schön, 1987) which has been so influential in recent years in teacher education and professional studies at all levels, and it also informs many of the dominant ideas and basic texts on professional development in further and adult education (see, for example, Minton, 1991, Kerry and Tollitt-Evans, 1992). For those who support such a conception of learning, CBET strategies must be regarded as anathema for they seem to be diametrically opposed to the tenets which are fundamental to this general approach. Instead of an holistic framework, CBET atomizes and fragments learning into assessable chinks; rather than valuing process and experience, CBET is concerned only with performance outcomes; and, most significantly, instead of encouraging critical reflection on alternative perspectives, CBET offers a mono-cultural view based on the satisfaction of narrow performance criteria and directed towards fixed and predetermined ends.

It is just these features of CBET which cause commentators such as Hodkinson, for instance, to suggest alternatives to the 'behaviouristic NCVQ model of competence' in the form of models which 'focus on beliefs and how we think, as well as on performance' and which view the teaching/learning process as 'central in the development of intelligent practice' (Hodkinson, 1992, pp. 34, 35). Certainly such alternative models are required in the area of professional education and development for there is a significant danger that, in reducing professional knowledge and skill to simplistic competence statements, professional development may be stifled as a result of the implication that competence is a once and for all achievement. It was just such a danger which prompted Eraut, in examining the suitability of the NVQ system for initial teacher education, to express the concern that, once trained, people might 'consider their competence as sufficient and ignore the need for further improvement' (Eraut, 1989, p. 181). What is required for professional and higher-level vocational courses is a model which allows for ongoing and continuous development and, in this respect, recent work on vocational 'expertise' seems to offer some valuable ideas.

In criticizing the NCVQ model, Eraut, following Dreyfus (1981), suggests instead a model of professional development which consists of a five-stage description of skill acquisition: novice advanced beginner, competent, proficient and expert (ibid. pp. 181–2). Unlike the NCVQ approach involving the assessment of competence at five discrete *levels* (NCVQ, 1991, p. 4), competence on this model is just one *stage* of development, and a 'competent' practitioner would only be around half-way to the realization of full potential in any particular occupational sphere.

This model of professionalism has been used successfully in the field of nurse education by Benner (1982), and Elliott (1989) has described a similar approach to the training of police officers. Incorporating such examples of good practice as 'empathising accurately with the concerns of others' and 'self-monitoring one's own conduct' (ibid. pp. 96–7), this expertise model seems to be particularly appropriate for courses of continuing professional development. The concept of expertise – defined by Tennant (1991, p. 50) as the 'knowledge and skill gained through sustained practice and experience' – has attracted wide attention in recent years and there is now a body of empirical work recording investigations in diverse occupational fields.

Summarizing a range of such studies, Chi *et al.* (1988) were able to identify a number of common characteristics of expertise evident across different spheres of activity. Experts were found to have a large amount of domain-specific knowledge, perceived large and meaningful patterns in their professional activity, were faster and more economical in judgement and decision-making and had strong self-monitoring skills. All of these characteristics seem to match well with the qualities of Schön's reflective practitioner mentioned earlier. However, in order to guard against professionals lapsing into the static role of 'infallible expert', Elliott (1991, p. 312) recommends in addition a commitment to the 'continuing reconstruction of . . . what constitutes relevant and useable knowledge' for 'shared reflection and dialogue with clients'.

Edwards (1993) has suggested recently that, in order to avoid being labelled as regressive Luddites, teachers in further and adult education need to formulate creative responses to NVQs in the form of programmes which can satisfy competence criteria and still foster active experiential learning. I would suggest that the perspectives offered by Hodkinson (1992), Eraut (1989) and Elliott (1991, 1993) represent such creative responses. Moreover, there are now good examples of development work in specific professional fields such as nurse education, medical education and social care which have attempted to locate NCVQ criteria within a framework which remains faithful to professional principles and practice.

Challis *et al.* (1993), for instance, recently completed a project which looked at ways of integrating competence outcomes within undergraduate medical training courses. The importance of using a wide range of assessment techniques and the maintenance of a primary emphasis on the specific professional context rather than the demands of the NCVQ system was clearly brought out in this research and confirmed in the project by Kelly *et al.* (1990) which looked at the implementation of NVQs in the field of social care. Criticizing the 'mechanistic' nature of standard NVQ procedures, the researchers urged professionals to secure 'ownership' of the change process and to stress the notion that 'NVQ needs to work for social care; not the other way around' (ibid. p. 94).

The NCVQ model is especially weak in relation to the teamwork and ethical dimensions of professional work. This debilitating 'individualism' of the competence model is picked out by Ashworth (1992) and by Chown and Last (1993) who also highlight the fact that NCVQ organization of functional outcomes into discrete units precludes the development of an 'overarching, integrating dimension of coherent professional practice' (ibid. p. 22). An attempt to remedy all these weakness can be found in the work of Winter (1992) on the ASSET programme, a competence-based degree-level qualification in social work developed by Anglia Polytechnic University in conjunction with Essex Social Services. Picking out inadequacies in the 'orthodox format' of the NCVQ approach (as represented by the competences specified in the Management Charter Initiative) such as insufficient attention to 'critical thinking' and lack of 'reference to any ethical dimension' of professionalism (ibid. pp. 107–8), Winter seeks to demonstrate that these deficiencies can be remedied by the incorporation of 'core assessment criteria' which give due attention to the knowledge, principles and values which characterize the work of professionals in the field. He concludes that the success of the programme resides in the fact that 'competences are not treated as product specifications but as learning goals'; and instead of 'quality standards' derived from an organizational mission statement there are 'educational criteria derived from an elaborated theory of the reflective practitioner' (ibid. p. 114).

CONCLUSION

The mechanical, atomistic and behaviouristic nature of CBET is at odds with the work of professionals and with the requirements of professional development. Criticisms of the TDLB have been referred to above, and similar criticisms of the 'behavioural-based approach' (Ramsay, 1993, p. 87) of the Management Charter Initiative are now emerging. Elliott (1993) offers a forceful analysis which provides a useful summary of the weaknesses of what he describes as the 'social market' model of professional development in which

> learning outcomes are conceived as behavioural, with an emphasis placed on the atomistic specification of discrete practical skills (competences). . . . The basic principle entailed by this social market perspective is that of behaviourism, with its implication that the significance of theoretical knowledge in training is a purely technical or instrumental one. Knowledge belongs to the realm of inputs rather than outputs. Its introduction can only be justified if it is a necessary condition for generating the desired behavioural outcomes of learning.
>
> (Elliott, 1993, p. 17)

Lecturers, trainers and other staff in the post-school sector committed to the development of professional knowledge, expertise and critical practice may legitimately claim to be interested in the outcomes as well as the learning processes and the knowledge and values constitutive of their fields of interest. This is perfectly proper so long as the outcomes in question do not overly predetermine content and methodology or foreclose learning options. Unfortunately, there is considerable evidence that CBET strategies simply *do* prescribe and restrict educational practice in just such a way.

As the TDLB standards are introduced into staff development programmes in further education and other spheres of education and training, it will be vital to ensure that the worst excesses of CBET are tempered by the critical and reflective dimensions of the models of professionalism recommended above. The NCVQ approach is concerned first and foremost with the generation and collection of *evidence* to satisfy competence criteria and, although this may be a useful activity, it needs to be distinguished sharply from the activity of *learning* and professional development. Programmes of professional education need to maintain a primary focus on learning *per se* rather than as evidence collected to meet competence requirements.

REFERENCES

Ashworth, P. (1992) 'Being competent and having "competencies"'. *Journal of Further & Higher Education*, **16**(3), 8–17.

Ashworth, P. and Saxton, J. (1990) 'On competence.' *Journal of Further & Higher Education*, **14**(1), 3–25.

Bartram, D. (1990) 'An appraisal of the case for adaptive assessment of knowledge and understanding in the delivery of competence-based qualifications.' In H. Black and A. Wolf (eds) *Knowledge and Competence: Current Issues in Training and Education*. Sheffield: Careers and Occupational Information Centre.

Benner, P. (1982) 'From novice to expert.' *American Journal of Nursing*, **82**(3), 402–7.

Broudy, H. (1975) *Towards a Theory of Vocational Education*. Columbus, Ohio: National Centre for Research in Vocational Education.

Bull, H. (1985) 'The use of behavioural objectives.' *Journal of Further & Higher Education*, **9**(1), 74–80.

Burwood, L. and Brady, C. (1984) 'Changing and explaining behaviour by reward.' *Journal of Philosophy of Education*, **18**(1), 109–14.

Callender, C. (1992) *Will NVQs Work? Evidence from the Construction Industry*. University of Sussex: Institute of Manpower Studies.

Carr, D. (1993) 'Questions of competence.' *British Journal of Educational Studies*, **41**(3), 253–71.

Challis, M., Underwood, T. and Joesbury, H. (1993) 'Assessing specified competences in medical undergraduate training.' *Competence & Assessment*, **22**, 6–9.

Chi, M., Glaser, R. and Farr, M. (1988) *The Nature of Expertise*. Hillsdale, New Jersey: Lawrence Erlbaum Associates.

Chitty, C. and Simon, B. (eds) (1993) *Education Answers Back*. London: Lawrence & Wishart.

Chown, A. (1992) 'TDLB standards in FE.' *Journal of Further & Higher Education*, **16**(3), 52–59.

Chown, A. and Last, J. (1993) 'Can the NCVQ model be used for teacher training?' *Journal of Further & Higher Education*, **17**(3), 15–26.

Clark, C. (1979) 'Education and behaviour modification.' *Journal of Philosophy of Education*, **13**, 73–82.

Collins, M. (1991) *Adult Education as Vocation*. London: Routledge.

Dearden, R. F. (1984) *Theory and Practice in Education*. London: Routledge & Kegan Paul.

Debling, G. and Hallmark, A. (1990) 'Identification and assessment of underpinning knowledge.' In H. Black and A. Wolf (eds) *Knowledge and Competence: Current Issues in Training and Education*. Sheffield: Careers and Occupational Information Centre.

DES (1991) *Education and Training for the 21st Century*. London: HMSO.

DES (1992) *The Reform of Initial Teacher Education*. London: Department for Education and Science.

DFE (1992) *Initial Teacher Training (Secondary Phase) Circular 9/92*. London: Department for Education.

DFE (1993) *NVQs: Lead Bodies and the Education Service*. Correspondence to the FEFC, 27 July 1993. London: Department for Education.

Dreyfus, S. E. (1981) *Four Models v. Human Situational Understanding: Inherent Limitations on the Modelling of Business Expertise*. US Air Force Office of Scientific Research, Contract No. 749620-79-C-0063.

Edwards, R. (1993) 'A spanner in the works: Luddism and competence.' *Adults Learning*, **4**(5), 124–5.

Elliott, J. (1989) 'Appraisal of performance or appraisal of persons.' In H. Simon and J. Elliott (eds) *Rethinking Appraisal and Assessment*. Milton Keynes: Open University.

Elliott, J. (1991) 'A model of professionalism and its implications for teacher education.' *British Educational Research Journal*, **17**(4), 309–18.

Elliott, J. (ed.) (1993) *Reconstructing Teacher Education*. London: Falmer Press.

Eraut, M. (1989) 'Initial teacher training and the NCVQ model.' In J. W. Burke (ed.) *Competency Based Education and Training*. Lewes: Falmer Press.

Fagan, E. (1984) 'Competence in educational practice: a rhetorical perspective.' In Short, E. (ed.) *Competence: Inquiries into its Meaning and Acquisition in Educational Settings*. New York: University of America Press.

FEU (1992) *Consultation on Qualifications Based on TDLB Standards* (RP712). London: Further Education Unit.

Field, J. (1993) 'Still waiting for the spring offensive.' *College Management* **1**(5), 5–6.

Fletcher, S. (1991) *NVQs, Standards and Competence*. London: Kogan Page.

Gibbs, G. (1988) *Learning By Doing*. London: Further Education Unit.

Gipps, C. V. (1993) 'Policy-making and the use and misuse of evidence.' In C. Chitty and B. Simon (eds) *Education Answers Back*. London: Lawrence & Wishart.

Glasgow University (1992) *National Standards for Training and Development within Masters Programmes*. University of Glasgow: Department of Education.

Gross, R. D. (1987) *Psychology*. London: Arnold.

Haffenden, I. and Brown, A. (1989) 'Towards the implementation of NVQs in colleges of FE.' In J. W. Burke (ed.) *Competency Based Education and Training*. Lewes: Falmer Press.

Hertzberg, H. W. (1976) 'Competency based teacher education: does it have a past or a future?' *Teachers College Record*, **78**(1), 1–21.

Hodkinson, P. (1992) 'Alternative models of competence in vocational education and training.' *Journal of Further & Higher Education*, **16**(2), 30–9.

Hyland, T. (1991) 'Vocational studies that won't work.' *Times Educational Supplement*, 20 September 1991.

Hyland, T. (1992a) 'Expertise and competence in further and adult education.' *British Journal of In-Service Education*, **18**(1), 23–8.

Hyland, T. (1992b) 'NVQs and the reform of vocational education and training.' *Journal of the National Association for Staff Development*, **26**(1), 29–36.

Hyland, T. (1993a) 'Outcomes and competence in higher education.' *Educational Change and Development*, **13**(2), 5–8.

Hyland, T. (1993b) 'Competence, knowledge and education.' *Journal of Philosophy of Education*, **27**(1), 57–68.

Jackson, B. (1991) 'Vocational council snubbed.' *Times Educational Supplement*, 13 December 1991.

Jarvis, V. and Prais, S. (1989) 'Two nations of shopkeepers; training for retailing in France and Britain.' *National Institute Economic Review*, **128**, 58–75.

Jessup, G. (1990) 'National vocational qualifications: implications for further education.' In M. Bees and M. Swords (eds) *NVQs and Further Education*. London: Kogan Page/NCVQ.

Jessup, G. (1991) *Outcomes: NVQs and the Emerging Model of Education and Training*. London: Falmer Press.

Kelly, D., Payne, C. and Warwick, J. (1990) *Making National Vocational Qualifications Work for Social Care*. London: National Institute.

Kerry, T. and Tollitt-Evans, J. (1992) *Teaching in Further Education*. Oxford: Blackwell.

Kolb, D. (1993) 'The process of experiential learning.' In M. Thorpe, R. Edwards and A. Hanson (eds) *Culture and Processes of Adult Learning*. London: Routledge/Open University.

Lewis, T. (1991) 'Difficulties attending the new vocationalism in the USA.' *Journal of Philosophy of Education*, **25**(1), 95–108.

Mansfield, B. (1990) 'Knowledge, evidence and assessment.' In H. Black and A. Wolf (eds) *Knowledge and Competence: Current Issues in Training and Education*. Sheffield: Careers and Occupational Information Centre.

Marshall, K. (1991) 'NVQs: an assessment of the outcomes approach to education and training.' *Journal of Further & Higher Education*, **15**(3), 56–64.

McAleavey, M. and McAleer, J. (1991) 'Competence-based training.' *British Journal of In-Service Education*, **17**(1), 19–23.

McHugh, G., Fuller, A. and Lobley, D. (1993) *Why Take NVQs?* Lancaster University: Centre for the Study of Education and Training.

Mezirow, J. (1990) 'A critical theory of adult learning and education.' In M. Tight (ed.) *Adult Learning and Education*. London: Routledge.

Minton, D. (1991) *Teaching Skills in Further and Adult Education*. London: City & Guilds/Macmillan.

Nash, I. (1993) 'UK set for training "disaster".' *Times Educational Supplement*, 17 December 1993.

NCVQ (1988) *Initial Criteria and Guidelines for Staff Development*. London: National Council for Vocational Qualifications.

NCVQ (1991) *Criteria for National Vocational Qualifications*. London: National Council for Vocational Qualifications.

Norris, N. (1991) 'The trouble with competence.' *Cambridge Journal of Education*, **21**(3), 331–41.

Otter, S. (1992) *Learning Outcomes in Higher Education*. London: FEU/Unit for the Development of Adult Continuing Education.

Radford, J. and Govier, F. (1980) *A Textbook of Psychology*. New York: Sheldon Press.

Raggatt, P. (1991) 'Quality assurance and NVQs.' In P. Raggatt and L. Unwin (eds) *Change and Intervention: Vocational Education and Training*. London: Falmer Press.

Ramsay, J. (1993) 'The hybrid course: competences and behaviourism in higher education.' *Journal of Further & Higher Education*, **17**(3), 70–89.

Schön, D. (1987) *Educating the Reflective Practitioner: Towards a New Design for Teaching and Learning in the Professions*. San Francisco: Jossey-Bass.

Smith, R. A. (ed.) (1981) *Regaining Educational Leadership*. New York: John Wiley.

Tennant, M. (1988) *Psychology and Adult Learning*. London: Routledge.

Tennant, M. (1991) 'Expertise as a dimension of adult development.' *New Education*, **13**(1), 49–55.

TES (1992) 'Government consults on training.' *Times Educational Supplement*, 18 September 1992.

Tuxworth, E. (1989) 'Competence based education and training: background and origins.' In J. W. Burke (ed.) *Competency Based Education and Training*. Lewes: Falmer Press.

Tysome, T. (1993) 'Vocational take-over bombshell.' *Times Higher Education Supplement*, 8 October 1993.

UDACE (1989) *Understanding Competence*. Leicester: Unit for the Development of Adult Continuing Education.

Whiteside, T. *et al.* (eds) (1992) *16–19 Changes in Education and Training*. London: David Fulton.

Winter, R. (1992) '"Quality management" or the "educative workplace": alternative versions of competence-based education.' *Journal of Further & Higher Education*, **16**(3), 100–15.

Wirth, A. G. (1991) 'Issues in the vocational–liberal controversy (1900–1917).' In D. Corson (ed.) *Education for Work*. Clevedon: Multilingual Natters Ltd.

Wragg, T. (1993) 'Ruled by the free market Stalinists.' *Times Educational Supplement*, 5 February 1993.

Wolf, A. (1989) 'Can knowledge and competence mix?' In J. W. Burke (ed.) *Competency Based Education and Training*. Lewes: Falmer Press.

Wolf, A. (1990) 'Unwrapping knowledge and understanding from standards of competence.' In H. Black and A. Wolf (eds) *Knowledge and Competence: Current Issues in Training and Education*. Sheffield: Careers and Occupational Information Centre.

Chapter 5

Professionalism and Competence

Phil Hodkinson

The debate about competence in this book is focused on the structures and conceptions of NCVQ, because their principles and procedures dominate both literature and practice in the United Kingdom. However, other conceptions of competence are possible (Elliott, 1991; Hodkinson, 1992). In this chapter I argue that the NCVQ model over-simplifies the nature of professional role performance and the contexts in which it takes place. To demonstrate this, I first explore a culturally grounded view of personal and professional development and compare the simplistic assumptions of NCVQ to it. I then go on to explore the possibilities for using competence attributes of a rather different character.

Recent work in social science sees the social world as complex, rapidly changing and reflexive. For some, the current situation is merely an extension of modern times, usually seen as beginning with the Enlightenment. Giddens (1990, 1991), for example, talks of 'late modernity'. For others, there is a substantive difference between an older modernity and the post-modernity they claim has now replaced it (Harvey, 1989; Beck, 1992). It is not my purpose here to engage in this complex debate. I merely wish to present some of the simpler principles of Giddens' analysis of late modernity to point up the inadequacy of a simplistic, technically rational view of competence and professionalism, and to draw from this rather different picture of the social world some suggestions for re-examining these issues.

LATE MODERNITY AND SELF-ACTUALIZATION

In analysing late modernity, Giddens (1990, 1991) claims that there is a dynamic interaction between the individual and social systems. He identifies

> the emergence of new mechanisms of self-identity which are shaped by – yet also shape – the institutions of modernity. The self is not a passive entity, determined by external influences; in forging their self-identities, no matter how local their specific contexts of action, individuals contribute to and directly promote social influences that are global in their consequences and implications.
>
> (Giddens, 1991, p. 2)

In this way, he claims, modernity is fundamentally reflexive. Individuals, institutions and culture are constantly changing through dialectical processes. Furthermore,

> One of the most obvious characteristics separating the modern era from any other period preceding it is modernity's extreme dynamism. The modern world is a 'runaway world': not only is the *pace* of social change much faster than in any prior system, so also is its *scope*, and the *profoundness* with which it affects preexisting social practices and modes of behaviour.
>
> (Giddens, 1991, p. 16)

This changing society offers individuals wider choices than would have been the case in more traditional societies. Thus, for example, there is choice over sexual and family relationships, resulting in a wide diversity of practice, so that self-actualization is an ongoing, reflexive process:

> The reflexive project of the self, which consists in the sustaining of coherent, yet continuously revised, biographical narratives, takes place in the context of multiple choice filtered through abstract systems. In modern social life, the notion of lifestyle takes on a particular significance. The more tradition loses hold, and the more daily life is reconstituted in terms of the dialectical interplay of the local and the global, the more individuals are forced to negotiate lifestyle choices among a diversity of options.
>
> (Giddens, 1991, p. 5)

Social structure restricts and enables these choices, but never totally eliminates them.

Giddens argues that self-actualization is a central and unavoidable facet of late modernity, and that its development, though strongly influenced by structural and cultural factors, retains a significant element of personal choice. For those working in the caring professions, self-actualization is important in two complementary ways. First, their own professional performance is rooted in their own identity (or, as some would have it, identities). Secondly, they are intimately concerned, in their work, with the self-actualization of others, be they pupils, other clients, or colleagues with whom they work, either in the same professional area or related ones.

CULTURE, SCHEMA AND HABITUS

Self-actualization can usefully be seen as deriving from culture. I am using 'culture' to describe the socially constructed and historically derived common base of knowledge, values and norms for action that people grow into and come to take as a natural way of life. In relation to such a view of culture, Clarke *et al.* (1981, pp. 52–53) claim 'a culture includes the "maps of meanings" which makes things intelligible to its members . . . Culture is the way the social relations of a group are structured and shaped; but it is also the way those shapes are experienced, understood and interpreted.' In this way, people make sense of the world they inhabit. Bourdieu uses the broader concept of 'habitus', rather than 'maps of meanings', to encapsulate the ways in which a person's schematic beliefs, ideas, preferences, etc., are both individually subjective but also formed by the objective social networks and cultural traditions in which that person lives. Habitus is 'that system of dispositions which acts as a mediation between structure and practice' (Bourdieu, 1977, p. 487).

Current work in social psychology on the nature of learning can help us take this a little further. From childhood, people amass schemata which serve as tools for understanding aspects of their experiences (Rumelhart, 1980). A schema structures what a person knows of the world, by filtering out irrelevancies and allowing sense to be made of partial information. In this way, two lights seen from a car in the dark can be turned into a cat or an approaching vehicle. A repertoire of schemata makes up the stock of knowledge in hand. As new experiences are gained, schemata are modified and developed and as they change so does what is recognized in the surrounding world.

Brown *et al.* (1989) argue that when we learn, concepts, actions and context are intricately interrelated. Knowledge and understanding do not simply underpin performance; the two are dialectically related and both are further related to the situation in which the activity takes place. To change any part of this complex web will cause changes elsewhere. Competence varies, chameleon-like, depending on who is performing, when and where.

As life progresses, although we cannot escape our past, changes in what we do or the context within which we do it alter what we know and understand. It also follows that if our schematic view of the world changes, this in turn alters the way in which we perceive the context in which we live and the actions that we take. In this dialectical way, the life history of the individual shapes and is shaped by his/her common-sense experience and horizons for action. By 'horizons for action' I mean what is possible, including that which is perceived as possible. In choosing any action, or in responding to the actions or initiatives of others, an individual uses his/her own schematic habitus. Habitus is, therefore, a result of a complex dialectical or reflexive interaction of the personal and the cultural or subcultural, with the contexts, experiences and actions undertaken, and with the structures of society as they are experienced.

This analysis suggests that, far from being a reified, definable and technical process, the performance of a caring professional, such as a teacher or social worker, is influenced by the life history and habitus of that professional, the context in which he/she works and his/her interactions with other workers, professionals, pupils or clients, each of whom also acts in ways influenced by the context, their own life histories and habitus and the actions of the professional with whom we started. What is more, these interactions are also influenced by social and institutional structures, which result in different stakeholders in the interactions wanting different things and having different priorities, while also possessing differing amounts of what Bourdieu called capital – cultural, symbolic and economic – which in turn gives differing potential power, which in turn is based partly on that distribution of capital. This whole, complex system is constantly changing, and changes to any one small part may have, often unpredicted and unmeasurable, influences on others.

In the realm of education, Brause (1992) shows how, in a typical American school, the perceptions of different managers, teachers and pupils interact together in an institutional context, in such a way that the combined effect is schooling that the majority of pupils 'endure', rather than enjoying or really learning from. She argues that anything less than the complex, holistic picture over-simplifies problems to the extent that action directed at one part in isolation from the rest is often ineffective and sometimes counter-productive. It is this holistic and dynamic complexity which the simplistic NCVQ competence model fails to address in numerous important ways.

THE INADEQUACY OF TECHNICALLY RATIONAL MANAGERIALISM

Such a view of the work of caring professionals raises questions about the currently rampant managerialism upon which NCVQ conceptions of competence are based. The links between technical rationality and managerialism are well known at a theoretical level (Habermas, 1971, 1972; Grundy, 1987). The links between NCVQ structures and managerial control can be seen in a variety of ways. The activity of the professional (or, indeed, any other worker) is prescribed by detailed standards of performance, determined by the lead bodies. Other conceptions of the role are outlawed, at least in relation to the achievement of the qualification upon which training and progression are to be based. The tight control of performance indicators for each unit and element of competence is a further manifestation of top-down managerialism, as is the complex verification process which is used to check the assessment processes. Often, for the individual worker, it is the line manager who carries out the assessment. As the NCVQ model develops, new occupational schemes have to adopt the competence units already designed for other areas, where titles are superficially similar. Increasing government insistence that funded courses must use the NCVQ competence structure reinforces the managerial approach. Finally, with its insistence on individual performance, the NCVQ approach focuses all the responsibility for professional activity on the isolated teacher or social worker. This underestimates the importance of collaborative and collective versions of competence, ignores power inequalities and (micro-) political struggles which have a major impact on the nature of professional provision, deflects attention from problems of context and makes it easy to blame the individual professional for any shortcomings in the system.

In relation to education, Ball (1990) argues that managerialism is neither inevitable nor neutral.

> The unchallengeable position of management effectively renders discussion of other possibilities for organisation mute. ... Management plays a key role in the ongoing process of reconstructing the work of teaching. ... In effect, control is to be exerted over teachers' work by the use of techniques of management ... Teachers are increasingly subject to systems of administrative rationality that exclude them from an effective say in the kind of substantive decision-making that could equally well be determined collectively.
>
> (Ball, 1990, p. 53)

Furthermore, the discourse based on management does not deal with all members of an institution equally, because

> concepts like efficiency are treated as though they were neutral and technical matters, rather than being tied to particular interests. The question of 'efficiency for whom?' is rarely asked. Efficiency itself is taken as self-evidently a good thing. The costs involved for workers in achieving greater efficiency (intensification, loss of autonomy, closer monitoring and appraisal, non-participation in decision-making, lack of personal development through work) are rarely considered.
>
> (Ball, 1990, p. 154)

Ball's analysis of managerialism, and therefore of any competence system derived from the same principles, is worrying for anyone concerned for the well-being of teachers and other caring professionals, not least because it disempowers the very people who have to provide a professional service. I will return to this point later, when examining the nature of professionalism further.

What is more, there is evidence from other sources that such managerial, technically rational approaches do not work in the ways their originators intended, even when evaluated in their own terms. Given the culturally and historically grounded complexity of social life, this is hardly surprising. Elliott (1991) reminds us that earlier attempts at competence-based teacher training in the USA in the 1970s were progressively abandoned. Work on innovation in schools consistently shows that top-down, managerial attempts to bring about change are largely ineffective, because they over-simplify the change process and ignore the cultural and personal transformations necessary if changes are to be 'owned' and absorbed (Rudduck, 1991). As Fullan notes,

> Change is a highly personal experience – each and every one of the teachers who will be affected by change must have the opportunity to work through this experience in a way in which the rewards at least equal the cost. The fact that those who advocate and develop changes get more rewards than costs, and those who are expected to implement them experience more costs than rewards, goes a long way to explaining why the more things change, the more they remain the same.

> (Fullan, 1991, p. 27)

Capper and Jamison (1993) show how the attempted use of the sophisticated industrial management tool, Total Quality Management (TQM), failed in improving quality for those members of the school population who were already disadvantaged. Rather the analysis resulted in suggestions to improve school performance by controlling the intake, in effect shifting responsibility for pupil failure on parents and the home background rather than the school. As well as illustrating some of the inadequacies of even the most sophisticated forms of managerialism, their article serves as a reminder that performance in the caring professions is intimately bound up in the needs of a widely diverse group of pupils or clients.

PROFESSIONALISM

In the opening chapter of this book, Hodkinson and Issitt suggested that concepts of profession usually contain notions of status preservation and boundary management through rites of passage. In Bourdieu's (1984) terms, professional structures are mechanisms to preserve and emphasize 'distinction' for those who belong. They are a means of maximizing capital, especially symbolic and cultural capital. As such, stronger traditional professions, such as law or medicine, control the discourse which in turn determines how some other groups see the field. As such, they exclude other professions, some of which might have valuable roles to play in the furthering of client interests. In teaching, such professional boundary maintenance and status protection occurs within the school between different teacher groups. Goodson (1984) and Sparkes (1990) show how subject status is of vital importance in the micro-politics of a secondary school.

A key purpose of this book, therefore, is to separate notions of professionalism from the ultimately divisive and self-serving activities of such professional groups. In attempting to do this, I am not advocating some utopia where we all stop defending our own interests, for Bourdieu would argue that the search for distinction is fundamental to social activity. But it is possible to base principles of practice and education in the caring professions around the conception of professionalism, without necessarily accepting the exclusivity of a profession. In the context of the argument thus far presented, a professional approach to teaching, social work or other similar caring roles, can be based on the principles of service to others, the striving for expertise, the empowerment of workers, both as individuals and collectively, and the adoption of a moral code. Each of these elements is complex, contested and controversial in ways that cannot be fully explored here. At this point, I simply wish to use such a model of professionalism as a tool to explore conceptions of competence rather different from that of the NCVQ. It is necessary, first, briefly to elaborate the model.

The prime focus of those working in the caring professions should be the service they provide to the clients and pupils they work with. The fundamental place of equality of opportunity issues in this agenda is explored by Issitt in Chapter 6. She and Jones (Chapter 7) stress the problematic and complex nature of providing such service in social work, and Harvard and Dunne (Chapter 11) show how in teaching, professional decision-making in the classroom is equally complex. As Giddens' analysis of late modernity stresses, we all have choices. Part of being professional is to deliberately maximize those (work-related) choices available to us in the best interests of the people we are employed to help. To be a professional means to develop expertise, in order to provide a high-quality service for society and for individual clients and pupils. The development of such expertise involves professional growth and independence. I choose to call such growth 'empowerment', for though this is now a highly contested term (Gore, 1992; Hodkinson, 1994), I can think of no other which is better. Empowerment, as used here, means maximizing the potential for action within whatever structural, economic or cultural constraints pertain. Such empowerment is inadequate on its own, for it is amoral and, in the complex world of social relations, neutrality is impossible. Hence there is a need for a clear moral and ethical dimension to professionalism, linked back to the original emphasis on service.

While always remembering that they must be positioned within clear ethical guidelines and focused on service, it is now helpful to examine empowerment and expertise a little further. I have argued elsewhere (Hodkinson, 1994) that empowerment is used in different ways by different groups. For believers in 'new right' individualism, empowerment was simply a matter of removing supposedly impeding legislations and regulation to allow 'free choice'. In vocational education and training, the main focus is on *doing*. For a period in the 1980s, it was fashionable to talk about 'enterprise', or the ability to 'make things happen'. Although this was usually linked explicitly to small-business growth and profit-making, I argued that the central idea could be separated from such ideological overtones, and be related to non-commercial activities such as running a playgroup, organizing a football team or planning a political demonstration. To distance myself from the overtones of enterprise, I labelled this form of empowerment *personal effectiveness*. On the other hand, to liberal educators, a sense of *critical autonomy* is the fundamental concern. Such thinkers do not use the term empowerment as such, but talk about the growth of autonomy. In the ongoing educational debates, such groups are highly suspicious of the practical forms of empowerment, which are perceived as maintaining the status quo, by rendering the question 'why?' silent in place of (for them) the less important question 'how?'. For others, empowerment is fundamentally a collaborative activity. For example, Ward and Mullender (1991) argue for what could be described as a mixture of personal effectiveness and critical autonomy, operating at group level as, for example, groups of women combine to combat the causes of oppression with communal action. Critical theorists are deeply suspicious of the individualism in empowerment, seeing it as a smoke screen which hides the real issues of power and inequality, and makes it easy to blame victims for their own misfortune.

While accepting that structural causes of inequality must also be addressed, I have further argued (Hodkinson and Sparkes, 1993; Hodkinson, 1994) that empowerment, as defined here, should be a holistic concept, including many of these different perspectives, which are complementary rather than mutually exclusive. This holistic version of empowerment can been seen as having three overlapping dimensions. They are personal effectiveness, critical autonomy and community. *Personal effectiveness* has already been described. An empowered professional should be able to perform expertly in a variety of situations, including the novel. This is predominantly what I take Schön (1983, 1987) to mean by reflective practice. Competence relates to personal effectiveness, but does not always address its essential proactive, initiating component. *Critical autonomy* describes the ability to think critically about one's own practice, the context in which that practice takes place, the purposes of that practice, the moral and ethical values which do/should underpin that practice. It is this dimension of empowerment that largely distinguishes the professional from the technician. *Community* is a clumsy term for that other essential dimension to professional empowerment, which takes it beyond the purely individual. It concerns teamwork and working with others, together with an understanding of the communities in which practice takes place. This includes recognizing conflicts between interest groups and the micro-politics that influence all our work. This holistic model of professional empowerment challenges the assumptions of managerialism that there are two distinctly different groups: managers, who consider broader issues of policy and context, and workers, who simply perform. The dimensions of critical autonomy and community remind us of the breadth of professional empowerment. All are essential to professionalism in their own right, for they complement performance, rather than being merely necessary for it.

Dreyfus (1981) gives a detailed analysis of what he calls expertise. He suggests that we can see professional development as progressing through five stages: novice, advanced beginner, competent, proficient and expert. Elliott (1991) suggests that this model might be adapted to develop a differing view of competence. Thus, it might be possible to define the attributes of competence and different levels of expertise. While Dreyfus saw these as developmental stages, they could also be seen as ways of distinguishing the quality of performance exhibited by experienced professionals. Elliott (1991), citing Spencer (1979), elaborates a procedure for analysing performance along these lines. Having consulted existing practitioners to identify a selection of the 'most effective performers of the job', hypothesized characteristics are developed to distinguish between superior and average performance. These differences then become the basis for identifying attributes of competence.

Klemp (1977) identifies three clusters of abilities that are commonly exercised by above-average performers in a range of occupations. These are 'cognitive abilities', 'interpersonal abilities' and types of 'motivation'. Although he claims these clusters can be applied in a range of professions, he does not see them as decontextualized transferable skills, but as situated understanding within the culture and context in which a professional is working. The cognitive abilities include discerning thematic consistencies, understanding controversial issues and learning from reflection on experience. The interpersonal abilities include empathy and promoting feelings of efficacy in others. In the motivations cluster come risk taking, goal setting, eliciting feedback, networking, goal-sharing and micro-political awareness.

Elliott (1991) uses Klemp's analysis to make a further point. While elements of competence in NVQs are discrete and can be assessed separately, 'the three clusters of abilities cited by Klemp exemplify what I have called "a structure of competence". Abilities are not isolated discrete elements but are linked together structurally' (Elliott, 1991, pp. 129–30). Such structural linkages relate rather better than the atomization of NCVQ to the complex, dynamic model of professionalism derived from habitus, interaction with others and with the context which I described earlier.

The view of practice contained in the technically rational, NCVQ competence model is restricted to parts of personal effectiveness, within tight external specification and managerial control. It pays little attention to expertise, and in seeing workers as technicians, disempowers them. In contrast, a model of professionalism based on empowerment and expertise stresses holistic judgements, made by practitioners themselves, working with others in the best interests of their pupils or clients. However, it would be a mistake to assume that competence has no place in the development of empowered professionalism. Rather, it is necessary to re-examine competence in this different context.

THE USES OF COMPETENCE

Given what has already been said about the nature of habitus and of a reflexive society, it is self-evident that no set of abilities or competence elements is anything more than one of many possible ways of analysing a professional role. Not only will different practitioners (and others) invest different meanings in the statements used in the analysis, but they will also find differing analyses ring more or less true, depending on personal perceptions through habitus and the particular situation they are in. Rather than ask the pointless question, 'Are these competence statements "correct"?', we would be better advised to concentrate on their *utility* in developing professionalism.

Within NVQs, the prime function of the competence framework is summative assessment. The elements, units and statements of competence are given meaning by the performance criteria and range statements that have to be met before the unit can be awarded. As Ashworth and Saxton (1990) point out, this atomizes the role so that the whole can only be seen as the sum of the separate parts, which although assessed in a working context, are also assumed to be context neutral in that they can be replicated in any relevant workplace. The analysis of the early part of this chapter contrasts starkly with such a simplistic view. I wish to suggest here that competence attributes, rather than being seen as the primary tools of summative assessment, may have four useful purposes as part, and only part, of a wider approach to professionalism. These purposes are: to aid learning, to clarify expertise, to aid assessment and to make more transparent the nature of professional practice. Whether or which competence attributes are used should be judged by how well these purposes can be fulfilled in practice. Let us now examine each of these in turn.

To aid learning

Getting to grips with the complexity of teaching or social work can be daunting for a novice. It is at least possible that some deconstruction of the role by competence attributes could make the whole more accessible to such learners.

To clarify expertise

We have already seen the emphasis placed on expertise by Dreyfus and Elliott. A set of competence attributes would serve a useful purpose if, within a given profession, they helped distinguish between levels of expertise. This might be done following the approaches cited in Klemp (1977). A similar structure of levels is used by Harvard and Dunne (Chapter 11) to help build in what they call 'state of the art' practice.

To aid assessment

While it is evident from the argument in this chapter that assessment of professional learning and/or performance should not be atomized and fragmented, it is possible that careful use of competence attributes might inform a more holistic assessment judgement, in the way that assessment criteria for an academic essay can fulfil the same role. A test of the appropriateness of any competence structure would then become the ease with which it aided such an assessment process. Note that to do this, it is not necessary for the statement itself to be measured or assessed directly. Returning to the Dreyfus model above, it might well be enough if such a framework reminded an assessor that, say, empathy was a key ability that should be present, alongside and as part of other factors. It is possible that competence attributes could aid the accreditation of prior learning in a similar, holistic fashion. Both Barnes (Chapter 9) and Maynard (Chapter 10) describe using competence statements to aid holistic assessment in this sort of way.

To make professional practice more transparent

One of the least defensible attributes of traditional professions is that they develop a mystique about what it is that members do. This is partly to do with exclusivity and hegemony and partly with the fact that specialist groups everywhere develop their own jargon as a means of easy communication between cognoscenti. It is possible that appropriate competence attributes might aid the process of demystification, thus making the workings of professional groups more open and transparent to others. In the caring professions, there are three groups who might benefit from this. They are the clients, other professionals who also work with the same pupils or clients, and prospective newcomers to the job.

I am not claiming that any set of competence attributes will necessarily be useful in these ways. Indeed, I have doubts that some of those currently being developed within the NCVQ framework will be so. They were, after all, designed for a different purpose. Nor am I claiming that these four purposes cannot be achieved in ways other than the use of competence attributes, for I am quite sure that they can. My point is rather to shift the ground upon which we make judgments about the value of competence attributes, or any other system of learning or assessment support, away from the focus on atomized performance measurement that currently dominates NCVQ thinking.

BROADENING THE PICTURE

There is a growing body of literature which focuses on the relationships between knowledge, understanding and performance in competence. For NCVQ and the Standards branch of the Employment Department, the first two are clearly subservient to the last.

> In the context of occupational competence, knowledge and understanding and associated cognitive skills, are part of performance not something separate from it.
> (Employment Department, 1993, p. 5)

In one sense, this is a truism which is entirely consistent with the culturally complex model of performance presented in this chapter. Of course knowledge and understanding influence performance, as in turn performance alters our knowledge and understanding. Much work is currently being done in many professions to enhance that interrelationship, often using the concept of reflective practice, made popular by Schön (1983, 1987). However, the NCVQ view of the relationship is grossly oversimplified, for it is extremely difficult to tease out precisely what knowledge and understanding directly contribute to performance, or in what way. Hyland, in Chapter 4, explores some of the limitations of the NCVQ view of learning in relation to this point.

In any event, what knowledge and understanding are necessary for performance is the wrong question to address. One of the advantages of the model of empowerment presented above is that it demonstrates the fallacy of assuming that the only purpose of knowledge and understanding is to underpin performance or personal effectiveness. Education of professional teachers, social workers and others needs to address wider issues of critical autonomy and community as well. Klemp's cognitive and interpersonal abilities partly bridge these dimensions, indeed 'understanding controversial issues' arguably focuses more on critical autonomy and community than on performance. It is hard to see how this could be tested or its content determined through performance, yet I would much rather my children were educated by professionals with that understanding than by those without. How much more true must this be for community workers and social workers.

Performance cannot be the sole focus of professional education, and neither should competence. There is no merit in using excessive energy and imagination twisting and adapting a competence system so that it can include everything, regardless of whether this is the most effective way of doing so. Approaches to course planning, teaching, learning and assessment can be mixed, as indeed many non-NVQ vocational and professional courses already are. We do not need to choose between competence or not competence, any more than between all group work and no group work, or between didactic instruction and learning through practice. Rather, we must weigh up the merits of including appropriate competence structures and learning styles as part of a larger package, in the way Maynard describes in Chapter 10. It may be as short-sighted to assert that competence can have no place, as to claim that it can do everything. In the infinitely complex and only partially understood worlds of teaching, youth and community work, we must shun over-simplification. Would that life were simple – but it is not.

REFERENCES

Ashworth, P. D. and Saxton, J. (1990) 'On competence.' *Journal of Further & Higher Education,* **14**(2), 1–25.

Ball, S. J. (1990) 'Management as moral technology: a Luddite analysis.' In S. J. Ball (ed.) *Foucault and Education: Disciplines and Knowledge.* London: Routledge.

Beck, U. (1992) *Risk Society: Towards a New Modernity.* London: Sage.

Bourdieu, P. (1977) 'Cultural reproduction and social reproduction.' In J. Karabel and A. H. Halsey (eds) *Power and Ideology in Education.* Oxford: Oxford University Press.

Bourdieu, P. (1984) *Distinction: A Social Critique of the Judgment of Taste.* London: Routledge & Kegan Paul.

Brause, R. S. (1992) *Enduring Schools: Problems and Possibilities.* London: Falmer.

Brown, J. S., Collins, A. and Duguid, P. (1989) 'Situated cognition and the culture of learning.' *Educational Researcher,* **18**(1), 32–42.

Capper, C. A. and Jamison, M. T. (1993) 'Let the buyer beware: total quality management and educational research and practice.' *Educational Researcher,* **22**(8), 25–30.

Clarke, J., All, S., Jefferson, T. and Roberts, B. (1981) 'Subcultures, cultures and class.' In T. Bennet, G. Martin, C. Mercer and J. Wallacott (eds) *Culture, Ideology and Social Process.* London: Batsford.

Dreyfus, S. E. (1981) *Four Models v. Human Situational Understanding: Inherent Limitations on the Modelling of Business Expertise.* US Air Force Office of Scientific Research, Contract No. f49620-79-C-0063.

Elliott, J. (1991) *Action Research for Educational Change.* Milton Keynes: Open University Press.

Employment Department (1993) *Knowledge and Understanding: Its Place in Relation To NVQs and SVQs.* Competence and Assessment: Briefing Series, No. 9. Sheffield: Employment Department.

Fullan, M. (1991) *The New Meaning of Educational Change.* London: Cassell.

Giddens, A. (1990) *The Consequences of Modernity.* Cambridge: Polity Press.

Giddens, A. (1991) *Modernity and Self-Identity: Self and Society in the Late Modern Age.* Cambridge: Polity Press.

Goodson, I. F. (1984) 'Beyond the subject monolith: subject traditions and sub-cultures.' In P. Harling (ed.) *New Directions in Educational Leadership.* Lewes: Falmer.

Gore, J. (1992) 'What we can do for you! What can "we" do for "you"?: Struggling over empowerment in critical and feminist pedagogy.' In C. Luke and J. Gore (eds) *Feminisms and Critical Pedagogy.* London: Routledge.

Grundy, S. (1987) *Curriculum: Product or Praxis.* London: Falmer.

Habermas, J. (1971) *Towards a Rational Society.* London: Heinemann.

Habermas, J. (1972) *Knowledge and Human Interests,* 2nd edn. London: Heinemann.

Harvey, D. (1989) *The Condition of Postmodernity: and Enquiry into the Origins of Cultural Change.* Oxford: Basil Blackwell.

Hodkinson, P. (1992) 'Alternative models of competence in vocational education and training.' *Journal of Further & Higher Education,* **16**(2), 30–9.

Hodkinson, P. (1994) 'Empowerment as an entitlement in the post-16 curriculum.' *Journal of Curriculum Studies* (forthcoming).

Hodkinson, P. and Sparkes, A. C. (1993) 'Prevocationalism and empowerment: some questions for PE.' In J. Evans (ed.) *Equality and Physical Education*. London: Falmer.

Klemp, G. O. (1977) *Three Factors of Success in the World of Work: Implications for Curriculum in Higher Education*. Boston: McBer & Co.

Rudduck, J. (1991) *Innovation and Change*. Milton Keynes: Open University Press.

Rumelhart, D. E. (1980) 'Schemata: the building blocks of cognition.' In R. Spiro, B. C. Bruce and W. F. Brewer (eds) *Theoretical Issues in Reading Comprehension*. Hillsdale, New Jersey: Lawrence Earlbaum.

Schön, D. A. (1983) *The Reflective Practitioner*. New York: Basic Books.

Schön, D. A. (1987) *Educating the Reflective Practitioner*. San Francisco: Josey Bass.

Sparkes, A. C. (1990) 'Power, domination and resistance in the process of teacher-initiated innovation.' *Research Papers in Education*, **5**(2), 59–84.

Spencer, L. M. (1979) *Identifying, Measuring and Training Soft Skill Competencies Which Predict Performance in Professional, Managerial and Human Service Jobs*. Boston: McBer & Co.

Ward, D. and Mullender, A. (1991) 'Empowerment and oppression: an indissoluble pairing for contemporary social work.' *Critical Social Policy*, **32**, 21–30.

Chapter 6

Competence, Professionalism and Equal Opportunities

Mary Issitt

This chapter is written from the perspective of a white, able-bodied woman with experience in the education and training of professionals in social work, youth and community work, and health. In addition to the secondary sources used, this perspective has been informed through discussion with Kerry Young, a black consultant and trainer. However, the interpretations and conclusions presented are those of the author alone.

INTRODUCTION

The main aim of this chapter is to begin to explore the relationship between competency-based education and training for person-centred professions and equality of opportunity. The term 'person-centred' professions here refers to education and 'welfare' based occupations such as youth and community work, social work, health education and teaching. The majority of those employed in these particular professions are salaried employees engaged upon work that is deemed necessary for the reproduction and maintenance of an educated, healthy and nurtured workforce. Even in these days of the application of market forces to public service, in the main, these professionals work in non-profit-making organizations which derive much of their funding directly or indirectly through the state (see Chapter 1).

The starting point and focus of this analysis will be social, youth and community work; however, the issues presented should have wider relevance to the other professions referred to above. In all of these work areas discourse and practice has developed which seeks to promote equality of opportunity for service consumers, and practitioners have increasingly seen themselves as operating in ways that 'empower', i.e. enable people to use and build upon experience in order to be more in control of their own lives (Mullender and Ward, 1985, 1989, 1991, 1993).

Moreover, within these occupations, efforts to link training to practice at both initial and post-qualifying levels have led increasingly to the development of competence-based assessment (Maisch and Winter, 1991; Issitt and Woodward, 1992). Much of this work has progressed concurrently with the activities of the National Council for Vocational Qualifications (NCVQ) and the Employment Department's Training, Employment and Education Directorate (TEED). These bodies are now beginning to address professional occupational levels whose training is normally delivered and/or validated by higher education institutions (see Chapters 3 and 4). In its own right, community work has engaged in this debate both inside and outside NCVQ structures. Since the late 1980s the work area has been represented on the Care Sector Consortium (CSC) and is currently undertaking the development of occupational standards. The outcome of this process will not only be of interest to social work and youth work, but also to other education and caring professions, and I refer to this later on.

This chapter seeks to contribute to the debate which must ensue as competence in relation to equal opportunities practice, as defined by the professional areas, is synthesized (or not) with NVQs. The promotion of equality of opportunity, a complex and disputed phenomenon, is central to the professional task in each of these occupations, as is evidenced by statements from the national bodies currently responsible for setting standards. Therefore, in order to begin to understand the complexities involved, I will first examine both discourse and action on equality of opportunity and consider their application in these professions in relation to current competence requirements. Secondly, the analysis briefly turns to the work thus far undertaken through NCVQ and discusses the implications of matching the NVQ framework and approach to competence for the aspects of these professional areas that are concerned with equality of opportunity.

EQUAL OPPORTUNITIES – DISCOURSE, TERMINOLOGY AND ACTION

Equal opportunities discourse and practice is wide ranging, and in this chapter I focus on those aspects that relate to policy and practice. Various terms are used to describe the level of action in which individuals and agencies are engaged and these reflect different ideological standpoints. In their research into the development of equal opportunities policies, Jewson and Mason show that

> participants in the policy-making process were using terms and concepts in a confused, arbitrary and contradictory manner (cf. Young and Connelly 1981). Sometimes this appeared to be a product of muddle and misunderstanding; on other occasions it appeared to be the result of more conscious and deliberate attempts to mislead and mystify opponents and outsiders.
>
> (Jewson and Mason, 1986 p. 308)

The confusion highlighted arises from a lack of understanding of the 'liberal' and 'radical' approaches to equal opportunities. The liberal approach essentially individualizes the collective experience of discrimination. It is concerned to develop fair and equitable rules, but fails to question the nature of such rules (which inevitably become complex and bureaucratic). The rules and procedures cannot address the wider structural inequalities, of which they are a part and which they may reproduce.

The 'radical' approach is less concerned with procedures that affect individuals but embraces the collective experience and outcomes leading to structural change. Radicals see even individual attributes of 'talent' and 'ability' as socially constructed and not morally or politically 'neutral', reflecting wider social inequalities. In the case of many middle class occupations, the demonstration of ability through educational qualifications demanded as entry requirements 'bears little relation to the tasks actually performed'. These qualifications are seen as 'screening devices' to preserve desirable occupations for the 'sons and the daughters of the bourgeoisie' (Jewson and Mason, 1986, p. 316). Thus in employment, the radical approach aims 'to politicise personnel decisions, particularly those of recruitment and promotion, and release a struggle for power and influence by disadvantaged groups. It calls for positive discrimination' (Cockburn, 1989, p. 215).

From both the liberal and radical perspectives, 'equal opportunities' is, therefore, an umbrella term that describes policy objectives, framework and intent. The majority of settings in which social workers, youth workers and community workers find themselves will have a policy statement regarding equal opportunities. However, the implementation and effectiveness of this policy will vary greatly from one setting to another.

DIFFERENCE AND IDENTITY

The confusion that Cockburn and Jewson and Mason have sought to unravel is further evidenced when policies are translated into statements of intent or action plans to combat 'disadvantage'. Service providers may be concerned about 'the notion of *disadvantage* and the need to guard against it – by avoiding disadvantaging certain people' (Thompson, 1993, p. 32). The result is that consumers of services may be forced to take on the label of 'disadvantage' in a way that conflicts with their own self-image (Cain and Yuval-Davis, 1990). 'Disadvantaged' groups may further become characterized as 'the other', posed as the opposite of the prevailing norm, for example, 'black v white', 'woman v man', 'people with disabilities v able-bodied' etc. As well as reducing those disadvantaged by discrimination to a group that is seen to deviate from the prevailing 'normality', individuals become subsumed into an 'all encompassing category both in terms of their treatment as well as their identity and empowerment' (Cain and Yuval-Davis, 1990, p. 23).

The assumption that follows is of homogeneity within each category that denies difference (Cain and Yuval-Davis, 1990; Aziz, 1992). 'Difference' should be acknowledge and celebrated and not only equated with disadvantage.

As equal opportunities policies have been put into practice, and sensitivity towards difference developed other terms such as 'anti-discriminatory practice', 'anti-oppressive practice', have entered the discourse and now require definition.

ANTI-DISCRIMINATORY PRACTICE

Thompson notes that 'Equality of Opportunity is closely linked to the notion of anti-discrimination and the anti-discrimination legislation which underpins it' (Thompson, 1993, p. 31). In spite of equal opportunities rhetoric and policy statements, agencies often 'fail' to promote equal opportunities. Services and workers may not be overtly discriminatory but subtly still discriminate against particular individuals or groups. Thompson's observation that 'social workers occupy positions of power and influence, so there is considerable scope for discrimination and oppression whether it is intentional or by default' (Thompson, 1993, p. 31), could equally be applied in educational and caring professions other than social work.

The term 'anti-discriminatory practice' is a multipurpose term used in a number of ways. It has been adopted by practitioners to acknowledge that they need to work towards eradicating both overt and covert discriminatory behaviour. It relates specifically to operating within the current legal framework and does not attempt to push back the boundaries of this framework further. The term may also be used generically to signal a commitment to tackling discrimination on all fronts rather than referring separately to anti-sexism, anti-racism, anti-ablism, anti-heterosexism, etc. As well as operating as a 'shorthand' it can also signal commonalities between different forms of discrimination, implying that there may be similarities in the anti-discriminatory practice required. A further application could be to indicate the will to acknowledge and celebrate difference.

ANTI-OPPRESSIVE PRACTICE

In equal opportunities discourse, anti-oppressive practice can include anti-discrimination and much more besides. Its use denotes that discrimination against particular groups is structurally determined by the society in which we live. Equality of opportunity cannot be brought about by merely working within existing frameworks and structures. From this perspective it is necessary to develop a practice that challenges and seeks to change. Generally this would involve a collective approach because change cannot be brought about by individuals alone. In acknowledging and celebrating 'difference' it would seek to collectivize the experience of different groups and communities, as well as linking together in common struggles.

The terms 'anti-discriminatory' and 'anti-oppressive' are often used interchangeably but in fact describe different forms and approaches to equal opportunities. Implicit in anti-oppressive practice is the radical agenda which requires collective action for social change. Anti-discriminatory practice fits into the 'liberal' agenda which may involve change for individuals but the means by which this will be achieved will focus on the construction of fair rules and procedures, which inevitably cannot address wider inequalities.

The radical/liberal dichotomy has been presented as offering a means of beginning to understand the complexity of discourse and action in respect of equal opportunities. In reality the approaches are intermingled and often radical outcomes are claimed for liberal procedures (Jewson and Mason, 1986). Cockburn believes that the dichotomy needs to be reconceptualized as a continuum of practice in terms of an 'equal opportunities agenda of shorter or greater length'. In the short term it would involve

> new measures to minimise bias in procedures . . . at its longest, its most ambitious it has to be recognised as a *project of transformation*. . . . It brings into view the nature and purpose of institutions by which the power of some groups over others is built and renewed. It acknowledges the need of disadvantaged groups for access to power . . . the radical approach. But it also looks for change in the nature of power, in the control ordinary people of diverse kinds have over institutions.
>
> (Cockburn, 1989, p. 218)

The transformative approach that she advocates

> tackles power itself. It recognises the capitalist mode of production with its class relations and its imperialist and racist history. It recognises a sex/gender system characterised by male supremacy that enables men as a sex to benefit economically, socially, and sexually from the oppression of women. It sees these systems as interacting in intricate ways. But it also sees that power, like the multiple subjects of disadvantage, is faceted and complex.
>
> (Cockburn, 1989, p. 219)

The generic term 'equal opportunities' covers a variety of different actions, descriptions and discourses, all of which have to be understood and applied sensitively. The whole range of the discourse and action described above can be identified within the statements emanating from the national bodies for social, youth and community work. These statements incorporate both radical and liberal perspectives and implicit within them are short and long agendas for action. Competent practice in relation to this may be judged differently by professionals wishing to promote equality of opportunity and those on the receiving end of the policies. A further complication in seeking to define competent practice turns upon the question as to whether the promotion of equal opportunities is about the removal of barriers to individual achievement or collectively challenging discriminatory structures in society, that is the 'transforming agenda' and this features further in the discussion below.

COMPETENCE – LIBERAL AND RADICAL PERSPECTIVES ASSESSED

Even with the limitations identified by Cockburn, the liberal/radical dichotomy applied above provides an entry into the debate about competence, and the arguments developed by Jewson and Mason (1986) in relation to equality of opportunity can also be applied to this concept. For liberals the shift from an 'input' model of vocational education and training, to an 'output' model that assesses competence not on the basis of educational qualifications but on the ability of an individual to do a job to the standard required in the workplace, in theory, allows individuals with the necessary talent to achieve (Jessup, 1990). What, then, has to be done to develop a fair set of rules and procedures to allow competence to be assessed to meet the needs of employment? Rather than occupying opposite ends of the continuum, there may be a convergence between some radicals and liberals around the 'short' agenda. Radicals may see competence to do a job as offering the means to accredit prior experience and learning in place of formal academic qualifications, as working positively in favour of disadvantaged groups (Banks, 1990).

There would still be a problem with the 'long' agenda, the difference between the two perspectives being that, as with equal opportunities, the liberal approach does not take account of structural inequalities and assumes that an objective system can be developed to assess competence. The radical approach has emerged from critiques of society which recognize that groups of people suffer structural disadvantage and are prevented from achieving their full potential. This can lead to the disempowerment of whole communities, with difference in culture or lifestyle not being accepted or fully valued. As in the case of equal opportunities policies, the radical approach would recognize that, while the lack of means to accredit competence is experienced at the individual level, the remedy lies in collective action to redress inequalities affecting the whole social group to which the individual belongs (Banks, 1990; Davies and Durkin, 1991; Issitt and Woodward, 1992).

EQUAL OPPORTUNITY AND COMPETENCE IN YOUTH AND COMMUNITY WORK AND SOCIAL WORK

In order to understand the relationship of equality of opportunity and competence in social, youth and community work, it is necessary simultaneously to consider two complex but linked concepts, each of which contains competing meanings in its own right. I will now demonstrate how this has become central in social, youth and community work.

The bodies that oversee the training of professionals in these work areas, namely, the Central Council for Education and Training in Social Work (CCETSW) and the National Youth Agency (NYA), identify the tackling of inequality as being a central part of the professional task, and both make reference to competence in the framing of requirements for professional qualification.

In its statement of 'Requirements and regulations for the Diploma in Social Work' the CCETSW (Paper 30; 1989) the promotion of equality of opportunity permeates all aspects of the professional social work role. To become professionally qualified, social workers must demonstrate competence which comprises knowledge and understanding, values and skills. Anti-discrimination is a key aspect of professional competence, and qualifying social workers must demonstrate *knowledge and understanding* through a critical awareness of structural inequalities and oppression and 'transcultural factors which affect clients' needs and social work practice'.

The *values* of social work are presented as 'a commitment to social justice and welfare, to enhance the quality of life of individuals, families and groups within communities, and to a repudiation of all forms of negative discrimination', both individual and institutional. Social workers should 'recognise the need for and seek to promote policies and practices which are non-discriminatory and anti-oppressive' (CCETSW, 1989, p. 15).

A range of *skills* is required to implement this knowledge and value base, these include the ability to 'recognise and work with personal, racial, social and cultural differences'. Competence for professional practice is demonstrated by the qualifying social worker's ability to integrate their knowledge, skills and values in all aspects of their work (CCETSW, 1989, pp. 15–17).

In youth and community work the importance of tackling inequalities is similarly expressed but couched more generally in terms of the promotion of equality of opportunity. In the report of the working group 'to define the definitive elements which form the core of all youth and community work training' (NYA, 1993) similar concerns are raised, and the tackling of oppression is explicit. The working party recognized that 'informal education' which is the profession's main purpose, 'is not a value-free exercise. It is fundamentally characterised by a commitment to equality of opportunity, justice and working against oppression', permeating both tasks and processes.

Professionally qualified youth and community workers will, therefore, be expected to execute the generic tasks and processes of informal education, and to fulfil the more specific 'purpose of youth work' which was defined at the second Ministerial Conference for the youth service as being:

> . . . to redress all forms of inequality and to ensure equality of opportunity for all young people to fulfil their potential as empowered individuals and members of groups and communities and to support young people during the transition to adulthood.
>
> (NYA, 1991, appendix)

The statement goes on to list a range of opportunities which youth work offers young people, one of which is:

> designed to promote equality of oppportunity – through the challenging of oppression such as racism and sexism and all those which spring from differences of culture, race, language, sexual identity, gender, disability, age, religion and class; and through the celebration of the diversity and strengths which arise from those differences.
>
> (NYA, 1991, appendix)

Although professional endorsement of community work has been linked with youth work, the occupation has always maintained separate organizations to act as fora for discussion and representation of interests. As well as contributing to the work of CETYCW and NYA, community work as a separate interest from youth work has promoted debate about the accreditation of training and experience for community work. Definitions require community workers to have an awareness of structural inequalities and to be at the leading edge of tackling oppression within the community, working alongside community groups to bring about social change, and to create 'new, more equal relationships between consumers and the providers of services'. Difference is positively acknowledged as the 'specific experience and contribution of Black people and women' (Federation of Community Work Training Groups, 1990).

To a greater or lesser extent the statements from all the bodies reflect the range of discourse and action on equal opportunities, both in relation to the terminology, and an incorporation of the liberal and radical aspects of the short and long agendas. Leaving aside for the moment the contradictions that these statements engender for practitioners, there are some commonalities. All have an underlying concern to promote 'justice' and 'equality' and imply a commitment to professional values, which combined with knowledge and skill are the components of competence. What more can we now learn about the definition of competence within the professional areas?

In both youth and community work and social work, the bodies that determine requirements at the point of professional qualification (the NYA and CCETSW respectively) have developed a generalistic, holistic notion of competence. Even within social work, whose statements are more specific about competence than in youth and community work, there is still considerable autonomy in the way competence is defined and demonstrated (Kemshall, 1993).

This competence includes commitment to the values, theoretical knowledge and understanding of, and practical skills in working to promote equality of opportunity. At the moment there is room at post-qualifying level in social work for the 'professional artistry' described by Jones (Chapter 7) and the more specific definition of standards using the functional analysis procedures (albeit modified) favoured by NCVQ and TEED, as exemplified through the ASSET programme (Maisch and Winter, 1991). At the level of initial qualification the definition of competence still may be unspecific and general in NCVQ terms, and is rarely defined down into units and elements of competence (*see* Chapter 1).

With respect to youth and community work the working party saw competence as a holistic process 'the core elements of which are two interrelated parts'. On the one hand are processes and values, and on the other 'functional competence i.e. the roles and responsibilities workers perform ... the group was very concerned that the two did not become separated and saw it as part of their task to ensure that they did not' (NYA, 1993, para. 6.1.5).

Within youth work and community work it is possible to identify the same autonomy and generalist approach to the application of competence. As Durkin (Chapter 8) shows, even on employment-based routes to qualification in the same national training programme it was possible to have schemes that were competence-based and those that followed a more traditional model. The NYA working party report quoted above reflects a shift towards competence-based assessment of ability to practice that has developed since the mid 1980s.

This was reflected in the *Guidelines for Endorsement* revised by the Council for Education and Training in Youth and Community Work (CETYCW, 1989) and written in a similar way to Paper 30. Here competence was predicated upon the importance of a person-centred approach, validating and building upon existing knowledge and experience (Bolger and Scott, 1984; Bainbridge, 1988). A number of training schemes for part-time workers who are the practitioners delivering most of the face-to-face work with young people in the community have used a broad-based competence approach. Only the Royal Borough of Kensington and Chelsea has undertaken a full-blown functional analysis and developed 'Standards for Youth Work' following a model based on NCVQ criteria (Royal Borough of Kensington and Chelsea, 1993). Although the scheme enables participants to gain awards through City and Guilds, in professional youth-work terms it is still only a local scheme, addressing the competence of part-time workers.

Community work as a separate entity from youth work, has gone further in seeking to define the occupational area within the NCVQ parameters. In its own right, community work has promoted programmes for the accreditation of learning and experience for community work based upon competence. These programmes have been professionally endorsed through the CETYCW/NYA system. At the conference 'Towards 2001' called by various community work organizations, it was agreed to work towards a separate body to oversee the development of professional standards and awards for community work (Federation of Community Work Training Groups, 1993).

Since the late 1980s the Federation of Community Work Training Groups (FCWTG) has been represented on the voluntary organizations group of the Care Sector Consortium (CSC). With the Convention of Scottish Local Authorities taking the lead, the FCWTG participated in a feasibility study of the community work occupational area. Through a consultation process held in different parts of the United Kingdom, a draft framework for a Functional Map of Community Work was developed (Care Sector Consortium, Voluntary Organizations Group, 1990). The FCWTG is now co-operating in the production of national standards for community work. The experience of this process will be referred to later in this chapter.

EQUAL OPPORTUNITIES VALUES AND COMPETENCE IN SOCIAL, YOUTH AND COMMUNITY WORK

At the time of writing, apart from the work undertaken within community work, the other professions considered here have not engaged in the national standards mapping exercise that will lead to the development of NVQs in their occupational areas. Both of these occupations are now poised to undertake this process in 1994–95. CCETSW has already initiated a review of the initial professional qualification for the Diploma in Social Work, and has awarded a contract for functional mapping and standards development for the occupational area (CCETSW, 1993a, 1994). The NYA hopes to undertake a similar exercise in relation to youth work even though a lead body has not yet been set up for education.[1] Concerns have simultaneously been expressed within youth and community work and social work about whether the holistic nature of both occupations will survive this process, and in addition whether the fundamental value base will be retained.

It is important therefore for the lessons that have thus far been learnt about the relationship between competence and equality of opportunity to be considered and the professional areas to move into the functional analysis process with the knowledge. I shall now consider important issues that have emerged from the professions themselves, and the implications for the development of national standards through the NVQ procedure will be discussed.

It has been suggested so far that workers in the professions of social, youth and community work are dealing with complex and contradictory phenomena in all aspects of their work. Jordan (1991) is concerned that within Paper 30 the liberal and radical approaches are presented alongside each other without comment. He suggests that the 'competence' implications of the contradictions and conflicts between the short and the long agendas of the whole social work task, to which equal opportunities is central, is not adequately considered.

> It is important that students should at least be allowed to acknowledge that there are contradictions in all this. To list these conflicting values and their associated competencies without such recognition is to invite them to a minefield without so much as a warning.
> (Jordan, 1991, p. 8)

This analysis of the contradictory situation in which practitioners may find themselves in relation to equal opportunities, and other values, is equally applicable to youth and community work. This would seem to fit into the arena of what Schön (1987) defines as 'indeterminate zones of practice', with the essence of professionalism being the ability to deal with these competently. Unfortunately these 'indeterminate zones of practice – uncertainty, uniqueness and value conflict – escape the canons of technical rationality' (Schön, 1987, p. 6). His definition of technical rationality in which 'practitioners are instrumental problem solvers who select the technical means best suited to particular purposes' (pp. 3–4), accords with the definition presented in the first chapter of this book. The challenge for professionals in any area of practice (and he draws examples from a wide variety of occupations, including medicine, music, engineering and architecture) is to find a creative way of dealing with these 'indeterminate zones'. What is required is a more holistic person-centred approach in which

We conceptualise professional knowledge in terms of 'thinking like a manager, lawyer, or teacher'. Students will still learn relevant facts but will also learn the forms of inquiry by which competent practitioners reason their way, in problematic instances, to clear connections between general knowledge and particular cases.

(Schön, 1987, p. 34)

Thus for Schön it is inadequate for practitioners to learn technical knowledge alone. They will also need to develop 'professional artistry' to deal with new situations and 'indeterminate zones'. This is gained through recognition of their engagement in transactions with their practice world and the development of the facility for 'reflection in action' to enable them to deal creatively with indeterminate zones.

There are many parallels between Schön's analysis of technical rationality and the critique of competence as being positivistic, behaviouristic and mechanistic, presented in this volume and elsewhere. This critique will not be repeated here, but competence-based approaches as developed within the professions under consideration will be examined to assess how they have helped deal with the indeterminate zones of equality of opportunity.

From her experience in the probation service, Kemshall (1993) argues that CCETSW's stated competencies are couched in behavioural statements, 'in order to secure the ground of objectivity'. However, the competencies that refer to attitudes and values, and clearly competence in respect to equality of opportunity comes within this sphere, 'are less amenable to manipulation by measurement, and are often not readily transferable into observable behavioural statements' (Kemshall, 1993, p. 38).

In relation to anti-discriminatory practice and dealing with oppression, she observes that a 'lack of consensus of what constitutes "good enough" practice' can lead to confusion over 'the nature of evidence required and conflict over what has been achieved'. It is her contention therefore that because competence statements cannot transcend the agency or the people engaged in the process of assessment then racism and sexism are likely to be perpetuated. Therefore for women competence that tends to be rewarded is that which confirms them in stereotypical work, 'fulfilling gender expectations of the subordinate, caring worker ... issues of competence for women do not normally arise until they challenge the patriarchy of the organisation or step out of role' (Kemshall, 1993, p. 42). The competence that is promoted is white and male.

She similarly illustrates how for black and Asian workers, both men and women, 'the reality of direct evidence for competence is likely to be that of the white, male, assessor.' The realities of black experience 'do not exist and they are not seen' (Kemshall, 1993, p. 42). Thus in the indeterminate zone of what constitutes competent practice for women, both black and white and for black men there appears to be little room for differential experience in terms of culture, colour or gender. Demonstrable competence reflects structural inequalities with the view of the most powerful prevailing, rendering the 'other' not fully competent.

In the development of competence-based assessment it is important, therefore, to guard against the assumption that because competence is divided into lists of behaviours that an objective framework is being created which does not perpetuate racist or sexist stereotypes. The capacity of competence frameworks to deal with both the 'short' and the 'long' agendas necessary for the promotion of equal opportunities may therefore be in question.

COMPETENCE FRAMEWORKS AND NVQs – CLARIFICATION OR CONFUSION OF THE PROFESSIONAL TASK?

It has been noted earlier that competence as defined by the bodies overseeing professional training in youth work and social work may be regarded as general and unspecific compared with definitions developed through the NCVQ functional analysis procedure. An important issue that is now of pressing concern for social, youth and community work, is whether NVQ competence frameworks can be fashioned to the requirements of the professional task, or will the professional task be distorted in order to fit with competence requirements? Before attempting to deal with this question, it will be necessary briefly to consider some of the work that NCVQ has supported in relation to equal opportunities.

The NCVQ itself has a clear, unequivocal position of commitment to the promotion of equal opportunities. In the context of NVQs and GNVQs, Elsa Dicks, the Assistant Director with special responsibility for equal opportunities, states that 'equal opportunities are fundamental to the NVQ/GNVQ system and to everyone involved in that system, whether candidate or provider' (Dicks, 1993, p. 3). She cites examples of NCVQ's readiness to learn from and develop good practice both in respect of organizations and individuals in the system. Lead and awarding bodies are required to have appropriate equal opportunities policies and statements, and there are individual performance criteria for assessors.

Work that has been undertaken through the Care Sector Consortium provides wider evidence that both in the development and assessment of NVQs, there has been a willingness to listen and respond flexibly to develop equal opportunities policy, and specifically to address the value-base required for those working in caring occupations. For example, the voluntary organizations group within the CSC initiated the setting up of an equal opportunities working group. This group was able to ensure wider representation and consultation, for example through the black perspectives group of the Local Government Management Board, and with various groups and organizations to address gender and disability issues. This has led to the development of policies and procedures that NCVQ regards as a model of good practice for other lead bodies (Employment Department, 1992). The black perspectives group has separately described the positive impact they were able to have on this process (Lyn-Cook, 1992).

The CSC has also addressed the issue of how underpinning values for the promotion of equality of opportunity can be consistently demonstrated. The Unit '0' – Promote Equality for All Individuals – is a detailed specification of how equal opportunities values can be demonstrated through good practice. It is to be used in conjunction with all the other units for the assessment of competence within care (Care Sector Consortium, 1991). Following on from its own work on equal opportunities, the CSC itself was able to recommend the commissioning of a research project into equal opportunities, with a remit to identify good practice and methods of dissemination (Employment Department, 1992). The ensuing report identified a series of recommendations in relation to equal opportunities for consideration by the Employment Department's standards methodology branch, and awarding bodies.

It would therefore appear that the NCVQ framework is able to adopt both a positive stance and structure on equal opportunities issues. It may well be therefore that the functional mapping process on which youth work and social work nationally are about to engage will enable the professions to deal with some of the problems highlighted by Kemshall above. A major issue for both areas will be to what extent professional knowledge, skills and values will be enhanced through a shift from generalized statements of competence, in which there clearly are anomalies in implementation and interpretation, as is the current situation, to a system which seeks to be more prescriptive and detailed in relation to required professional behaviours.

There are some indications that there is cause for concern that the central task as defined by the professions themselves may become altered by the standards mapping process. Two examples from youth work and community work illustrate this problem.

As there is currently no education lead body through which the standards for youth work would expect to be determined, some local authority youth services have felt that they are missing the tide in terms of equipping their part-time youth leaders with NVQs. Therefore the Royal Borough of Kensington and Chelsea, in conjunction with City and Guilds have developed 'Standards for Youth Work' (Royal Borough of Kensington and Chelsea and City and Guilds, 1993). Although this project has aroused considerable interest, these standards have only local currency as there are no national standards for youth work.

In spite of this, Kensington and Chelsea adopted the NVQ functional analysis procedure, and, in line with NCVQ requirements, utilized relevant units of competence from another occupational area. Those adopted are from the lead body for management – the Management Charter Initiative. Therefore the key roles of youth work in the Kensington and Chelsea scheme are all defined in management terms. This has led to concern within the wider profession as workers see a high profile scheme defining youth work as management and thus, for many, distorting the professional task.

Examination of the experience of the Community Work Standards development project also shows that concern is not unfounded. Following the feasibility study referred to earlier, the Federation of Community Work Training Groups gained funding through the Training Education and Enterprise Directorate of the Department of Employment (TEED) to develop national standards for community work.[2] It is important to note that the 'Key Purpose' for community work as defined in the functional model presented in the original feasibility study is as follows:

> To work with people who experience inequality, discrimination and injustice in order that they may take collective action which challenges their oppression, achieves change and improves the quality of their lives.
> (Care Sector Consortium, Voluntary Organizations Group, 1990, p. 15)

This broad purpose is further broken down as follows:

- Engage with the community
- Promote the development of autonomous groups
- Determining the basis for action
- Manage the resources of the employing agency
- Promote community work
- Review the community work process
> (Care Sector Consortium, Voluntary Organizations Group, 1990, p. 15)

These six functions are further subdivided into twenty-two units of competence shared between them.

The following is also noted on the model: 'All functions underpinned by: analyse the nature of inequality, injustice, discrimination and other forms of oppression' (Care Consortium, Voluntary Organization Group, 1990, p. 15).

In undertaking the standards development work those involved from the community work occupational area encountered problems. First, as with the Kensington and Chelsea example quoted above, NCVQ requires that relevant units developed in other occupations have to be used. These had to be imported in whole units of competence, whereas only a few elements were required. This led to a disproportionate number of units being defined in management terms than might have been anticipated through the original feasibility study.

Criticisms came from TEED about the technical correctness of the standards themselves. When this was pursued further by the FCWTG it was difficult to find a technical expert among those versed in the process of standards development who could be precise in the criticism. Within the occupation there was agreement that the standards were a good reflection of the work area and had been arrived at through careful consultation with the community work field. Funding was temporarily withdrawn but, with the support of the project steering group and CCETSW, the FCWTG has once again managed to secure support from TEED to continue the process. The outcome of the standards development procedure will be relevant to youth workers and social workers, who will wish to learn from the community work experience.

Although this was not explicit, it may be that community work encountered an incapacity within the standards development procedure to cope with the long-term radical agenda in relation to equal oppportunities that is central to the key purpose of community work. Perhaps it is not possible for a technically rational process to be usefully applied to the disaggregation of a key purpose that is concerned with social transformation in order to tackle inequalities. Many practitioners in social, youth and community work will be concerned if engagement in the process of standards development leads to a technically rational response that requires them to exclude the collectivist and oppositional aspects of their role. It is this that has often brought about change and led to equal opportunities issues being central to the professional task.

Further understanding may be gained by examination of the '0' unit referred to earlier. This 'value' base unit is applicable to every other unit in the framework. It is an integral part of every qualification (Care Sector Consortium, 1991). It contains five elements of competence, with 46 performance criteria between them, requiring evidence from all other units of competence within a particular qualification. Apart from the complications of administering and cross-referencing necessary for the candidate to demonstrate competence, these criteria are constructed in terms of individual performance by the worker in relation to an individual client. The notion of collectivities of workers or consumers with competing demands and interests in relation to equal opportunities is not accommodated in this assessment model. If competence is only expressed in individualistic terms does this mean that only anti-discriminatory practice can be assessed? Will the collective dimension of anti-oppressive practice come to be seen as outside the realms of competence and therefore not a legitimate activity for a 'competent' professional to be engaged in? This may be the heart of the challenge of competence for equal opportunities!

WHITHER COMPETENCE, EQUAL OPPORTUNITIES AND PROFESSIONALISM?

The aim of this chapter was to raise issues for debate in relation to equal opportunities and competence for practice in relation to 'person-centred' professions. The debate will be rife as feasibility studies and occupational mapping take place within social, youth and community work, and these standards come to be implemented.

Equal opportunities knowledge, skills and values provide a major testing ground for the application and development of competence-based assessment procedures. The 'person-centred' professions have always been riven with contradiction both at the individual and collective levels as they walk the tightrope 'in and against the state' (Bailey and Brake, 1977; London to Edinburgh Weekend Return Group, 1980). The breadth of discourse and action between 'radical' and 'liberal' approaches covers many aspects of professional values and these are epitomized in respect of equal opportunities. The challenge for competence will be whether, with the best will in the world, and the rigour and intentions of NCVQ are not here being questioned, the essentially technically rational approach can deal with or merely exacerbate these contradictions.

Equal opportunities discourse and action has been shown to be a complex and disputed area, an 'indeterminate zone of practice' in which it is difficult always to identify the right answer. In presenting itself as a means of objectively measuring the values of professional practice, does the inevitably individualistic, technically rational response perpetuate structural inequalities while giving an illusion of tackling oppression? In dealing with the complexities of discourse and action in relation to equal opportunities, the NCVQ solution is to be more specific and prescriptive about competent behaviour as is the case with the '0' unit. The paradox may be that the specification of competent behaviour becomes so detailed and mystifyingly complex that it becomes inaccessible to those for whom assessment of qualification by competence promised entry to a wider range of occupations.

Furthermore, as defined in the professional task of social, youth and community work, the promotion of equality of opportunity involves, in part, question and challenge to unequal structures within society. The competence that is required here is often that of the group rather than the individual. The challenge for the NCVQ standards development process will be whether it can include the collective dimension, or will this be defined as outside the range of individualistic, competent practice, which is restrospective and reflects the status quo? The question for professionals will be, do they want this activity to be incorporated into a national standards framework? On the other hand, recognition of complexity of discourse and action in relation to both equal opportunities and competence, is not an excuse for perpetuating oppressive practice. The temptation to hide behind equal opportunities rhetoric, and to use arguments which might be described as elitist about the professional task being too complex to be disaggregated is to eschew the challenge of competence which offers professionals the chance to reappraise what they are doing and to examine the rationale, content and effects of their practice in relation to equal opportunities.

Within the 'person-centred' professions there is already considerable experience and debate about competence. Practitioners need to be assertive about this during the development of national standards. In relation to equal opportunities values, much of this may turn around the assessment process as subjective or objective, and the negotiability of competence to take account of difference while adhering to high professional standards. A further dimension will be to re-appraise the validity of the shift to 'output' measures of competence. It may be that meaningful debate leading to the development of high professional standards needs to revisit and not ignore the resources, knowledge and process that form the 'input' aspect of the equation in order to identify truly competent practice for the late twentieth and early twenty-first centuries. Alternatively, we may need to reject the 'input/output' equation and find an alternative that builds upon best practice both within these professions and within the NCVQ processes.

Acknowledgements

I am grateful to Rooney Martin, Kerry Young, Julie Griffiths and Jean Spence for their comments on an earlier draft of this paper.

NOTES

1. The NYA announced its intention to seek funding from TEED to undertake a feasibility study to identify the standards for youth work, at a conference held on 10 November 1993, at their offices in Leicester.
2. This information comes from a workshop on standards development in community work given at the same conference.

REFERENCES

Aziz, R. (1992) 'Feminism and the challenge of racism'. In H. Crowley and S. Himmelweit (eds) *Knowing Women*. London: Polity.

Bailey, R. and Brake, M. (eds) (1977) *Radical Social Work*. London: Edward Arnold.

Bainbridge, P. (1988) *Taking the Experience Route*. Leicester: CETYCW.

Banks, S. (1990) 'Accreditating prior learning: implications for education and training in youth and community work.' *Youth and Policy No. 31*, November 1990.

Bolger, S. and Scott, D. (1984) *Starting from Strengths*. Leicester: National Youth Agency.

Cain, H. and Yuval-Davis, N.L. (1990) 'The Equal Opportunities Community and the Anti-Racist Struggle'. *Critical Social Policy*, **29**, 5-26.

Care Sector Consortium, Voluntary Organizations Group (1990) 'Commission Work Feasibility Study on behalf of the Care Sector Consortium: Recommendations for the way forward in the identification of standards linked to vocational qualifications'. London: Care Sector Consortium.

Care Sector Consortium (1991) *Unit 0 Promote Equality for All Individuals*. London: NCVQ.

CCETSW (1989) *Requirements and Regulations for the Diploma in Social Work*. CCETSW Paper 30. London: CCETSW.

CCETSW (1993) *DipSW to be Reviewed*. London: CCETSW autumn 1993, No. 10.

CCETSW (1993b) *Report of Council Meeting*, 18 November 1993. London: CCETSW.

CCETSW (1994) *Review Draws Huge Response*. London: CCETSW February 1994, No. 11.

CETYCW (1989) *Guidelines for Endorsement*. Leicester: CETYCW.

Cockburn, C. (1989) 'Equal Opportunities: the short and the long agenda.' *Industrial Relations Journal*, **20**(3) autumn 1979.

Davies, B. and Durkin, M. (1991) 'Skill, competence and competencies in youth and community work.' *Youth and Policy*, **34**, September 1991.

Dicks, E. (1993) 'Equal opportunities and NVQs.' *NCVQ Monitor*, June 1993.

Dominelli, L. and McLeod, E. (1991) *Feminist Social Work*. London: Macmillan.

Employment Department (1992) *Equal Opportunities and the Development of NVQs and SVQs*. Sheffield: Employment Department, Research and Development Series, Report No. 10.

Federation of Community Work Training Groups (1990) *Learning for Action*. Sheffield: Federation of Community Work Training Groups.

Federation of Community Work Training Groups (1993) *Towards 2001*, Conference Report. Sheffield: Federation of Community Work Training Groups.

Issitt, M. and Woodward, M. (1992) 'Competence and contradiction.' In P. Carter, T. Jeffs and M.K. Smith (eds) *Changing Social Work and Welfare*. Buckingham: Open University Press.

Jessup, G. (1990) 'National vocational qualifications: implications for further education.' In M. Bees and M. Swords (eds) *National Vocational Qualifications and Further Education*. London: Kogan Page.

Jewson, N. and Mason, D. (1986) 'Theory and practice of equal opportunities.' *Sociological Review*, **34**(2), March 1986, 307–34.

Jordan, B. (1991) 'Competencies and values.' *Social Work Education*, **10**(1), 5–11.

Kemshall, H. (1993) 'Assessing competence: scientific process or subjective interference? Do we really see it?' *Social Work Education*, **12**(1), 36–45.

London to Edinburgh Weekend Return Group (1980) *In and Against the State*. London: Pluto.

Lyn-Cook, S. (1992) 'The impact of the Black Perspectives Group on S/NVQ developments in the social care field'. In S. Burton, R. Dutt and S. Lyn-Cook (eds) *Black Perspectives in S/NVQ*. London: National Institute for Social Work.

Maisch, M. and Winter, R. (1991) *The Functional Analysis Method as Applied to the Description of Professional Level Practice*. Paper presented to the National ASSET Conference, March 1991. Chelmsford: Essex Social Services and Anglia College of Higher Education.

Mullender, A. and Ward, D. (1985) 'Towards an alternative model of social groupwork'. *British Journal of Social Work*, **15**, 155–72.

Mullender, A. and Ward, D. (1989) 'Challenging familiar assumptions; preparing for and initiating a self-directed group'. *Groupwork*, **2**, 5–26.

Mullender, A. and Ward, D. (1991) *Self Directed Groupwork: Users Take Action for Empowerment*. London: Whiting and Birch.

Mullender, A. and Ward, D. (1993) 'Empowerment and oppression: an indissoluble pairing for contemporary social work.' In J. Walmsley, J. Reynolds, P. Shakespeare and R. Woolf (eds) *Health and Welfare Practice*. London: Sage.

NCVQ (1988) *The NCVQ Criteria and Related Guidance*. London: NCVQ.

NYA (1991) 'Background papers', the *Third Ministerial Conference for the Youth Service*. Leicester: NYA.

NYA (1993) *The Core of Youth and Community Work Training: The Report of the Working Group to define the Distinctive Elements which form the Core of all Youth and Community Work Training*. Leicester: NYA.

Royal Borough of Kensington and Chelsea Youth Service (1993) *Standards for Youth Work*. London: Royal Borough of Kensington and Chelsea.

Schön, D.A. (1987) *Educating the Reflective Practitioner*. San Francisco: Jossey Bass.

Thompson, N. (1993) *Anti-Discriminatory Practice*. London: Macmillan.

Young, K. and Connelly, N. (1981) *Policy and Practice in the Multi-Racial City*. London: Policy Studies Institute.

Chapter 7

'Professional Artistry' and Child Protection: Towards a Reflective Holistic Practice

Jocelyn Jones

INTRODUCTION

At the end of the 1980s social work education and training underwent considerable change with the introduction of the new qualifying award, the Diploma in Social Work (CCETSW, 1989). At the same time, consultation was taking place about the future shape and direction of post-qualifying education and training to supersede CCETSW-approved, college-based study programmes and *ad hoc* in-service training courses. The first edition of Paper 31 was published in December 1990 (CCETSW, 1990), and it outlined an ambitious new infrastructure for the implementation of a UK-wide social work post-qualifying framework. This chapter focuses on the context of learning at this level, the meaning of competence, and its assessment. Questions are raised about the resourcing of the infrastructure, and the roles of assessor, supervisor and mentor. The chapter concludes by urging all those employed in social work post-qualifying education and training to create a forum to debate the nature of professional competence, and particularly in the challenging field of child protection.

COMPETENCE AND CCETSW'S TRAINING CONTINUUM

The Central Council for Education and Training in Social Work (CCETSW) has developed a training continuum with three main elements: National Vocational Qualifications (NVQs) or Scottish Vocational Qualifications (SVQs); the Diploma in Social Work; and two awards at post-qualifying and advanced level. As Tony Hall, CCETSW's Director has said: '[The training continuum] is designed to provide an unbroken ladder of qualifications to equip staff for social work and care tasks from the most simple to the most highly complex and specialised' (Hall, 1993, p. 1). At the lower levels in the continuum the NVQ definition of competence predominates, and is defined as, 'the ability to perform work activities to the standards required in employment' (NCVQ, 1988) However, as one travels up the continuum the definition of competence appears to change and new meanings evolve but in an *ad hoc* way. At the qualifying level CCETSW (1989, p. 17) indicates that:

> Competence in social work practice is the product of knowledge, skills and values. Qualifying social workers must demonstrate their competence in practice to: assess needs, strengths, situations and risks; plan appropriate action; intervene to provide an initial response; implement action in a particular area of practice within the relevant legal and organisational structures; evaluate their work; transfer their knowledge and skills to new situations; and take responsibility for their professional practice.

Clearly the definition of competence employed here is much wider than the NCVQ definition, and because of the subtle interplay of knowledge, skills and values, its assessment can no longer be based on seductive notions of objectivity and value-freedom. The definition at this level is much closer to that offered by the Training Agency:

> Competence is defined as the ability to perform activities within an occupation. Competence is a wide concept which embodies the ability to transfer skills and knowledge to new situations within the occupational area. It encompasses organisation and planning of work, innovation and coping with non-routine activities. It includes those qualities of personal effectiveness that are required in the workplace to deal with co-workers, managers and customers.
>
> (cited in CNAA, 1991, p. 12)

As Issitt and Woodward (1992, p. 46) point out, embodied within this definition are notions such as initiative, originality, and the transferability of skills in situations which require increased levels of knowledge, understanding, and personal effectiveness. Thus competence 'can be taken to mean quite separate things, namely role competence, transferable competence or personal competence'.

At the advanced level, personal competence is given a high profile in the working paper on child care (CCETSW, 1993a, p. 2): 'Candidates should have a high level of personal attributes. They should be energetic, enthusiastic, sensitive, thoughtful, creative, supportive of others, possess a breadth of vision, a degree of self direction, and be self motivated and able to motivate others.' Thus competence at this higher level is quite removed from the NCVQ notion indicated previously and begins to touch on the holistic nature of professional expertise.

Using staff consultation and functional analysis, the ASSET programme (Maisch and Winter, 1991) and CCETSW's Scottish Office (CCETSW, 1993b) have attempted to generate competence statements at the post-qualifying level in child care and child protection respectively. In the Scottish Office report, five units are broken down into 24 elements of competence. Each element is then further subdivided into performance criteria, of which there are nearly 200 in total. CCETSW's working papers on child care produced by its London office (CCETSW, 1993a, c) use a different method with the much broader Paper 31 post-qualifying and advanced level requirements (CCETSW, 1992) being defined as competences. These are then broken down directly into performance criteria. No debate has yet taken place on definitions of competence at the higher professional levels, and whether assessment of competence at this level is feasible or desirable. Some of the difficulties of competence-based assessment are hinted at by Issitt and Woodward (1992, p. 48): 'It seems that by breaking down the whole performance into constituent parts, it is impossible to assess the whole person in action, which more accurately demonstrates the interaction of skills, abilities, experience, intuition and knowledge.'

COMPETENCE AND CHILD PROTECTION PRACTICE

The importance of having 'competent' practitioners in child protection cannot be underestimated: failure to make the correct decision about a child can have fateful consequences. It is therefore a highly relevant area in which to test the application of 'competence'. The need for professional competence is hinted at in the Kimberley Carlile Inquiry (London Borough of Greenwich, 1987, p. 96): 'It is never enough simply to comply with the letter of the state of procedures. ... There is always an overriding professional duty to exercise skill, judgement and care.' Not only does this message apply to social workers, but to all other child protection professionals. In order to protect children from permanent psychological harm or death, front-line workers have to develop an holistic practice which goes beyond the procedures and adult explanations of a child's injuries or 'disturbed behaviour', however plausible or authoritative. Such a practice connects intuitively with the world as experienced by the child, and requires a child-centred practice philosophy, theoretical knowledge of all types of abuse, and skills and experience built up over several years. It is the analysis and synthesis of these elements, and how they are then applied in an assessment which distinguishes outstanding practitioners from average practitioners, and ultimately a child's life from death.

This 'whole person in action' concept embodies all the qualities described by Issitt and Woodward (1992) above. Barnett (1993, p. 3), in her practice portfolio[1] for the award of Diploma in Child Protection Studies, Leicester University, begins by giving an overview of the value system and principles which inform her practice:

> My approach to all the pieces of work reflects my value system and the key principles that underpin my practice with adults and children.
>
> They are:
>
> i)   value the strengths in people i.e. all people have skills, understanding and ability;
> ii) people have rights, including the right to be heard and the right to control their own lives (which includes choosing what kinds of intervention they will accept in their lives, on the basis of full information about the alternatives);
> iii) a person's problems can never be understood if they are seen solely as a result of personal inadequacies. Issues of oppression, social policy, the environment and the economy are major contributory factors.

> It is my experience that these principles are constantly challenged when working in the field of child protection and the pieces of work [in the portfolio] highlight the tensions/contradictions in trying to maintain these value positions. For example in [one] case I was working in partnership with the parents, but their rights to self-determination were in tension with the child's welfare as paramount. I am also aware that often because of limitations in services to children and families (especially a lack of preventative services) I am constricted to work in ways which seem to focus on the child or parent as 'the problem', and so by implication pathologise individuals e.g. providing a groupwork programme to adolescent girls which singles them out for 'treatment' rather than being able to offer a package that includes the whole family. A great deal of my work is intervening in the lives of young children and I do have a strong children's rights perspective. This

often becomes uncomfortably juxtaposed with an adult view of what is best for a particular child. It is not an easy task representing children's interests and rights and resisting paternalistic assumptions of what is in their 'best interests' e.g. insisting that a child be given the right to decide whether or not to participate in a group (regardless of the views of the referrer) and the right to define their own issues and take action on them.

Figure 7.1 *Summary of principles for decision-making in child care. Based on Department of Health (1989).*

1) Children and young people and their parents should all be considered as individuals with particular needs and potentialities.
3) Children are entitled to protection from neglect, abuse and exploitation.
4) A child's age, sex, health, personality, race, culture and life experiences are all relevant to any consideration of needs and vulnerability and have to be taken into account when planning or providing help.
6) Parents are individuals with needs of their own.
7) The development of a working partnership with parents is usually the most effective route to providing supplementary or substitute care for their own children.
20) All children need to develop self confidence and a sense of self worth, so alongside the development of identity, and equally important is self esteem.
21) Since discrimination of all kinds is an everyday reality in many children's lives, every effort must be made to ensure that agency services and practices do not reflect or reinforce it.
23) Young people should not be disadvantaged or stigmatised by action taken on their behalf, e.g. as a result of admission to care or to special residential provision.
25) Young people's wishes must be elicited and taken seriously.
35) . . . a balance must be struck between offering carers support (thus building confidence) and holding them accountable for the child's well-being.

Many of the principles Barnett describes can be found in Department of Health (DoH, 1989) guidance on the Children Act where 42 principles which should inform decision-making in child care are outlined, some of which are summarized in Figure 7.1. These principles are described as 'colours on the social worker painter's palette to be used in the combinations and patterns required for each picture painted/child care case handled . . . The range and quality of colour helps to produce a good painting, but it is the painter's skill which makes or mars the picture' (DoH, 1989, pp. 6, 17).

The list offers some guidance to practitioners and managers and helps them analyse their decision-making in this complex ethical field. However, it is only when the principles are applied to specific cases that potential conflicts between people's needs, potentialities, rights and responsibilities become apparent. In the same way as the worker's whole interactive performance is of value, so too are the combinations of principles. By themselves, and applied in a mechanistic way like competences, they are of little value. A social worker's skills with children, young people and adults and the use of self are also of importance in explaining these principles to clients, so that they too have an opportunity to influence and/or understand the reasons why decisions are made. At the receiving end the consumer or client does not evaluate a practitioner's competence in performance criteria which are systematically ticked off. Rather performance is evaluated in its entirety, both intellectually and emotionally. Once again it is the 'whole person in action' who is valued, and this is best expressed in the words of H, a 16-year-old survivor of sexual abuse, in her evaluation of Louise Barnett's practice:

> The best bits I liked about working with Louise was when we started to write stuff out, trying to sort things out, but most of all [I] loved doing the drawings, looking and talking

about what they meant and what they said about me and how I was feeling. Sometimes I would just talk, talk, and talk and she would just listen. I could say what I liked and it did not matter how I said it, if I wanted to swear I could, I would always [say] sorry afterwards, Louise did not mind. I could be so open, sometimes it would scare me. She would see things I would never let anyone see and I didn't care if she did see. I could cry also, sometimes I wish she had given me a hug when I sat there crying. But the day I did really cry she did sit there and cuddle me and I cried my heart out.

I learnt a lot from Louise. Working with her she has helped me so much by listening, caring, talking, helping me feel better about my self and [she] gave me a lot of encouragement all the time. Telling me I am an OK person and even now when she writes, her letters always seem encouraging in one way or another. Also when I asked questions about what happens after she has seen me, she would tell me which was brill[iant].

(Barnett, 1993, Appendix F)

Lists of principles help to emphasize the ethical aspects of child protection decision-making, but perhaps minimize the emotional effects of such decision-making for both practitioners and managers. It is difficult, if not impossible, for managers and front-line staff not to be affected by the work they do. Coping strategies, formal and informal support systems and supervision play an important role in helping to counteract the effects of stress. Such support systems form a crucial part of the infrastructure in the 'whole person in action' concept of an holistic, empowering practice.

However, organizational culture can be a significant impediment to reducing stress among staff in agencies, where to raise vulnerability and fear may result in the labelling of a practitioner as incompetent:

Unfortunately when it comes to the myths and beliefs around the management of stress, many of the most fundamental survival messages have been along the lines of 'don't feel, be strong, don't admit mistakes and coping is professional' . . . It is precisely these messages that create added stress to staff.

(Morrison, 1990, p. 255)

The infrastructure of any organization is an important aspect of the way in which stress is managed and how staff are encouraged and supported in the professionally and personally demanding work they do. Through it opportunities are offered for staff to receive education and training.

THE POST-QUALIFYING EDUCATION AND TRAINING INFRASTRUCTURE

The post-qualifying education and training framework, with its flexible, modular, work-based 'pathway' approach, appears to be very much designed with the needs of the individual candidate in mind. It could therefore justifiably be considered as part of a supportive infrastructure for an empowering practice. However, a closer examination of exactly whose interests are being met by the framework reveals that it is those of the employer which will be paramount during this decade. The bureaucratic and regionally based consortium structure comprising colleges and agencies 'will negotiate, but not necessarily provide, all training needs at both levels within constraints imposed by local needs, resources and UK-wide standards' (CCETSW, 1990c, p. 3).

The wider context of collaboration between educational institutions and employers merits fuller consideration. When the framework was first envisaged resources were not as constrained as they now are, but Paper 31 (CCETSW, 1992, p. 9) makes several references to implementation being dependent upon them:

> The requirements deliberately do not prescribe a set programme so that employers can make immediate use of existing and new opportunities of varying lengths and style in a local area as is feasible within resource and other constraints.

Due to such resource constraints affecting not only employers, but also universities and colleges, it is my view that the framework will not be implemented in the original manner in which it was intended. Indeed, in a world increasingly dominated by market forces and devolved budgeting, collaborative arrangements may become far more difficult.

The individual candidate's needs for advanced level learning may become lost in the under-resourced bureaucratic machinery of a consortium comprising different agencies, some with competing agendas, and all struggling for financial advantage, or mere survival in an increasingly competitive market.

Individuals will also face more difficulty in choosing a post-qualifying programme within a university of their choice, particularly where resources are limited and budgets devolved. In addition, the finance now reserved for centralized CCETSW fees bursaries is going to transfer to consortia as they become approved. For candidates wishing to undertake more specialized, away-based learning opportunities leading to the advanced award, the move towards workplace assessment and in-service training within their own employing authority will prove particularly frustrating. More seriously, will there be sufficient resources to offer learning opportunities and assess candidates beyond the post-qualifying award?

With a focus on cost and the employer's needs rather than the individual candidate's, it is argued that the direction of social work post-qualifying education and training in the 1990s will mirror the direction vocational training took in the 1980s:

> The system must be planned and led by employers as it is they who are best placed to judge skill needs; it must actively engage individuals of every age, background and occupation, because they have much to gain from appropriate investment in their own training and skills; it must co-operate with the education service.
>
> (Department of Employment, 1988, p. 33)

Davies and Durkin (1991, p. 7) provide a powerful warning to colleges and individuals on the allocation of power within this triangular relationship:

> In charge is the employer with her or his needs paramount. Then, as an unavoidable necessity is the 'engagement' of the individual worker, in so far as his or her interests are useful to the employer. And, finally very much as the poor relation is the education service.

How will this tension between the employer's needs, the employee's needs and the role of higher education be resolved? A key person at the interface between the employing agency and the individual worker is the line manager who may, under CCETSW's regulations, also be the candidate's supervisor at post-qualifying level. When resources are limited, to combine these different roles makes sound economic sense. However, the potential difficulties of combining the two roles need to be examined.

THE ROLE OF SUPERVISOR AT POST-QUALIFYING LEVEL

Supervision is a key component of the support infrastructure for social work staff, and the balance between its various objectives deserves closer scrutiny.
Supervision may be defined as:

> A process in which one worker is given responsibility to work with another worker(s) in order to meet certain organisational, professional and personal objectives. These objectives are competent, accountable performance, continuing professional development and personal support.
>
> (Morrison, 1993, p. 13)

Texts on supervision often quote three major functions of supervision (Kadushin, 1976; Pettes, 1979; Payne and Scott, 1982):

> The management function: ensuring that agency policies and practices are understood and adhered to; prioritising and allocating work; managing the workload; setting objectives and evaluating the effectiveness of what is done.
> The educational function: helping staff to continue to learn and to develop professionally, so that they are able to cope with societal and organisational demands and to initiate fresh ways of approaching the work, according to changing needs.
> The supportive function: enabling staff to cope with the many stresses that work entails.
> (Richards and Payne, 1990, p. 13)

Richards and Payne (1990) and Morrison (1993) add a fourth category, the mediation function, which emphasizes the multi-agency dimension to current practice where professionals are required to work collaboratively. The mediation function is concerned with representing staff needs to higher management or other agencies and negotiating the co-ordination of services. Analysed in this way, the role of the first line manager can be seen to demand a range of skills and knowledge. Morrison then breaks down each of the four functions into aims. A closer look at these aims begins to reveal areas of potential conflict. Competence-based training is presented with a rhetoric of flexibility for the individual candidate, but the earlier discussion has indicated that it is employer-driven. There may therefore be an inherent tension between the following aims, as described by Morrison (1993): ensuring the overall quality of the worker's performance (the management function); developing the professional competence of the worker (the educational function); validating the worker both as a professional and as a person (the supportive function); and briefing higher management about resource deficits while allocating existing resources in the most efficient way (the mediation function). In the current political and economic climate, the assessment of competence-based learning in the workplace could become yet another managerial tool for monitoring workers' performance, rather than improving their professional competence or providing personal validation.

A qualitative study of child protection supervision, undertaken by Gadsby Waters (1992, p. 100), confirms the direction in which supervision seems to be heading. The results of her exploratory study reveal that for the majority of participants supervision was perceived to be managerial with the focus on 'behaving correctly' as distinct from 'behaving effectively' – doing things right as opposed to doing the right things. She argues that the educational and supportive functions of supervision need to be given a much higher profile to 'ensure good confident practice by social workers to best serve the needs of children suffering or at risk of abuse'. There is also the added danger that, for a worker who wants to appear competent for appraisal purposes, the disclosure of fear and vulnerability to their post-qualifying line manager/supervisor, may affect the outcome of both the appraisal and the competence-based assessment depending on their line manager's involvement in the assessment process. The definitions of other roles, such as those of the assessor and independent verifier, are also of importance: the influence of organizational culture cannot be ignored and impact on the whole process. Morrison's (1993) survival messages 'don't feel, be strong, don't admit mistakes and coping is professional' become more real in an organizational culture where to admit vulnerability may affect assessment of a worker's competence, and ultimately their future career.

Gadsby Waters (1992) concludes by arguing that if a worker-oriented approach cannot be incorporated within formal supervision, then it is necessary to offer other opportunities to meet professional and personal needs if workers are going to be enabled to practise confidently and competently. It would seem that the logical step would be for post-qualifying supervisors not to be line managers.

If the supervision of staff becomes more centred on the management and mediation functions, particularly regarding the allocation of resources within devolved budgets, then it may become more difficult for such workers themselves to demonstrate the enabling and empowering aspects of supervision at the post-qualifying level and management at the advanced level. There is also the question of assessment and how different qualities and perspectives are perceived within an organizational culture.

Assessment of competence in social work and child protection requires fuller consideration. There is a clear need to ensure that assessment processes and procedures reflect the anti-oppressive requirements of CCETSW itself. If workers experience supervision as oppressive, unsupportive and overly managerial, what then are the implications for their own support and for the development of an holistic, empowering practice with service users?

ASSESSMENT OF COMPETENCE

Kemshall (1993, p. 37) focuses on the 'human and social process of assessing', and like Ashworth (1992), she questions the supposed value freedom of competency-based assessment. However, she also questions the malleability of 'competences' in the organizational context:

> Competences may reflect little more than an agency's priorities and values, with no meaningful definition outside of the agency practices and context within which they are demanded and observed. This observation of competences also has its limits, and is a product of a complex relationship between agency practices, organisational context, and the relationship between supervisor and supervisee. Competence is the point at which the supervisee's performance 'fits' with the subjective view of the assessor and the organisational goals of the agency.

She argues that the 'occupational culture' of social work remains male and white, despite the recruitment of women and people from minority ethnic groups to the lower professional grades. It is in this organizational culture and context that the assessment of workers and students takes place:

> Crucial to [workers' and students'] experience of assessment are the values and perceptions they bring with them, how these fit with those of the organisation and the assessor, and the recognition and genuine appreciation those values are given by the assessor.
>
> (Kemshall, 1993, p. 39)

Who assesses the competence of the mentor, the supervisor and the assessor? Here the clash of two organizational cultures becomes more apparent. At one level there is the more 'feminized' culture of the front-line team members. However, the higher levels of management are frequently dominated by 'macho' management styles where senior managers are striving to become more businesslike in their emulation of the private sector (Kemshall, 1993). Within a competence-based employer-driven training structure, it is likely to be the more business and budgetary-oriented culture which influences the competence statements, and their assessment at the higher levels.

THE CHALLENGE OF COMPETENCE

The challenge of competence in child protection is to create organizational cultures which support and empower practitioners in the difficult decisions they have to take both with and on behalf of clients.

Barnett (1993, p. 15) had the back-up of a psychologist to help her if she felt over-whelmed by H.'s self harm and thoughts of suicide, which she discussed with H. The necessity for such support systems are vital to an holistic, empowering practice:

> My approach to H.'s experience of sexual abuse, was informed by an analysis of power and a view of sexual abuse as being interconnected with the experience and process of oppression. In other words, H.'s 'victim' experience related to the coercion/force of the abuser and his treatment of her as an object. I therefore attempted to respond to H. in an empowering, holistic way. On the whole I worked in a non-directive way, using whatever 'material' H. chose to bring to a session and utilised H.'s strengths and coping mechanisms as a survivor, including tapping into her creative abilities. My 'counselling' of H. aimed at her empowerment and development of self-confidence and helping her gain more control over her life. I did not view myself as the 'expert' with H., rather a container, supporter and enabler i.e. being present with H. in a firm, accepting way and not being afraid of the strong feelings during H.'s process of self-exploration. I worked explicitly with H., sharing recording, intended actions and models of understanding.
>
> The challenge of working anti-oppressively was highlighted during the time H. self-harmed. Giving H. choices was weighed against her need for protection as a young person in crisis and risk.
>
> (Barnett, 1993, p. 15)

Thus the complexity of practice and the selection of principles, 'like colours on the social worker's painter's palette' (DoH, 1989, p. 16) in a continually evolving practice canvas are highlighted in one worker's performance. A performance which demands the 'weighing-up' of principles involving child protection and risk, the consideration of a young person's individuality, their potentialities and wishes and feelings, the development of their self-esteem, and anti-oppressive practice (Figure 7.1).

It is the holistic, processual, intuitive and often personal nature of professional competence at the higher levels that differentiates adequate performers from outstanding performers. It is these qualities when considered *as a whole* that are valued by service users. This is confirmed by H.'s final sentence in her evaluation of Louise Barnett's practice (Barnett, 1993, Appendix F): 'I think Louise is brilliant at her job but also as [a] person.'

The challenge to competence in post-qualifying and advanced level education and training lies in developing definitions, empowering organizational cultures and ways of assessing competence which capture and nurture the 'professional artistry' (Schön, 1987, p. 22) of a highly experienced, competent practitioner in action. There is an urgent need to debate the nature of professional competence at the higher levels so that the holistic and reflective nature of competent performance may be recognized in the same way as H. evaluated and appreciated the variety of ways in which she had been helped by her social worker.

Whilst this chapter has focused primarily on individual competence and child protection social work, it should not be forgotten that child protection is above all a multi-agency activity, and we are reminded of this in *Working Together under the Children Act 1989* (DoH, 1991, p. 53):

> Effective child protection depends not only on reliable and accepted systems of co-operation, but also on the skills, knowledge and judgement of all staff working with children in relation to child protection matters.

While the holistic performance of all workers as individuals is emphasized, the real challenge of competence in child protection is to develop ways of facilitating and assessing outstanding co-operation and competence in a group of workers from different professional backgrounds. The 'whole person in action' concept is translated into a 'whole system in action'. If we can develop imaginative ways of defining and assessing holistic and collective performance across professional boundaries, then there is a possibility that competence in child protection could transcend its current individualistic context. This would be a real step forward in the interest of abused children and their families.

Acknowledgements

I would like to thank my friend and colleague Meg Bond for her comments on an earlier draft of this paper. I would also like to express my gratitude to Louise Barnett and H. for their permission to use extracts from Louise Barnett's practice portfolio. This 5,000 to 6,000 word submission (excluding appendices, bibliographies etc.) is one of four assignments which seek to demonstrate different aspects of the advanced level requirements (CCETSW, 1992). It comprises critical analysis and documentary evidence (e.g. thirty minute video-tape, reports, recording, and written evaluations from colleagues and service users etc.)

REFERENCES

Ashworth, P. (1992) 'Being Competent and Having Competencies'. *Journal of Further & Higher Education*, 16(3), 8–17.

Barnett, L. (1993) 'Practice portfolio submitted for the award of Diploma in Child Protection Studies', unpublished assignment. University of Leicester.

CCETSW (1989) *DipSW: Requirements and Regulations for the Diploma in Social Work*, Paper 30. London: CCETSW.

CCETSW (1990) *The Requirements for Post Qualifying Education and Training: A Framework for Continuing Professional Development*, Paper 31, 1st edn. London: CCETSW.

CCETSW (1992) *The Requirements for Post Qualifying Education and Training: A Framework for Continuing Professional Development*, Paper 31, 2nd edn. London: CCETSW.

CCETSW (1993a) 'Draft working paper on child care practice at the advanced award level'. Unpublished. London: CCETSW.

CCETSW (1993b) 'Competence in child protection: post qualification'. Final Report. Edinburgh: CCETSW.

CCETSW (1993c) 'Draft working paper on child care at the post qualifying level'. Unpublished. London: CCETSW.

CNAA (1991) *Competence-Based Approaches to Teacher Education*, Committee for Teacher Education. London: CNAA.

Davies, B. and Durkin, M. (1991) ' "Skill", "competence" and "competencies" in Youth and Community Work'. *Youth and Policy*, **34**, 1–11.

Department of Employment (1988) *Employment in the 1990s*. London: HMSO.

Department of Health (1989) *The Care of Children: Principles and Practice in Regulations and Guidance*. London: HMSO.

Department of Health (1991) *Working Together Under the Children Act 1989: A Guide to Arrangements for Inter-Agency Co-operation for the Protection of Children from Abuse*. London: HMSO.

Gadsby Waters, J. (1992) *The Supervision of Child Protection Work*. Aldershot: Avebury.

Hall, T. (1993) 'The training continuum: ascending the ladder'. *Community Care*, **981** (inside supplement), 1–2.

Issitt, M. and Woodward, M. (1992) 'Competence and contradiction'. In P. Carter, T. Jeffs and M.K. Smith (eds) *Changing Social Work and Welfare*. Milton Keynes: Open University Press.

Kadushin, A. (1976) *Supervision in Social Work*. New York: Columbia University Press.

Kemshall, H. (1993) 'Assessing competence: scientific process or subjective interference? Do we really see it?' *Social Work Education*, **12**(1), 36–45.

London Borough of Greenwich (1987) *A Child in Mind: Protection of Children in a Responsible Society, The Report of the Commission of Inquiry into the Circumstances Surrounding the Death of Kimberley Carlile*. London: London Borough of Greenwich and Greenwich Health Authority.

Maisch, M. and Winter, R. (1991) 'The NCVQ functional analysis method as applied to the description of professional level practice'. Paper presented to the National ASSET Conference, Chelmsford, March 1991.

Morrison, T. (1990) 'The emotional effects of child protection work on the worker'. *Practice*, 4(4), 253–71.

Morrison, T. (1993) *Staff Supervision in Social Care*. Harlow: Longman.

NCVQ (1988) *The NCVQ Criteria and Related Guidance*. London: NCVQ.

Payne, C. and Scott, T. (1982) *Developing Supervision of Teams in Field and Residential Work*, Paper 12. London: National Institute for Social Work.

Pettes, D. (1979) *Staff and Student Supervision: A Task-Centred Approach*. London: Allen and Unwin.

Richards, M. and Payne, C. (1990) *Staff Supervision in Child Protection Work*. London: National Institute for Social Work.

Schön, D. (1987) *Educating the Reflective Practitioner*. San Francisco: Jossey Bass.

Chapter 8

Competence and Curriculum in Youth and Community Work Training

Mary Durkin

In 1989 a National Youth and Community Work apprenticeship scheme was established in 24 local authorities across England and Wales. One of the principal reasons for the establishment of such a project was to draw into full-time youth and community work groups of people who were seen to be under-represented, for example, women, people from minority ethnic groups, people with disabilities. An important objective was to recruit a group of people younger than those who become qualified through other routes to professional qualification. A further important consideration was that these young people would become qualified and work within their own communities (Sinclair, 1987).

The scheme was known as 'Youth Leaders for the Inner Cities' and 'Youth Leaders for the Valleys' in England and Wales respectively. The training was centrally funded through Education Support Grants (ESG), and was overseen by a national steering committee which reported to the Parliamentary Under Secretary of State for Further and Higher Education (DES, 1988, 1989).

BACKGROUND TO THE NATIONAL SCHEME

Much of the thinking behind the scheme was based on work observed in San Francisco and recorded by HMI (DES, 1987, unpublished) on neighbourhood, peer-led, community work in which young people identified as leaders or activists in their own communities were given training to work professionally with their peers. Although the ESG schemes were a development of this thinking, in that participating young people in England and Wales would be trained to full qualifying level in youth and community work, the emphasis on local community-based experience of the United States scheme, and the fact that the participants' academic background would probably be minimal, remained central.

The schemes were apprenticeships; that is, the learning was to be undertaken 'on the job', rooted in the everyday realities of local authority and voluntary youth and community work, not based in a college with students making occasional forays into the field. The young participants were to be employed by the local authority for the duration of the scheme, and obliged to abide by the terms of employment covering all local authority employees, although with special contracts to allow for the pursuit of training. It was stressed by the DES from the beginning that this innovative training offered to a younger group of indigenous workers was expected to produce a fresh approach to youth and community work (DES, 1988). The participants would not merely reproduce the sorts of youth and community work from which they were learning, but would identify new projects and methods of tackling old problems (Sinclair, 1989).

The initiative was welcomed by many in the youth service and representatives of the 24 participating authorities came together in the early stages to plan their schemes. This was by no means the first initiative of its kind – apprenticeship schemes had been operating for many years in the profession – but the scale of this scheme, and the central Government funding focused professional thinking. Most influential on those planning the curricula for local schemes was the work of Bainbridge (1988) on validating learning from experience, and Bolger and Scott (1984) on a competence-based route to training for part-time youth workers. The thrust behind these publications was that youth and community work skills could be developed practically, building on life experience and drawing their theoretical base from that experience. Core youth and community work 'competences' were identified, which could be developed through guided experiential learning. Evidence of this learning was gathered in a portfolio, and on this portfolio was the participant to be judged.

This model was believed to be far less oppressive than conventional, college-based routes to training, in that it allowed the possibility of challenge to what could be seen as an elitist college curriculum, it avoided over-emphasis on academic work, and in validating the student's own experience and perception in working with black people it mitigated the effects of white cultural imperialism and promoted equality of opportunity. The term 'apprenticeship training' was used because it was seen to be more meaningful to people from working class communities.

The national scheme responded to another trend in which local authority youth and community services were becoming increasingly concerned to determine the training of those people whom they would be employing in a full-time professional role. The ESG thus gave youth and community services the opportunity to develop schemes to meet the needs of their service. Although the bulk of the funding came from central Government through the ESG, local authorities were free to develop the detail of their own scheme within a standard model with guidance from the National Steering Committee.

The model required that participants from each local authority should be between 18 and 25 years of age who would not normally be seen to have the necessary qualifications to gain entry to higher education. The apprentices, who become known as 'workers in training' to distinguish them from students on conventional courses, would be engaged on the same national qualification route. Each scheme required the local authority to develop the local training in conjunction with an Institute of Higher Education (Training Agency). Sixty per cent of the 'worker-in-training' time was to be spent learning 'on the job', guided by a qualified youth and community worker as supervisor; 40 per cent of the time was to be spent learning 'off the job', guided by a tutor from the training agency. Each local authority scheme appointed a co-ordinator, responsible for the overall coherence of the scheme. The training took three years (although an exception was made for two authorities which ran for only two and a half years) and workers-in-training were to be judged at exactly the same level as students on college-based courses.

Positive action was an important feature of the model and guidance was issued to local authorities as to the recruitment of 'under-represented groups'. Positive action measures included additional help with child care to enable young parents to participate in the schemes.[1]

THE APPRENTICESHIP MODEL AND EXISTING TRAINING

Before looking at the use of the competence model on the schemes it is necessary to give an outline of the apprenticeship model in relation to youth work and community work training. The traditional route to initial qualification as a full-time professional worker is through courses at institutes of higher education, and universities. The academic level of the work varies from Certificate of Higher Education to degree or postgraduate level . Increasingly the professional award is made at the level of Diploma of Higher Education. Indeed that transition happened during the course of the apprenticeship schemes, but for reasons unrelated to the development of work-based training. Normally college-based schemes recruit students with two or three years of experience in the youth and community work field either on a voluntary or paid basis, normally with five or six 'O' levels and sometimes with 'A' level qualifications or equivalent for mature students. The course will last for a minimum of two years and will involve college-based work as well as placements in youth or community centres. The balance will be roughly 60 per cent of students' time spent in college and 40 per cent 'on the job'. Professional endorsement was through the then Council for Education and Training in Youth and Community Work (CETYCW), now the National Youth Agency, and validated academically through the same channels as any other higher education course. The 40 per cent of time spent 'on the job' is supervised by an accredited supervisor, and the supervisor's report in conjunction with the college tutor's visits and personal knowledge of the student will be taken as evidence of the student's achievement on the job. Additionally under normal circumstances the student's work at college will be expected to reflect the growth of experience, and theoretical understanding should be fully applied. The academic work will be assessed through the usual academic methods. These are principally essays and reports, sometimes group and project work, and occasionally through formal examinations.

The apprenticeship schemes were developed by the local authorities in close co-operation with the institutes of higher education. This made an interesting combination. The local authorities often had very highly developed training services for part-time workers and volunteers. These services had been influenced, as outlined earlier by Bainbridge (1988) and Bolger and Scott (1984), by competence-based training and by the accreditation of prior learning. The thrust of this work was to build on the experience of the worker and to avoid the imposition of an academic curriculum which may easily be culture bound and not relate to the worker's needs.

The training agencies, on the other hand, were accustomed to working from a more formal syllabus broadly following the academic conventions. Most were very open-minded about the ideas developed through local authorities. All were anxious to extend access to previously excluded students, and all were interested in new methods of teaching and assessing where these were available. Most were already very familiar with many of the methods employed in the local authorities' part-time training. There was nevertheless a tension in some of the schemes between the two strands of thinking. Generally, this was productive, although occasionally it became problematic and serious mistrust developed between the interested parties (Issitt, 1991).

By no means all of the apprenticeship schemes decided to adopt the competence-based methods already developed in the training of part-time and voluntary workers. Some did and had very strong feelings about it; other schemes were equally clear that the methods were not suitable for initial training level. This chapter describes three schemes which took different stances on the matter. In all three, sound education and training was delivered to the young people appointed and there were no serious worries at any stage about the standard or content of that training.

THE THREE APPROACHES TO APPRENTICESHIP TRAINING

Scheme A

Ten local young people were employed through this scheme, none of whom under normal circumstances would have been accepted in a college of higher education, on the grounds of their youth and lack of formal academic qualifications. The scheme was developed by the local authority's principal youth officer and training officer, and fully supported by the education-related departments within the authority. Officers in the authority had been centrally involved in the development of much of the work on competence mentioned earlier in the training of part-time workers and volunteers, and there was a real commitment to extend this understanding to the initial training of youth and community workers (Bainbridge, 1988).

There was additionally a very strong resolve to train local people, capitalizing on local knowledge and experience and, in particular, to recruit local black people to work on issues of the gravest importance within their own communities.

Finally, there was a commitment that the curriculum should be responsive to the experience and understanding of the local people and not an imposition upon them. Skills were to be identified and accredited as well as developed and underpinned theoretically through the experience of the workers in training.

The authority appointed a scheme co-ordinator, a very experienced youth worker, who after appointment became centrally involved with the principal youth officer in the development of the course. Unusually among the apprenticeship schemes, the authority decided not to work with the local institute of higher education, but with the Open University (OU). This was a new departure as the OU at that time did not operate its own course for training youth and community workers. The link with the OU was seen to be appropriate as the CETYCW had already collaborated with the OU on the training of part-time workers and volunteers and upon the validation of learning from experience. An additional part of the thinking was that the OU was already very experienced in developing learning materials for students from an unconventional background and this could be fruitfully applied. A tutor was appointed on a part-time basis.

Scheme B

This programme was developed by the youth and community work service again with co-operation from the Local Education Committee as well as voluntary organizations in the area. This authority also had a strong grounding in competence-based work for part-time workers and volunteers. Unlike scheme A, scheme B chose to work with its local college of higher education and, in conjunction with that college of higher education, developed the apprenticeship training. The college of higher education already had a broad range of well-established college-based professional training for youth and community work.

Unusually among the apprenticeship schemes, scheme B worked closely with disability resettlement officers and other disability rights organizations and attracted a very high number of young people with disabilities to the scheme. Out of ten successful candidates, five on scheme B were young people with disabilities.

The scheme was deeply committed to a competence-based model on the grounds that this was the best method to validate the experience of young people themselves and to allow them to develop their skills without what was seen as the impediment of a superimposed theoretical framework. It should be stressed, however, that in neither scheme A nor scheme B was theory considered irrelevant. It was simply seen as something that should be drawn from the practice rather than imposed upon it.

The scheme B co-ordinator was the local authority training officer, who was responsible for designing the scheme and for linking the practical, or what became known as the on-the-job work, with the off-the-job training. The college working with scheme B appointed a part-time tutor to work with the apprentices, responsible for most of the off-the-job teaching and the assessment procedures and working very closely with the scheme co-ordinator in matters of student welfare and development of individual learning.

Scheme C

This scheme was designed by senior officers in the youth and community work department, with some involvement from most of their full-time workforce in the borough. The borough co-operated very closely with the local institute of higher education in the design and delivery of the scheme. As with the other schemes, ten local young people were appointed, most of whom would have found formal higher education inaccessible for one reason or another. Those managing and developing scheme C were very strongly opposed to employing competence-based teaching methods. They considered the method too limiting and too mechanistic and they firmly believed that their workers in training were entitled to the same theoretical foundation as other students. They feared that competence-based training might lead to a second-class service for already disadvantaged people. Much of this thinking came from a history of good relations with their local institute of higher education. This college had for some years run initial training for youth and community workers and had prided itself on attracting a cohort of mature working class people without standard entry qualifications for higher education who had benefited from professional training in the higher education context (Issitt and Spence, 1988). Both the college and local authority maintained that, without in any way dismissing the life experience of working class participants, their intellectual and experiential horizons had been extended by exposure to the theoretical framework of their work, and to a grounding in related academic disciplines (sociology, economics and politics).

All three schemes were physically housed by their local authorities. They had two or three rooms (known as 'the base') where some teaching would take place each week and from which on- and off-the-job learning was organized. The base also acted as a contact point for supervisors and as the apprentices' workplace. In the case of schemes A and B almost all of the off-the-job training was undertaken in the local authority base. In the case of scheme C, of the two days a week off-the-job training, one day was spent at the local authority base but the other was spent at the institute of higher education involved. On this day the workers-in-training on the scheme would work with apprentices from a neighbouring authority and would be taught by the full staff team of the youth and community work department of the college. In line with ordinary college practice, the apprentices would have a personal tutor responsible for individual academic development, and for liaison with the scheme co-ordinator and with the on-the-job supervisor.

The level of academic validation varied among the three schemes. Scheme A was validated through the OU at Certificate of Higher Education level. There was grave reluctance on the part of the OU to give academic credit for on-the-job learning. This meant that 60 per cent of the apprentices' time would effectively be seen merely as a back-up and practice for the validated work. The scheme and the authority were unhappy with this situation, on the grounds that youth and community work as a vocational course should be judged as a whole, not simply on the academic understanding of the process. Accordingly scheme staff went directly to the CNAA with the work of their apprentices and sought validation on an individual basis for the apprentices' work at Diploma of Higher Education (DipHE) Level. In every case the application to the CNAA was successful.

Scheme B was initially validated by the college at Certificate of Higher Education level. When it was perceived that some students were achieving beyond this mark, a facility was written into the scheme for allowing those students who felt so inclined to proceed to DipHE level by undertaking an extra module. This module was academically based and really comprised a long assessed essay. A minority of students on this scheme availed themselves of this. All who did passed.

Scheme C was validated at Certificate of Higher Education level. There was strong feeling that this was the traditional and appropriate level for training in youth and community work. There is now, however, some evidence that had the scheme been presented for academic validation at DipHE level it may well have passed, and indeed subsequent comparable work at the college has been accepted as DipHE level.

The background of the apprentices on all three schemes was remarkably similar. The average age on starting was 20. Out of the 30 apprentices, just over half were women and six were severely disabled. Under half were black and these were mainly clustered on scheme A although all schemes had some black apprentices. Most apprentices had English as their mother tongue, although for some it was their second language, their first being Urdu, Punjabi, Gujerati or British Sign Language. The only participants facing significant difficulty with English as a foreign language were the two profoundly deaf workers in training on scheme B for whom translation from sign into English remained problematic throughout the scheme. Workers in training on two of the schemes had difficulty with literacy. This was not in any way related to whether or not English was their mother tongue. All workers in training had some experience of youth and community work before appointment and had lived most of their lives in the local authority. All were appointed as trainees on the same salary level. Many of them had young children in their care.

The understanding of 'competence-based training' on the two schemes particularly wedded to the method differed to a significant extent. What was common was an understanding of the method as expounded in manuals for the training of part-time workers and volunteers. At its simplest, this was a new method of assessment and in this sense the development of the training became assessment led. People were judged on what they do and how well they do it rather than how much they know and how thoroughly they understand it, although no exponent of competence-based training would argue that theoretical understanding was unnecessary. The equation would use the Bainbridge formula that competence equals knowledge and understanding underpinned by values (Bainbridge, 1988).

On all three schemes the major areas of the curriculum and, therefore, the major areas in which competence had to be demonstrated were largely pre-identified by in the first instance the guidelines produced for professional endorsement (CETYCW, 1989) and secondly by Bainbridge's core competences. While these may have been expressed differently on the three schemes, written work was compulsory and assessed conventionally.

The difference was seen in the assessment of on-the-job work. On scheme C, the curriculum-based scheme, this was assessed through continuous assessment by the supervisor, the co-ordinator and the apprentice, using the criteria laid down and refined through the curriculum document and the individually developed learning contract. In the other two schemes it was assessed through concrete evidence of achievement (contained in the portfolio) of a long list (over 60) of essential 'competences', which could be achieved at different levels. The assessment of the supervisor was secondary to this independent demonstration of competence.

The differences were more axiomatic than real. Scheme C apprentices had evidence of their fieldwork other than the reports produced, and in the other two schemes reports were often used to support the portfolio. Other than the language used it would have been difficult for the intelligent outsider to spot the difference.

It should be pointed out that regardless of the teaching method and assessment method used, each scheme was endorsed professionally, and validated academically according to the same processes as required for other qualification routes. No allowance within both of these judgements would be made for different teaching approaches. With a similar cohort and similar objectives, therefore, it should be possible to trace the differences in the progress of the three schemes.

From the outset the biggest problem was one of fragmentation. The week was split, and the workers-in-training related variously to tutors, supervisors and co-ordinators. Line management could be confused with academic accountability. Guidance for the worker-in-training who may never before have been in full-time employment and had almost certainly no post-16 education, could come from a variety of sources, or all parties might assume it was coming from elsewhere. On all 24 schemes the co-ordinator was the single person with an overview of the scheme and became absolutely pivotal. Within that role was concentrated knowledge of on- and off-the-job training; local authority management procedures; academic regulations; individual development of the workers-in-training; and other matters which, under normal circumstances, had they been lodged anywhere, would have been lodged with the personnel department. Where the role of co-ordinator broke down schemes became chaotic, and workers-in-training disproportionately found difficulty in finishing the course. On the three schemes concerned, co-ordination did not break down, to the credit of the three individuals concerned.

It must be said, however, that the detailed breakdown of professional achievement into very specific competences was not necessarily helpful to the workers-in-training. In a fragmented world they at times served to add to the fragmentation rather than clarify the task. Classic scenarios emerged in which one worker-in-training, who was working well, complained that on- and off-the-job learning were progressing as planned 'but the competences were a bit confusing'. There were times then when the system appeared an impediment.

However, local authority A, as stated above, firmly believed that a competence-based model was the best suited to achieve these ends and staff on the scheme were committed to what they called a more holistic approach to initial training, with more creative links and cross-fertilization between on-the-job and off-the-job learning; between theory and practice; between prior experience and the learning process; and between the range of departments and agencies (statutory and non-statutory) involved in working with young people and community groups. Training was the acquisition of generic core competences which underpinned the curriculum of scheme A.

In both towns the advantage of a competence-based method was seen to be the continual review of learning and learning objectives, in the light of each individual student's personal background and current learning. The level of competence would be continually assessed until a satisfactory level had been reached and bench marks would be established individually for each worker in training on a regular basis. Learning contracts would become the main vehicle for this assessment and developmental process. In the case of scheme B, a competence grid developed by Ian Ledgerwood at Bradford and Ilkley College was used for the assessment of competence.

Scheme C described its method in fairly similar terms. They refer to an integrated learning experience covering practical work experience, theoretical study, tutorial and group work. They refer to the importance of the partnership between Sunderland Polytechnic and the local authority and emphasize that the key to this relationship will be the individual learning contracts which will review and record progress and determine short- and long-term objectives. They stress that the learning will develop from experience and practice to organizing and conceptualizing through to theory and on to (changed) experience and practice. They do not, however, refer to competence or core competences and they present their course as based on an established curriculum.

In all three cases a significant amount of time was set aside for the development of study skills, and work in small groups, with intensive support in particular from the co-ordinator, the base line. The two competence-based schemes, in addition to the scheme co-ordinator, academic tutor and work supervisor, offered support to each 'worker-in-training' through a personal learning tutor. This role was identified in *Starting from Strengths* (Bolger and Scott, 1984) and is equivalent to that of mentor in the development of national vocational qualifications. The personal learning tutor was to be outside of the assessment and learning process and had at heart educational and professional development of the workers-in-training. It was in conjunction with the personal learning tutor that a personal learning path should be plotted. These tutors were paid on a sessional basis and the amount of use was varied.

The major criticism that proponents of the non-competence model would make of the competence model was that the teaching was outcome-based and assessment-led, and that little account was taken of growth, development and understanding. The major criticism that the competence model would have of the curriculum-based model would be that a curriculum was being imposed upon the workers-in-training regardless of the demands of the workplace, the experience of the workers-in-training and their immediate learning needs. Competence-based schemes might also argue that their use of assessment as a continuous process to affect learning meant that assessment became an integral part of the learning process and a tool with which to develop understanding, rather than an imposition imposed by academic authorities divorced from the needs of the student or the workplace. Adherents of the curriculum-based approach might reply that the competence-based schemes tied the worker-in-training far too rigidly to the demands of the workplace and that the assessment method continually imposed a mechanistic skill-based framework on the worker-in-training, stultifying development and inhibiting imaginative application of new ideas and new theory.

The portfolio was the vehicle through which the worker-in-training demonstrated evidence of competence. The portfolio is a record of youth and community work practice of the worker-in-training which may well include documentation of experience prior to coming on the scheme. It also records their personal development and will include recordings, photos, press cuttings, testimonials, written assignments and any other evidence that the worker-in-training in conjunction with her or his tutor might see fit to present. Like the learning contract, portfolio building was seen as a tool in enabling workers-in-training to assess their own learning needs and plot their own learning.

For its part, scheme C did not rely heavily on a portfolio. However, it referred to the central importance of learning through assessment. The assessment of the individual trainee is an integral part of the delivery aims of the overall scheme. It is through a varied but structured assessment process that trainees will make the necessary connections between their own experience and new learning activities, which in turn lead to the development of professional practice. The methods of assessment identified were: individual learning contracts and tutorials as self-assessment, group tutorials and end-of-year assessment, group and peer assessment, continuous assessment of work practice reflected in the revision and recording of individual learning contracts, reports from placement supervisors, reports by the trainees themselves on their practical work, a report on this work overall by the co-ordinator, the assessment of course assignments, for example, of essays, reports, a final end-of-year *viva voce* formal assessment process. It remains to be seen whether the portfolio as a tool amounted to any more or less than the vehicle for the presentation of the documentation which would anyway be presented by scheme C.

As the schemes progressed, over the three years, there were inevitably peaks and troughs in both training methods. In all three schemes the pivotal role became that of the scheme co-ordinator who was the person with oversight of all scheme elements. The role of workplace supervisor, which had initially been seen as central in the scheme design, in all three cases became on occasions problematic again. Specific training had been offered for all workplace supervisors, who were generally well-qualified and experienced practitioners. The training met with various success, depending upon the experience and interest of the supervisor concerned. However, the demands of the workplace often militated against the fullest involvement of the workplace supervisor and the role was sometimes seen as prohibitively onerous. Where the relationship worked well, however, the supervisor in both competence-based and curriculum-based schemes was centrally involved in the development of the worker-in-training's learning contract and at times, in individual interim sessions with the worker-in-training, played a part in integrating the experience of the workplace with the theoretical work delivered through institutes of higher education.

The integration of theory and practice in this way was crucial and common to all three schemes. According to a competence-based model, theory will emerge from the learning needs of the individual worker-in-training and will, therefore, be seen in context and as a tool for development rather than an academic exercise. A curriculum-based scheme would argue that the theory was there and must be understood and applied to practical work as appropriate. In effect all three schemes were obliged to produce a schedule for the off-the-job learning, which was applied on base days through the co-ordinator, to the practical work as appropriate. These clear 'outcomes' were not sufficient in themselves but required a supporting structure of 'inputs' into the learning process.

To say that the learning contract would dictate the teaching for each individual worker-in-training was a council of perfection. There were ten workers-in-training on each scheme, all with different individual learning needs which were to be met by part-time tuition from an institute of higher education. While every effort was made to integrate theory with practice on base days, and while to a great extent this was successful, workers-in-training on both competence-based schemes often referred to the disjunction of the two elements. It seems inevitable that this would be the case. The only difference between these two and the curriculum-based scheme was that no pretence was ever made on the curriculum-based scheme that this disjunction would not happen. The curriculum-based scheme went a step beyond this. In an interview, the co-ordinator made very clear her view that while much of the discussion and the focus of the group work was negotiable according to the students' needs, the lion's share was thought through in advance by the co-ordinator. She did not believe that responding to the immediate concerns of any individual worker-in-training was necessarily the best means of teaching. She referred to this as responding to crisis which she said might result in a sticking plaster approach to education.

Both competence-based schemes acknowledge this dysfunction, which was remedied, in part, through the personal learning supervisor. However, the principal means through which individual workers-in-training were enabled to bring the two parts of their learning together, was when they were in the work setting with their work supervisor and the base days with the scheme co-ordinator. On neither occasion was there formal input from the HE Institution. Scheme A, however, quickly acknowledged the limitations of the competence-based model for learning theoretical work and adopted more conventional methods for assessment in this area.

The difference became one of emphasis and one of terminology. As well as the ordinary process of rigorous assessment instituted by the colleges of higher education concerned, all three schemes were subject to rigorous review by two external examiners. Academic and professional standards were carefully scrutinized throughout the three years. While examination board meetings and reports from external examiners were never unadulterated praise, there was at no stage in the process of any of these three schemes, any doubt that the academic and professional standards would ultimately be met. That is not to say that all of the workers-in-training concerned would eventually be awarded the initial training qualifications and indeed on two of the schemes there was a less than 100 per cent pass rate. This proportion was comparable with that on conventional training schemes.

CONCLUSION

It would have been a simple matter to look at less successful schemes, and demonstrate how either, on the one hand, the competence model was cumbersome and mechanistic, or on the other, that the curriculum model was subjective and imprecise; that the competence model valued personal experience and challenged an oppressive curriculum, or that the curriculum-based model extended horizons, moved beyond personal experience offering education, not training. This would have been to skew the evidence that, notwithstanding the ideological positions, good sensitive teaching overrode the difference of approach. In practice there were more similarities than differences both in outcome and process. A question must remain as to the extent to which, if the key roles of co-ordinator, personal training and academic tutors had been poorly executed, the deficiencies in either model would have been highlighted.

NOTE

1. During 1989 the National Steering Committee for Youth and Community Work Apprentices Tips issued a series of guidance notes to local authorities participating in the scheme and 'The Recruitment and Selection of Workers Training' was the title of one such paper.

REFERENCES

Bainbridge, P. (1988) *Taking the Experience Route*. Leicester: Council for Education and Training in Youth and Community Work.
Bolger, S. and Scott, D. (1984) *Starting from Strengths*. Leicester: National Youth Bureau.
Bolger, S., Jackson, M. and Young, K. (1989) *Handbook for Personal Training Advisers*. Leicester: Council for Education and Training in Youth and Community Work.
DES (1988) *Education Support Grant Notification to Local Authorities*. London: Department of Education and Science.

DES (1989) *Education Support Grants. Guidance Notes to Local Authorities*. London: Department of Education and Science.

Issitt, M. (1990) 'The tensions between the employer and the training agency on apprenticeship training.' *Youth Leaders for the Inner Cities and the Valleys*. Conference for Employers Participating in the Education Support Grants.

Issitt, M. and Spence, J. (1988) 'An exploration of the relationship between community education and higher education.' *Journal of Community Education*, 6(4), 14–19.

Sinclair, T. (1987) 'Apprenticeship Training'. *Youth and Policy*, 21, 4–7.

Sinclair, T. (1989) *Towards a Vision*. Conference paper circulated by the National Steering Committee for Youth and Community Work Apprenticeships, Leicester.

Chapter 9

The Use of Competence in an Articled Teacher Scheme

Elaine Barnes

We are now in a period where the social and political context of state-provided schooling in Britain is reminiscent in a number of ways of the climate of reaction in the 1860s. There is a growing emphasis upon tighter accountability; a required core curriculum and a concentration upon basics. The role and strength of the inspectorate is being reappraised and changes can be expected in the ideology and practice of inspection at all levels. Both teacher training and the work of teachers in schools are to be subject to more surveillance and to the application of more specific criteria for the assessment and evaluation of competence.

(Grace, 1985, p. 13)

The PGCE (Articled Teacher) Course at Crewe and Alsager College of Higher Education (1990–93) was one of the first teacher education courses in the country to adopt a competence-based approach. This chapter looks at the nature of PGCE (Articled Teacher) schemes in general terms and goes on to consider how the Crewe and Alsager pilot developed the use of competences in relation to its course. Improvements which have been implemented since the pilot began are summarized, and the lessons learned from this competency-based pilot scheme are considered. The chapter as a whole presents an example of how teacher education in one institution has responded both to the external influences of the last decade as outlined by Grace (1985) and to the carefully considered views of a group of teacher educators committed to enhancing the quality of student experience.

BACKGROUND TO THE PGCE (ARTICLED TEACHER) SCHEME

Various Articled Teacher (AT) schemes began in September 1990 as the result of a Government initiative to encourage the piloting of this school-based partnership approach to teacher training. Students enrolling on the two-year PGCE course were to spend 80 per cent of their time in school and 20 per cent in college, with all courses required to meet the existing criteria relating to primary teacher education as specified by the Council for the Accreditation of Teacher Education (CATE) in Circular 24/89. Applications for inclusion in this pilot scheme had to be jointly presented by institutions of higher education and local education authorities, and this Government requirement represented the first formal indication of its desire to increase the involvement of schools and teachers in the training process, thus also reducing the role of higher education institutions.

Fourteen consortia comprising such local education authority and teacher education institution partnerships were originally granted Department of Education and Science (DES) approval and support, and each of these schemes, while meeting the same basic criteria and the same underlying principles, was designed to suit the needs and interests of those partners involved, often taking account of local priorities or initiatives. Some, for instance, concentrated on recruiting candidates who could offer community languages, others on early years' education, and some secondary courses focused on shortage subject areas. This variety, plus the number of different approaches to course recruitment and design, provided the DES with many models of school-based training for evaluation purposes. In comparison with the other 13 pilot schemes, the distinctive feature of the course developed by Crewe and Alsager/Tameside was that it adopted a competence-based approach.

This scheme was aimed at intending primary teachers and focused primarily on developing the partnership between school and college, and between tutor and teacher. It aimed to produce teachers who were competent, confident, reflexive and professional. In addition to being an early example of such a training partnership and of a school-focused approach to teacher education, the scheme was also the first offered by Crewe and Alsager which was based on competences and was underpinned by the use of a Professional Development Profile.

THE DEVELOPMENT OF CREWE AND ALSAGER'S COMPETENCES

Cogan (1973) described the teacher education process as 'the development of the professionally responsible teacher who is analytical of his own performance, open to help from others and withal self-directing'. During the late 1980s a working party of staff within Crewe and Alsager College had been meeting to consider the relative merits of adopting a competence-based approach to teacher education in an effort to develop the type of teacher Cogan (1973) describes. The use of competences within other training routes and an increasing awareness of the potential of competence approaches gained through consideration of developments in other professions had prompted this work, and this, together with a recognition that the existing teaching/learning relationship within teacher education might soon be restructured and redefined, had led staff to consider innovative approaches.

This working party identified 26 competences, using the CATE criteria as a basic starting point, and the group faced a particular challenge in identifying teacher competences which were general without being vague, but also specific without being silly, as in 'can hold chalk'. As a result the competences were not exclusively behavioural but related to those aspects of knowledge, skills and attitudes that a professional teacher might be expected to demonstrate, recognizing the importance to the teaching role of the affective domain. In this sense it can be seen that the notion of competence in teacher education was interpreted more broadly and descriptively than in current NVQ-based vocational schemes.

The competences needed to be more than performance indicators, and their use was, and is, seen as central to an ongoing process of development. For this reason the criteria statements were not a set of behavioural objectives to be considered as achieved and completed once demonstrated. Rather the competences were intended to be descriptors which would apply to teaching performance both during initial training and also during the rest of a teacher's professional career.

The process of self-evaluation against the competency criteria was considered to represent a major shift in both the initial and the continuing professional development of teachers which could also be related to the growing use of Records of Achievement in secondary education and the introduction of appraisal in teaching. Students completing Records of Achievement during their secondary education are engaged in a process of identifying and making explicit their knowledge and experiences, and the majority of applicants for undergraduate courses use such records to support their applications. At the end of their training these students would be regularly involved in appraisal exercises as professional teachers. There was an undeniable logic which demanded the bridging of the higher education 'gap' in this personal and professional continuum, and this logic gave further support to the development of a competency model involving self-assessment and presentation of evidence.

THE USE OF THE COMPETENCES IN THE CREWE AND ALSAGER ARTICLED TEACHER (AT) SCHEME

The 26 competences which had been identified by the working party became the central focus of the whole course. They helped to determine the planning, delivery, assessment and evaluation of the AT training programme, and provided a 'mission statement' for all those involved in the partnership.

In practical terms the 26 competences represented the main element in the students' Professional Development Profile. Students took an active role and were required to evaluate and assess their own development each half-term against the list of competences, and to identify their strengths and their professional and personal targets for the following half-term period. School-based mentors also made use of the competences in analysing student performance, and the comparison of the student's self-assessment and the mentor's assessment became the basis for professional discussion and the planning of future school- and college-based experiences.

A basic decision which had to be taken at a very early stage in the course related to whether all 26 competences should be introduced to students from the first day of their training, or whether the competences needed to be phased in during the course. It was decided that the course should meet student needs by focusing on various aspects of education in turn. The total list of 26 competences were grouped into those relating to:

1. the classroom, and teaching and learning issues;
2. issues relating to whole school policy;
3. the wider educational issues which needed to be considered by intending professionals.

Each group became the primary focus of one phase of the course. As the whole course lasted two years or six terms, each of these phases was equated with a two-term period. Consequently, terms 1 and 2 became Phase 1, and 13 competences applied. During terms 3 and 4 the focus was extended to cover the whole school dimension, and a further four competences were added to the original 13. The focus was shifted to wider educational issues in the final two terms of the course, and all 26 competences related to this period.

The plan was that students should use this list of competences by ranking their own development against a given scale which originally was a five-point scale as shown in Figure 9.1.

This pilot scheme attracted considerable attention, both as an example of a new route into teaching *and* as a competence-based model of teacher training. Regular visits by Her Majesty's Inspectors, interest expressed by the Council for the National Accreditation of Awards (CNAA), and internal evaluation and quality control mechanisms plus a funded external evaluation all provided information as to the development of the course.

As the use of competences was central, considerable attention was focused on this aspect. The number of professionals involved in this scheme, both as participants and as observers, helped to inform developments through ongoing evaluation and regular discussion. Termly visits were paid, for example, by a team of HMI, and regular debriefings were held after such visits. Both the scheme itself and the competence-based approach benefited from this close scrutiny, and a number of changes were made as a result.

DEVELOPMENTS IN THE USE OF THE COMPETENCES DURING THE PILOT SCHEME

The recording of competence and the use of the Professional Development Profile (PDP)

In assessing their development, students were originally asked to rate their level of competence for each of the relevant competency criteria against a five-point scale. Since 1990 this has gradually been refined, initially to a four-point scale, then to a two-category model, and finally, in 1994, to a point where the need for a scale is being questioned and reviewed. In addition to the completion of this 'tick list', students were also required to identify, at the end of each term, their professional strengths and their targets for the following term. Together these two elements formed the basis of a student's PDP.

This original idea of a student ranking their own competence on a tick list was found to be less efficient than it first promised to be. The evolution of the tick list as previously described has also been accompanied by a move towards students augmenting this summary approach with supporting evidence. This development, which occurred during the early part of the course, resulted from one student showing us the way forward. She decided in the first term that the tick lists and summary sheets alone were not sufficient for meeting her needs, and she started to write a paragraph on each competence each term, offering an explanation for the decision she had reached. This written justification and the provision of written evidence to support the final decision proved so informative and so useful in encouraging the type of reflexivity towards

TERM 2 COMPETENCY CRITERIA	SUPERIOR	HIGHLY SATISFACTORY	SATISFACTORY	NEEDS ATTENTION
①. Adequate and appropriate subject knowledge including National Curriculum requirements.				
②. Ability to set appropriate aims and objectives.				
③. Ability to plan coherent and progressive sequences of work.				
④. Skills in classroom management and organization.				
⑤. Establishment of good order and good working relationships with pupils.				
6. Competent in the delivery of subject(s) and/or curriculum experiences.				
7. Ability to select and use appropriate settings and resources for learning.				
8. Use of information technology.				
9. Ability to employ a range of teaching methods appropriate to children's needs and abilities which also reflects a concern with equal opportunities.				
10. Ability to provide for special educational needs.				
11. Skills in evaluation and assessment of children's progress.				
12. Understanding of the cognitive development of children in the appropriate age-range.				
13. Awareness of the value of self-appraisal and appraisal by others.				
Phase 1. End				

Figure 9.1 *Example of competency criteria.*

which the course was aiming that this has since been accepted as the best way forward. The tick sheets have, to date, remained but are augmented by the presentation of supporting evidence. The demand for more explicit written and verbal justification raises the level of deliberation and thought, and therefore enhances the learning opportunities this activity provides.

This shift in the use of the PDP reflects a revised view of the approach in that the value has now been focused on the *process* of deliberating, reflecting, assessing and evaluating rather than solely on the *product* or the tick list. The instigators of this approach always intended that the process should be the focus in order to develop the student's reflexivity, but the system that was established needed refining before this facilitated the intended outcome.

Our experience shows that students, particularly undergraduates, when completing tick lists can either deliberate about their decision for a long time and prove reluctant to commit their thoughts to paper, or they can find it easy to complete the profile with little depth of analysis. The process benefits considerably when supported by a system which requires students to present evidence to support their views, and a system of mentoring or tutoring which offers students the opportunity to discuss their progress in a professional manner with someone who is familiar with the process. In the AT scheme this function was served by school-based 'mentors' and in order to extend this benefit to other ITE (Initial Teacher Education) routes a system of 'professional tutors' has been established. Students meet their professional tutor at least once per term for a discussion to support the development of their professional reflexivity.

The identification of key competences

The philosophy behind the development of the criteria was that each competency was an important aspect of teaching that would be expected in a competent, confident, reflexive professional. All 26 competences were therefore listed as of equal importance, and the numbering of these only represented an organizational device. No hierarchical arrangement was thought to be appropriate.

In any programme of professional training it is necessary for all those involved in the course to be able to identify those students who are progressing in a satisfactory manner, and those, if any, who fail to reach an acceptable level of competence. The need to identify 'key competences' arose from HMI advice, as it was felt that a minimum threshold level of competence needed to be established which would have to be met in order for a student to pass the course. Several aspects of this development caused subsequent concern.

It was decided that those involved with the course would identify ten of the competences as 'key competences' and that each student would need to be rated at least at the satisfactory level for each of the ten identified key criteria. This proved a very difficult task, as the various contributors to the course all differed slightly in their selection of the ten 'most important' competences, but eventually consensus was reached and the ten key criteria were identified with a circle around the competence number (*see* Figure 9.1).

The fact that such variety existed in this identification of key competences reflects how experience, expertise and context influence an individual's view of the most important elements of the teaching role. The professionals had no difficulty in agreeing that all the competences were important and relevant, but there were understandable differences in placing such competences into a hierarchy. For example, one mentor who was responsible, within her school, for the special needs work considered this to be one of the key competences, whereas others selected different criteria which they considered more essential. Total agreement would therefore be highly unlikely, but a general consensus was all that was deemed necessary.

Within the pilot scheme the identification of certain criteria statements as representing 'key' competences later led to some misunderstanding about the relationship between those ten competences which had been identified as the 'core' and the remaining 16. This caused several students to believe that all competences were equal but that some were more equal than others. It appeared that the circling of the ten competences had served to draw the reader's eye and attention towards these to the detriment of the others and further work was needed to reinforce the idea that all competences merited equal consideration. Staff began seriously to question whether the identification of the minimum threshold was of any real benefit.

The assessment of professional competence

The assessment of whether a student teacher has reached an acceptable level of competence in the classroom has been a central part of initial teacher education for many years. This is generally a holistic judgement based on classroom observation of the student's teaching performance by experienced practitioners, and mechanisms exist to standardize this process and ensure that the subjective judgement is augmented by the collection of evidence, often with a set of criteria to support the decision and to ensure some degree of objectivity.

There was a great deal of discussion within the AT scheme as to whether such a holistic approach to judging classroom 'competence' could or should be replaced by the notion of students reaching a minimum threshold in a number of identified competences. It was decided to maintain the holistic judgement of student performance alongside the competency approach as it is theoretically possible for a student to prove satisfactory or even successful at various aspects of the teaching role (i.e. individual competences) and yet still be unable to teach in a truly effective manner. The whole is definitely more than the sum of the parts.

The reluctance of the professionals involved in the course to abandon the holistic judgement in favour of the minimum threshold of competence approach signified an instinctive and intuitive reaction which only later became rationalized. The model of competence was initially adopted in order to support and inform professional development in a formative manner and it was not designed as an assessment tool, particularly not in an external and summative sense. The use of the competence model reflects a philosophy which recognizes the importance and the value of involving the student in monitoring and assessing his/her own professional development. Responsibility for and ownership of this approach rests with the student and no formal judgement is made of the student's ability to evaluate personal and professional development. Where the mentor or professional tutor might not fully agree with the student's self-assessment a useful discussion might ensue, but ultimately the completion of the

PDP is done according to the student's informed self-appraisal. Thus it is the student's involvement in the competency process which is deemed to be important and the formative nature of this which supports and informs future practice.

The decision was therefore taken to keep the competency approach and the final and summative assessment of professional classroom competence separate, although, of course, any professional judgement at a holistic level is closely related to an interpretation of the various competences which contribute to effective teaching and quality learning in the primary classroom.

The understanding of the relevance of context

The use of the competency criteria and the five/four category scale initially caused major concerns to all those working on the course. Students found it difficult to take account of the stage of their training and of the context in which they were working when they assessed their own performance and it had to be constantly stressed that the decision related to an assessment at a specific point in the course, and in a specific context. Thus to achieve the 'satisfactory' rating in the first term of a course needed a lower level of competence to be demonstrated than for the same classification at the end of the two years.

Another associated feature of this was that a student's performance might appear to regress rather than progress if either the context altered significantly or if the student became more aware of the demands of the teaching/learning process. That this was quite normal and only to be expected did take some explaining, and a lot of support was needed in discussing this aspect of professional awareness with all of the course members.

Leat's (1993) attempt to provide a conceptual model of competence indicates this importance of context by identifying three components of teacher competence: cognitive, affective and behavioural. He represents the complex links between these components by using a Venn diagram (shown in Figure 9.2).

Leat's explanation of this conceptual model of teacher competence illustrates the importance of context.

> ... the three are inextricably linked. They are related to one another, but they are also partly independent, they may respond at different rates as teachers learn. The links between them are myriad and complex, but may be loosely described as intellectual and emotional processes. Where the three overlap may be thought as competence, in that context. I deliberately imply that competence is context specific. Moving schools can unhinge the synchrony and, within a teacher's timetable, one class can induce the dislocation of one or more components.
>
> (Leat, 1993, p. 36)

Understanding of the terms used

The mentors were all primary teachers who had had limited experience in working with students in such a manner prior to their appointment to this role, and both students and mentors wanted further detail to support their interpretation of the competency

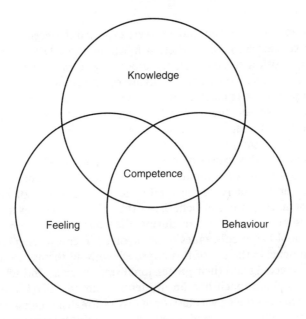

Figure 9.2 *A conceptual model of competence.*

statements. This was partly caused by the simplicity of some of the competence statements and the way, described earlier, that the statements needed to be interpreted according to context and stage of the course.

An attempt was made to provide descriptors to break down the statements of competence into a developmental sequence of skills, and this also helped students and mentors to interpret the level of competence that was being demonstrated. These descriptors were offered for the ten key competences and were considered to be a very useful addition to the assessment process. Everyone involved recognized and accepted that this task needed to be further reviewed and developed.

THE BENEFITS OF THE COMPETENCE-BASED APPROACH IN THE AT SCHEME

One of the major benefits of the competency approach on this type of partnership course was the fact that the criteria provided all of those involved in the scheme with a common language and a shared 'mission statement' which evolved through regular discussion about the interpretation and meaning of the individual criteria. Such shared understanding is vital to the success of any scheme which involves close and effective partnership but was particularly important in the AT scheme which included a large number of constituent members: students, class teachers, mentors, head teachers, LEA advisers and college tutors. The scope for slippage or misinterpretation of the scheme was potentially enormous, yet all those involved felt that this was averted by the central role played by the use of competences and the PDP.

The competences provided a publicly stated and widely available description of the knowledge, skills and attitudes the students were expected to develop and demonstrate, and the regular consideration of the criteria within the PDP enabled the teacher educators to adopt both a reactive role in responding to meet each individual's identified targets, and a proactive role in arranging opportunities and experiences which would facilitate the student's personal and professional development according to both the phase of the course and the student's projected future needs. For example, the course addressed the basic aspects of identifying and responding to special educational needs and included a short placement in a special school. A student who identified a perceived weakness in this aspect of her work was also provided with opportunities to 'shadow' a special needs co-ordinator within the school to enhance her understanding of the issues and to increase her confidence in this aspect of teaching.

One of the unplanned but major benefits of this pilot scheme was identified by class teachers, mentors and head teachers during the course evaluation. It had proved impossible for school-based colleagues to be involved in considering competences and supporting the students in the use of this approach without themselves taking a critical view of their own teaching and their professionalism. Teachers and schools found that the competence-based approach had an influential and beneficial impact in terms of raising staff awareness of their own classroom professionalism, enhancing the teachers' ability to reflect critically on this, and in providing a useful framework for professional discussion and debate.

Interestingly, in this pilot course the early benefits of the competence-based approach were for the teachers, mentors and tutors using the competences rather than for the students themselves. The students accepted this aspect of the course without question, and were soon developing the skills this approach required. When questioned by HMI and others about the value of a competence-based approach they found difficulty commenting, because as they put it, they knew no other type of course design and had no means of comparing their experience with that of others. What was soon natural to them was new to all the others involved in the scheme, and it was the necessity to take a fresh look at what teaching should involve which proved beneficial to the professionals involved.

During 1992/3 the students from the first cohort were interviewed as part of the course's externally organized evaluation process. Many of them had obtained teaching jobs by this time and they reported that they felt themselves to be better equipped than their fellow newly qualified colleagues to identify and to meet their own professional needs. It appeared that the confidence and reflexivity which the course had aimed to develop had certainly been taken forward into their teaching careers.

Although, in the early stages, the students were not able to verbalize the benefits they gained from the use of competency criteria and the PDP it was of great value for them to know, from the outset of their teacher training, exactly what was expected of them and what their expected goal should be. The model of the teacher on which the competences were based became fixed in their minds, and the regular assessment against the criteria helped to build their confidence and to reinforce the qualities of professionalism and reflexivity which were central to the course.

CONCLUSION

In conclusion, the general principle of the competence-based approach to teacher education and the use of the Professional Development Profile have served to enhance the quality of the course in a number of ways.

First, they have enabled students to recognize and accept the clear and obvious links to be made between the many and various elements of teacher education. The connections between theory and practice, the relationship between college-based work and its practical application on school experience, the ways in which study of primary curriculum subject areas and degree-level academic work interrelate have all been made more visible by the competency approach.

Secondly, they have enabled all those involved in educating intending teachers to have a shared metalanguage related to teaching competence.

Thirdly, the involvement of students in self-assessment and evaluation and in professional discussion about their individual development from the very beginning stages of their training has helped to develop reflexive practitioners in a way that was not possible with more traditional course design.

Fourthly, this active involvement of each student in his/her own learning process has resulted in college staff being able to apply to professional training within higher education many of the same principles which they applied in their own classrooms as primary teachers such as clearly communicating the purpose of activities, encouraging independence within a supportive atmosphere and so on.

Fifthly, our experience has shown that the use of a competence-based approach needs to be supported by a system of skilled mentoring or professional tutoring if it is to be successful.

Finally, the debate continues as to what the wording of teaching competences should be and how professional development should be recorded. In the light of recent developments both within our institution and in the country as a whole, our original list of competences and the way in which they were used now seem rather naïve and clumsy, but as we were among the first to attempt such work this is hardly surprising. Since our PGCE (Articled Teacher) scheme began, the Government has adopted the idea of competence-based teacher education and Circular 9/92 expressed the minimum competences required for the approval of secondary Initial Teacher Education courses, with Circular 14/93 serving the same purpose for primary courses. Staff at Crewe and Alsager are now facing the challenge of building upon the work to date, and designing new courses for both undergraduate and postgraduate entry into the teaching profession. We are undertaking this work secure in the belief that it is the actual *use* of competences which is of value, rather than the exact wording of the competency statements themselves, and although refinements to the actual format may help those involved with the scheme to some extent, the overall value is in the process rather than the product.

Developing the Articled Teacher PGCE with its innovative approaches to teacher education was a challenging task, but one which brought us many benefits. The lessons we learned during the pilot scheme have provided us with a firm foundation on which to base future changes and our experiences will enable us to face the present and impending developments in teacher education confidently and with a clear idea of how we want to proceed. We firmly believe that a competence-based approach can enhance the quality of professional development within all Initial Teacher Education courses.

REFERENCES

Cogan, M. L. (1973) *Clinical Supervision*. Boston, MA: Houghton Mifflin.
Grace, G. (1985) 'Judging teachers; the social and political contexts of teacher evaluation.' *British Journal of Sociology of Education*, 6(1), 3–16.
Leat, D. (1993) 'A conceptual model of competence.' *British Journal of In-Service Education*, 19(2), 35–40.

Chapter 10

Competency in Practice – Cheshire Certificate in Education: Further Education

Carol Maynard

The Cheshire Certificate in Education: Further Education, was validated by CNAA in June 1991, with 75 teachers graduating from the programme in September 1993. The scheme was devised by colleagues from six further education (FE) colleges in Cheshire and supported by a higher education (HE) institution. There are many reasons why the scheme was developed; the one relevant to this chapter is that previous FE teacher training programmes did not meet the needs of Cheshire teachers. This chapter is in three parts: first an overview of the development, strengths and weaknesses of the programme will be given, then I will compare and contrast this programme with Training and Development Lead Body (TDLB) awards, followed by comment on broader issues associated with competency-based approaches.

DEVELOPMENT OF THE PROGRAMME

Staff working in the further education sector come from a diverse range of academic, vocational and professional backgrounds, many having received little or no teacher training. Further education institutions deliver education and training programmes to post-16 students of varying abilities. Programmes range from Access into HE to Basic Skills, with the majority of training being in the vocational areas, for example, engineering, business studies, construction. In order to be responsive to the varied needs of further education students, colleges must recruit staff who are flexible and adaptable as well as appropriately qualified in their particular academic, vocational or professional fields. This often means that staff are recruited for their vocational and academic background and knowledge rather than their ability to teach. Therefore, teacher training in FE has been an integral feature of in-service staff development to enable staff to be trained adequately. FE teachers in Cheshire, prior to the new programme being introduced, were offered a range of teacher training programmes in-house, at county level and at neighbouring HE institutions, some leading to accreditation. The programme was disjointed and *ad hoc*, and did not provide a structured approach to professional development. Therefore, following a review of existing teacher training programmes in the area, a working group formed to develop a scheme which had the following features as its central focus:

- coherence
- flexibility
- increased access and progression opportunities
- equality of opportunity
- experiential learning highly valued
- the development and accreditation of work-based learning
- provision of a coherent framework of professional development
- teaching and learning strategies which mirror current FE provision

The programme needed to be coherent in order to offer FE teachers a planned programme of professional development linking teacher-training skills, professional up-dating and management training together. Flexibility was required to enable staff to receive training when and where they needed it. Previous programmes had been course-specific with days away from the workplace. The organization of such training was often inflexible with rigid attendance requirements including weekend sessions. Such an approach did not suit FE institutions as staff timetables made attendance difficult. Part-time and female staff were also disadvantaged by such inflexibility. Therefore, the new programme had to increase access and progression opportunities through flexible delivery and attendance modes. The new programme had to value experiential learning in the current teaching of students, and also previous experience deserved recognition. Finally, the programme had to be designed in such a way as to reflect current practice in FE, such as the progressive introduction of NVQs and GNVQs. To take this all into account, the new FE Certificate in Education was competency based, using the NCVQ model as its starting point.

Change in the funding of teacher training was a minor factor leading to the development of a competency-based programme. There was a possibility that the current system of mandatory awards for teacher training might be withdrawn in favour of finance through the Training and Enterprise Councils for programmes leading to NVQs. In consideration of this the Cheshire programme content was defined in terms of units and elements of competence in a similar manner to other NVQs (see Figure 10.1). In this way the Cheshire scheme was prepared for further modification to fit with NVQs should a different source of funding be necessary, although the educational rationale for the competence-based approach had already been established.

While the format mirrored that of NCVQ programmes, the way the programme was devised differed. At the time of devising the Cheshire scheme some lead bodies were using a task analysis approach (Mitchell, 1989) where routine occupational skills and tasks were thought to form the basis of vocational training and standards. This resulted in a rather narrow and mechanistic view of work roles (Mansfield, 1989), therefore, NCVQ and the Training Agency recommended that functional analysis should be the method for the development of the standards. The working group rejected both approaches and started planning the programme using the assumption that teachers require a body of knowledge, a theoretical base, as well as the need for occupational competence to become professionals. The need to plan an initial teacher training scheme which aimed to produce 'reflective practitioners' (Schön, 1987) was considered to be paramount. The main influences were Schön

CERTIFICATE IN EDUCATION: FURTHER EDUCATION

Units and Elements of Competence

Unit Code and Title 3. Programme Design

Design programmes/sessions to achieve curriculum and syllabus objectives.

Element Code and Title 3.1

Write a scheme of work based on identified student learning needs.

Performance Criteria

3.1.1 Identified needs of learners have been taken account of.

3.1.2 Syllabus/curriculum has been broken up into manageable units of learning.

3.1.3 Outcomes and content have been ordered and structured to provide for progressive learning.

3.1.4 Accreditation suitable for learning outcomes has been identified and agreed, and requirements of appropriate external authorities has been met.

3.1.5 Programme has been set out in a form understandable by all parties.

3.1.6 Feedback on the appropriateness of structuring has been sought from colleagues and students.

Range Indicators

Scheme/programme to cover 10 sessions or 30 hours.

Assessment Specifications
Performance/Product Evidence

Scheme of work/programme which meets the learning needs of a defined group, expressed in learning outcomes, leading to accreditation where possible and appropriate.

Supplementary Evidence

Written aims and objectives reflecting the needs of learners.

A rationale justifying the components of the programme produced.

Figure 10.1 *An example of a course element.*

(1987), Rogers (1983) and the Further Education Unit's model of curriculum development.

The basic structure of the course is as follows. Following an initial review an action plan is agreed between student and tutor which sets up the parameters for the programme. Students can negotiate their learning programme based on preferred learning styles and opportunities for collection and assessment of evidence. Such activity is reviewed regularly with the core themes integrated into the programme overall. The units and elements of competence forming the content of the programme, i.e. what a student should know and be able to do at the end. In Phase 1 students provide evidence of competence in practical teaching skills as well as associated knowledge and understanding of the underlying principles of teaching and learning. Phase 1 units of competence were devised to cover identification of needs, programme design, delivery methods, assessment, use of resources, and review and evaluation in addition to keeping up to date with professional issues. Phase 2 units were devised to encourage progression and development within three complementary and overlapping strands:

1. the student should develop as a reflective, professional practitioner;
2. the student should develop an understanding of increasingly wider contexts;
3. the student's competence should grow from being primarily situation-specific to encompass a broad range of further education contexts.

Phase 2 units have been devised to develop these three strands in response to student demand. The range reflects the need for education and training for specific FE developments for broader areas of an FE teacher's role. The range reflects the varied needs of students, who include health professionals, prison lecturers, adult education tutors, as well as FE college lecturers. For example, guidance is introduced in Phase 1 within the context of a tutor's usual duties relating to tutorial support. In Phase 2, 'Guidance' as a unit broadens the context so that students are aware of the importance of guidance within the FE sector overall in terms of funding, retention rates, etc. In Phase 1 the development of learning materials is covered as part of programme design and use of resources. The Phase 2 unit, 'Open/Flexible Learning' extends knowledge and understanding further through the production of learning materials which can be used in a variety of teaching and learning contexts. This unit also focuses on research in the field which students must critically evaluate. Students must complete six units in Phase 2, and it is hoped that the choice of such units matches their professional development needs, building on interests developed in Phase 1. Students' line managers may contribute to the discussion regarding Phase 2 choices so that institutional needs are considered too.

The programme aims to balance assessment of competence within a work-based environment with assessment of theoretical aspects of teacher education. The external examiner highlighted the tensions this caused in one of his reports.

> There are, however, obvious tensions in the prescription of the holistic conception of reflective practice operating alongside a competence-based scheme based on the premise that the professional role can be reduced to discrete (though connected) components.

The working group aimed to reduce such 'tensions' through the assessment methodologies within the programme. These have been refined and developed since the start of the programme and now comprise:

1. observation of natural performance where classroom teaching and other areas are assessed in addition to accreditation of competences;
2. assessment by portfolio, evidence compilation (including Accreditation of Prior Learning) related to units and elements of competence with supplementary evidence (underpinning knowledge) supporting portfolio artefacts;
3. assessment activities devised by course teams to enable students to demonstrate their competence and knowledge, e.g. seminars, micro-teaching, workshops;
4. the completion of a Learning Record throughout the programme.

It is the fourth assessment strategy which aims to bridge the divide between occupational competence and professional development. Through completion of the Learning Record, students are expected to maintain a critical log of both academic and topical reading; review and evaluate their teaching on a regular basis, with the emphasis on analysis rather than description; comment on and evaluate 'taught' aspects of their programme; and chart their professional development as a result of the education and training they are experiencing. Of all the assessment strategies, this has been the most difficult to develop.

STRENGTHS AND WEAKNESSES OF THE PROGRAMME

The programme has developed and been modified since 1991 following extensive review and evaluation activities. The content, assessment strategies and format are still being developed and this process will continue as part of the quality assurance mechanisms at course and institutional level. Evaluation evidence compiled since the programme commenced points to several conclusions.

Language

Most students and tutors have expressed their dissatisfaction with the language used in the units and elements of competence. There are two aspects to this issue. First, students and tutors who are unfamiliar with NCVQ, or other competency-based programmes, find the terminology and format used in the programme difficult. It has a jargon of its own which is not programme-specific, but relates to NVQ-type competency-based learning overall. To be confronted by performance criteria, range indicators and elements of competence is daunting for any student embarking on the programme, as it may be unlike any other course studied previously.

An example from Unit 4 illustrates the difficulty. By the end of this unit the student should be able to 'implement learning programmes to meet organization's curriculum objectives and make effective use of a range of methods and techniques'. In simple terms this means 'Can you teach effectively?'. Students are confused until they have received thorough instruction in the terminology. This is now a feature of the induction programme of the Certificate in Education (as with other NVQ programmes in FE), when the terminology is clearly defined before the students collect evidence. This has not overcome the dislike of the language used on this competency-based programme but has provided a vehicle for staff development for students and tutors.

This has proved a valuable learning experience for both students and tutors involved with the programme. Eventually all FE staff will be working with students on competency-based schemes, and their awareness and knowledge will be greatly enhanced if they have been through a similar process themselves. Those students on the Certificate in Education programme who have already been involved with NVQ delivery, for example, hairdressing and catering teachers, adapt well to the language and format as it is familiar to them. The second language problem is less complex. Some Certificate in Education terminology, for example, 'manufacture' instead of 'make' resources, is too stilted and jargonistic, and this will be monitored and altered accordingly as the programme develops.

Volume of work

Another area of concern identified by both tutors and students was the amount of work which had to be completed. While accepting that students often complain about their workload, tutors do need to take particular notice of their concern in this instance. In the first two years of the scheme tutors may have been too demanding over the submission of evidence to cover every element of competence. There are two possible explanations for this. First, tutors themselves were not too familiar with the programme and possibly over-assessed due to lack of confidence and experience. A second explanation has also been given by staff working on NVQ programmes. Assessors on NCVQ programmes can only accredit the element when all performance criteria have been met. This sometimes results in a rather tedious interpretation of the criteria with a piece of evidence required for each. It is possible that this happened during the early stages of the Cheshire scheme despite our intention that evidence should be used for several elements, assessed collectively. There has to be a balance between rigour and rigid adherence when assessing performance criteria. The Definitive Course Document outlines this clearly: '. . . this course is concerned with the holistic development of FE teachers and course tutors will focus on the general competence of teachers as opposed to a detailed checklist approach' (C. and A., 1991, p. 28).

Accreditation of Prior Learning

Accreditation of Prior Learning (APL) is an integral part of the course because as a strategy it offers individual students an opportunity to use and have valued and recognized prior learning and experience. This is important to those FE staff who may be experienced in a range of vocational and educational contexts and as such attempts to offer equality of opportunity by meeting the needs of all individuals through the recognition of experience and preferred learning styles.

Since the course began there have been few APL submissions. This is because of tutor inexperience and student perceptions of APL. Some tutors have not encouraged the submission of APL evidence due to their own lack of confidence in identifying and assessing appropriate evidence. This is currently being addressed through staff development sessions and regular verification meetings where APL submissions are assessed by other team members. As tutors become more confident in supporting APL, students may wish to be more proactive in compiling portfolio evidence which is not current. Some students have perceived APL as the easier route and have perhaps confused it with exemption. For example, one student submitted a letter from her line manager which stated that she had been teaching in his department for three years and that she met the requirements of most of the Phase 1 units. The letter did not provide details of any contexts in which the competences were demonstrated and there was no matching of activity to performance criteria. When this was discussed with the student she realized that more detail was required and the rationale for it. The line manager required more persuasion believing that his opinion 'that she is a good teacher and therefore meets the requirements of Phase 1' was being challenged. This situation has now been resolved but it took considerable time to explain the differences. Course teams need to emphasize that evidence must match up to objective criteria instead of being based upon opinion.

Some students felt aggrieved that their attendance on previous teacher training programmes did not normally count as exemption. This was only possible if they were able to provide evidence of competence as a result of attending such courses, for example, previously assessed work or teaching observations, which could then be submitted for APL. These misconceptions have had to be dealt with sensitively and in future more detailed guidance will be given at the induction and action planning stages.

In practice, despite simplistic assumptions by some students, submission of APL evidence has often been more complex and rigorous than assessment of current competence. As the programme is new, tutors have been over-anxious and possibly too demanding when assessing prior evidence. Such practice is being reviewed in order to decrease the anxiety of both students and tutors.

APL within the Certificate in Education context is different from that on other NVQ programmes where artefacts are solely assessed against the performance criteria with no requirements for reflective practice. This may be appropriate for some skills-based areas, such as catering, but needs careful consideration when being applied to management or teacher training: 'It is no accident that professionals often refer to an "art" of teaching or management and use the term artist to refer to practitioners unusually adept at handling situations of uncertainty, uniqueness and conflict' (Schön, 1987, p. 16).

With APL evidence it is sometimes difficult to ascertain the learning and development which has taken place as a result of activities which happened some time ago. To be presented with a set of artefacts which do not always provide evidence of reflection and self-development can be problematic. The best solution is to insist on cross-referenced explanations in the Learning Record, which also ties APL evidence into the rest of the programme.

Group learning

One of the criticisms of competency-based programmes is that they reduce the need for group and/or taught sessions. However, tutors and students on this programme have both identified group learning as a strength. Course teams always wished to maintain group and peer contact but with such an individually based programme this cannot be a compulsory element. However, colleges structure group sessions as part of their programmes and these are generally well attended. As well as focusing on particular theoretical aspects, and underpinning knowledge, these sessions are used as tutorials or seminars where ideas, opinions and concerns are shared. This is an essential part of the holistic approach to the programme. Colleagues from Croydon College also believed group dynamics and peer group learning to be paramount when planning their own competency-based curriculum. An HMI report (1990) had previously identified such teaching and learning strategies as invaluable.

Tutorial support

Initially, tutors raised concerns about the amount of tutorial time needed to run this particular programme, yet evaluative evidence suggests that students value the amount and quality of tutorial support. It is possible that in the early stages of the programme, course teams were having to provide more tutorial support than is usual on other teacher training programmes. Issues relating to jargon, use of language and unfamiliarity with APL have been raised earlier as possible initial inhibitors at the start of the programme. There is no doubt that as tutors have become more familiar and confident with the programme, the time needed for individual support has decreased. Tutors have devised flexible modes of delivery to facilitate student learning, and budget-holders in the colleges need to understand this. This programme is not delivered in a traditional, didactic manner, and recognition needs to be given to the demands placed upon tutors. Most colleges operate a case load approach to ensure fairness, with team members organizing support, taught sessions, observations and review sessions, based on the needs of individuals.

Tutors will need to build on and extend their skills in developing students' abilities to take responsibility for their own learning thus lessening tutor dependency. Some students have found it difficult to self-review and manage their own learning programme. This is not surprising if they have previously experienced only more traditional forms of teaching and learning. Careful preparation of students at the start of this type of programme needs to take place alongside staff development for tutors. This should minimize a reactive, crisis management approach being adopted at a later stage.

In conclusion, students and tutors have acknowledged the benefits of reflective practice. They still need support in compiling and assessing Learning Records; however, this aspect has been recognized as being as valuable as observation of teaching, for assessment purposes. It is this aspect which is not explicit in NVQ programmes. There is no requirement for reflective practice, only compilation of evidence to meet the performance criteria. The next section compares the Cheshire Scheme with the Training and Development Lead Body (TDLB) awards and expands this issue further.

COMPARISON BETWEEN THE CHESHIRE CERTIFICATE IN EDUCATION AND TRAINING AND DEVELOPMENT LEAD BODY (TDLB) AWARDS

The TDLB was set up in 1989 with support from the Training Agency to set standards and provide the basis for vocational qualifications for all those with a training and development responsibility. The aim has been to define standards that will apply to anyone in a training and development role.

The standards were published in 1991 (TDLB, 1991) and are currently being revised. Since 1991 the main cohort of students registering for such awards has been those involved in the delivery of NVQs and GNVQs, with two of the units (D32 and D33) being essential requirements for assessors working on NVQ and GNVQ programmes. Within the FE context, D34 (Internal Verifier) and D36 (APL Adviser) are units which are being acquired by course co-ordinators and staff involved in APL assessments. These units are also essential requirements for NVQ and GNVQ programmes. Most FE institutions are running staff development programmes focusing on the acquisition of these four units of competence. FE staff could convert the units into a NVQ Level 3 qualification if they acquire further units, but at the time of writing these have not been specified.

Both the Cheshire Certificate in Education and TDLB awards are competency-based qualifications. However, there are two fundamental differences. The Cheshire Certificate in Education programme has been developed to acknowledge and recognize the breadth of the role of FE teachers. The outline of the development and content of the programme should demonstrate this. The current TDLB awards being acquired in FE are appropriate to specifically defined areas of a teacher's role, namely, assessment of evidence, internal verification and APL practice. At present these particular areas are appropriate only to those staff working on NVQ and GNVQ programmes.

The other difference between the two qualifications concerns the nature of assessment. As the TDLB awards relate to specific areas of an NVQ/GNVQ teacher's role, the evidence required is narrowly defined. The format and language is the same as that used in the Certificate in Education programme, but there is no requirement for reflective practice. Once evidence is presented which meets the performance criteria this is accepted as competence. In the Certificate in Education programme students are required to demonstrate their knowledge of underlying principles through completion of a Learning Record which charts their professional development. The Certificate in Education programme is concerned with the holistic development of FE staff, whereas the TDLB awards cover a limited range of activities associated with the current job of an FE teacher. In 1993 the Cheshire Certificate in Education added the unit 'Assessment of Competence' to its Phase 2 portfolio. This covers assessment for D32 and D33. However, in addition to the compilation of evidence, for the TDLB awards the students must demonstrate their knowledge of the advantages and disadvantages of competency-based assessment. They are required critically to evaluate competency with reference to their own experience and current research in the field.

Looking to the future, there is pressure for TDLB awards to be the preferred training qualifications in FE. The Government has set ambitious National Education and Training Targets (NETTS) and is steering FE institutions, through funding regulations, to accelerate the achievement of such targets. Training and Enterprise Councils are currently supporting the acquisition of TDLB awards, and it is likely that this will continue to enable them to achieve their own targets relating to NETTS. With the absence of a lead body for FE teacher education, it is possible that the TDLB will take on the role thus moving the TDLB awards and Certificate in Education closer together, with the possibility that Certificate in Education programmes in their current form may disappear. The Cheshire Certificate may survive with little modification as it can encompass TDLB awards and competency-based assessment. However, funding of the Certificate in Education may be threatened if TECs will only support NVQ outcomes, and mandatory awards for FE teacher training are withdrawn. The aspects of the Cheshire programme which support the holistic development of staff may be considered expensive frills. This would pose a serious threat to the scheme and would undermine the key features of the programme. It would also undermine the professionalism of FE college staff.

CONCLUSIONS

This final section attempts to link the lessons learned from the Cheshire scheme, as outlined in the first section, with findings within the field of competency.

Currently, there is much criticism relating to competency-based qualifications. Eraut (1989), Hyland (1992) and Smithers (1993) have produced scathing reports on the new vocational qualifications believing that the underlying assumption of such qualifications is the application of behaviourism. Their main concern is that such an approach assumes that if students can show they are capable of carrying out specified tasks, they must have acquired the necessary knowledge and understanding. The City and Guilds of London Institute in a letter of response to Professor Smithers' criticisms of NVQs and GNVQs emphasizes that 'knowledge is an integral part of competence and is separately assessed in NVQs where this is necessary to confirm competence'. The FEU in its critique of TDLB standards (FEU, 1992) indicated that in field trials the standards did not appear to relate to the process of learning and recommended that appropriate interpersonal skills could be included to support the learning cycle. The same report highlighted similar concerns already expressed in this chapter relating to the language of NVQ programmes and in particular to that associated with the TDLB standards. These standards are being revised, and it is hoped that such a revision will encompass the broader picture of self-review and critical evaluation (Leigh, 1992) as well as product evidence and direct observation. Edmonds and Stuart (1992) in a critique of Management Charter Initiative developments stated that management is not the easiest area in which to specify competence as judgements about performance are rarely clear cut. They are concerned that under a competency-based system contingency situations, understanding and transferability to different contexts would be difficult to assess. These features are part of managers' roles and need to be included in any professional development programme. Such comments are applicable to the training of teachers. Similarly, Schön (1987), Edmonds and Teh (1991) and Leigh (1992) all advocate reflection, creativity and the development of personal competence so that the individual can develop his/her own style whilst demonstrating job/skill competence. The Cheshire scheme works within such a framework.

Fletcher (1992) argues that traditional courses have produced employees who only know what to do, with employers complaining that their employees cannot actually do the job. Fennell (1989) informs us that the interweaving of off-the-job and on-the-job learning is being widely adopted in Europe. He maintains that management training in most EC countries is rarely studied as a generic, totally academic discipline but within the context of the profession which is to be managed. The Cheshire scheme provides training which adopts the European model with the intention of producing employees who have knowledge and job competence.

So, within the context of teacher training is there some middle ground between the NCVQ approach and that of the more traditional academic models? Hodkinson (1992) argues that an interactive model of competence combines the theory and the process of learning with performance so that the learner makes sense of his/her experience with the support of a mentor or facilitator. This model of competence enables the learner to adapt, be flexible, change according to the context because it focuses upon reflection of practice. The ability to draw on and learn from experience to meet new situations (Schön, 1987) is encompassed within this model thus reducing the risk of task analysis or the somewhat reductionist approach encompassed by NCVQ. Perhaps the new vocational 'A' levels (GNVQs) are attempting to combine the best of these two approaches by promoting an interactive model of competence.

Does the Cheshire scheme fit this model? In theory it does; the underlying principles and key features fit well into such a model. Evidence presented in this chapter suggests that in practice the programme is moving towards an interactive model of competence. Course teams are striving to develop the programme so that it is holistic rather than behaviouristic providing a 'mixed diet' (Hodkinson, 1992) for teachers so that they, in turn, may develop their own teaching and learning in a similar way.

Taking into account that the Cheshire scheme needs to improve in certain areas, evidence suggests that this competency-based programme provides the necessary balance between behaviouristic competence and theoretical study. Through 'intelligent practice' (Hodkinson, 1992) the programme fits the interactive model of competence. The following quote, taken from a questionnaire completed by a tutor working on the programme, summarizes this chapter well.

> The combination of specific criteria for assessment and a learning record in which course members reflect critically on all aspects of the development ensures that this Certificate in Education: Further Education covers a broad range of objectives and produces practitioners who can examine their own performance in depth.

REFERENCES

C. and A. (1991) *The Certificate in Education: Further Education*. The Definitive Course Document. Crewe: Crewe and Alsager College of Higher Education.

Edmonds, T. and Stuart, D. (1992) 'Assessing competence at higher levels: the management experience.' *Competence and Assessment*, **15**, 6-8.

Edmonds, T. and Teh, M. (1991) 'Personal competence: where does it fit in?' *Competence and Assessment*, **13**, 6-8.

Eraut, M. (1989) 'Initial teacher training and the NVQ model'. In J. W. Burke (ed.) *Competency Based Education and Training*. East Sussex: Falmer Press.

Fennell, E. (1989) 'Vocational qualifications in Europe – shake down or shake out.' *Competence and Assessment*, **9**, 9-11.

FEU (1992) *TDLB Standards in Further Education*. FEU.

Fletcher, S. (1992) *NVQs Standards and Competence*. London: Kogan Page.

HMI (1990) *Training for Teaching in Further and Adult Education*. London: DES.

Hodkinson, P. (1992) 'Alternative models of competence in vocational education and training.' *Journal of Further & Higher Education*, **16**(2), 30-39.

Hyland, T. (1992) 'Lecturing profession or occupation?' *NATFHE Journal*, **17**(3), 10-11.

Leigh, A. (1992) 'The assessment of vocational and academic competence.' *Journal of Competence and Assessment*, **17**, 18–20.

Mansfield, R. (1989) 'Competence and standards.' In J.W. Burke (ed.) *Competency Based Education and Training*. East Sussex: Falmer Press.

Mitchell, L. (1989) 'The Definition of Standards and Their Assessment.' In J.E. Burke (ed.) *Competency Based Education and Training*. East Sussex: Falmer Press.

Rogers, C. (1983) *Freedom to Learn for the 1980s*. Oxford: Merrill.

Schön, D.A. (1987) *Educating the Reflective Practitioner*. San Francisco: Josey Bass.

Smithers, A. (1993) *All Our Futures – Britain's Education Revolution*. London: Channel 4 Television.

Training and Development Lead Body (1991) *National Standards for Training and Development*. London: Department of Employment.

Chapter 11

Competences and Partnership

Gareth Harvard and Richard Dunne

> The *T. J. Hooper* and the ship it was guiding got into trouble in the Atlantic Ocean when a sudden storm blew up. The storm damaged the ship and caused injury and property loss to its clients, who promptly sued. At that time common practice among tugs was to get weather information via hand signals from shore. Although radio had been introduced it was not in common use. The *T. J. Hooper* did not use radio, but if it had, the tug-master would have known of the danger. . . . the courts ruled that, when important matters are at stake, the legal obligation is to use the state of the art.
>
> Reynolds (1989, preface)

INTRODUCTION

Eraut has summarized the current consensus about 'competence' as 'The ability to perform to an agreed standard, a specified set of tasks, processes and functions over an agreed range of contexts and situations' (Eraut, 1993, Appendix 1) and indicates (ibid. p. 1) that it is useful 'to discuss evidence of professional competence under two main headings: performance and capability'. In recognizing capability as 'the potential to perform [comprising] the knowledge, skills and qualities which enable performance' (ibid. Appendix 1) he appears to divert criticism of the competence movement as 'reductionist' and 'mechanistic'.

In teacher education it has become acceptable to discuss the 'competences' of teaching, but with some suspicion. The idea is disparaged by Elliott (1993, p. 17) when they are 'outcomes that are construed as quantifiable products which can be clearly pre-specified in tangible and concrete form ... conceived as behavioural, with an emphasis placed on the atomist specification of discrete practical skills', yet applauded by the same author (ibid. p. 78) when they focus on 'those abilities which are manifested by good performances in the kinds of unstructured practical situations service professionals frequently have to respond in'. Eraut's description of the organic relationship of 'performance' and 'capability' initially appears to be an elegant anticipation of Elliott's concerns, yet we are further concerned that the very plausibility of Eraut's phraseology will encourage rather simplistic versions of competence to be adopted, seemingly legitimized by the unexamined assumption that 'capability' exists waiting only to be either specified or identified in current practice. There is a danger that the 'performance and capability' conjunction will mask the well-known and complex problems of 'transfer'. Some notion of transfer is implicit in Eraut's assumption that capability underpins future performance: the question of how learning in one situation comes effectively to be utilized and developed in another situation (transfer) cannot unproblematically be deflected by resort to the vocabulary of 'capability'.

Debling (1990, p. 8) has recognized this in referring to competence as

> ... the ability to perform the activities within an occupation ... a wide concept which embodies the ability to transfer skills and knowledge to new situations within the occupational area. It encompasses the organisation and planning of work, innovation and coping with non-routine activities. It includes those qualities of personal effectiveness that are required in a work place to deal with co-workers, managers and customers.

The crucial question that needs attention is about the conditions that facilitate transfer. It is clear that little work is being done within the competency movement to identify and specify the predicates of transfer (such that Blagg *et al.* [1993, p. 1] report that they noted confusion and disagreement between practitioners and experts about core skills and transfer issues) in order that courses should have carefully designed elements to develop skills, described in terms of performance, that are transferable. There is certainly considerable enthusiasm for transfer with Slee (1989), for instance, declaring that

> disciplines must be seen not as an end in themselves but as a means to a series of ends. Process must be made as important as product. And the process which characterises every discipline should be developed as the prime vehicle for developing the transferable personal skills that will come to characterise work.
>
> (Slee, 1989, p. 67)

This is a bold claim. Not only does it assume the transferability of skills but also predicts a revolution in how work is conceived, with the 'common denominator of highly qualified manpower ... [as] ... the ability to think, learn and adapt' which makes 'personal transferable skills – problem-solving, communication, teamwork ... the stabilizing characteristic of work' (Slee, 1989, p. 67).

A major problem is now brought into sharp relief: the ambitious, general aspiration to enable people to 'think, learn and adapt' is translated into the assumption not only that transferability is desirable but that it is 'problem-solving, communication, teamwork' that are the central items. We do not deny that these abilities are worth having: what concerns us is the assumption here, and it is widespread, that these abilities are 'skills'; that they are transferable just for the asking; and that they are of the same type as each other. It matters a great deal that the competence debate has proceeded without serious examination of the nature of the item that is the subject of such expensive and vigorous development; in particular, the extent to which lists which (typically) include 'problem-solving, communication, teamwork' exhibit the problem of the 'category mistake' that Ryle (1949) so elegantly examined. There is not the space here to rehearse this debate (see Dunne and Harvard, 1993) beyond indicating that our work has developed on the basis that 'communication' is so different in kind from 'problem-solving' that it is misleading to conjoin them in the phrase 'communication and problem-solving'. We will show how we have developed management, communication and subject matter knowledge (being in the same category) as generic competences while we would regard 'problem-solving' and 'teamwork' as workplace applications (that is, if we thought they in any case needed identifying as distinctive applications – which we do not, as they are more likely to prove as elusive as phlogiston and the ether in chemistry and physics).

This problem of transferability and the definition of what constitutes successful practice is reasonably familiar to course designers in the initial education of teachers. In recognizing that classrooms are complex environments that need rapid decision-making on the basis of uncertain information, teaching has been characterized as 'problem-solving', 'decision-making' and 'a reflective practice'. Such views of teaching are popular in the training institutions and among teachers; so much so that challenges to this are dismissed as uninformed and regressive. When cabinet ministers criticize the quality of courses in initial teacher training they tend to refer to the need for training to be undertaken in schools so that the realities of on-the-job experience provide an antidote to and make irrelevant the theoretical work that is assumed to be the basis of university courses. Recent legislative moves (DFE, 1992) to ensure that the practice element of teacher training is given a high priority include the specification of minimum amounts of time to be spent on a school site; the involvement of school-teachers in course development and delivery; the characterization of teaching in terms of competences; and the requirement that initial training institutions do their work in partnership with schools. This chapter will examine these demands, making particular reference to the nature of competences in teaching and the uncertain notion of partnership.

THE NATURE OF COMPETENCE IN TEACHING

In our work in recent years we have given detailed attention to how to represent and develop the classroom performance of student-teachers. This attention to performance has been maintained with an overarching emphasis on the manner in which teachers make decisions in their work: we characterized this as a need for teachers to make principled decisions. This carried the imperative for us to specify what constitutes principled decision-making, relating both to the ways in which decisions are taken and on what they are based. One particular aspect of this question of principled decision-making will be noted immediately: is adherence to common practice sufficient, or is it necessary for teachers to take into account the state of the art? (Reynolds, 1989; see extract at the beginning of this chapter). In other words, can teaching methods be defended as 'principled' if they are based solely on conventional wisdom (that is, common practice) or must they in contrast be based on the coherent understandings that distinguish the more productive teachers from the less productive ones (the state of the art)? It is not our intention in referring to 'state of the art' to suggest that principled decision-making in teaching relates to modernity or novelty, or even to the most recent piece of research; on the contrary, we think that the absence of detailed consideration of how to define state of the art has allowed undue emphasis on modernity to masquerade as principle in teaching. In placing 'state of the art' in a pivotal position we want not to nominate particular approaches or concepts as state of the art but to indicate the need for the teaching profession to establish ways of indexing and evaluating their emergence. We will show that our characterization of competence in teaching demands reference to the state of the art as recognizable and recorded paradigms that engage the attention of teachers.

In claiming that teachers must take into account in their work more than common practice, that they must refer in principled ways to the state of the art, we are making a strong claim. Our approach to the question of competence in teaching rests on an acceptance of this as a basic tenet. If this is accepted a number of interesting consequences follow, and these will be teased out through a description of some of our work.

Our overall concern is to describe the nature of being a teacher, which includes as one part of it the nature of teaching (i.e. classroom work). In order to capture the nature of teaching we have listed these kinds of teacher activities and labelled them the *nine dimensions of teaching*. This is shown in Figure 11.1.

Figure 11.1   *The nine dimensions of teaching.*

Dimension 0 – Ethos
Dimension 1 – Direct instruction
Dimension 2 – Management of materials
Dimension 3 – Guided practice
Dimension 4 – Structured conversation
Dimension 5 – Monitoring
Dimension 6 – Management of order
Dimension 7 – Planning and preparation
Dimension 8 – Written evaluation

The nine dimensions of teaching summarize what teachers do in their observable classroom work. We do not expect it to be clear simply from reading the list what is meant by each of 'direct instruction', 'guided practice' and so on, but this does not matter for the present purpose. What might be surprising is that although we have already emphasized how much of the classroom work of teachers involves taking decisions, this does not appear as one of the nine dimensions. There is good reason for this. When teachers take decisions they take them *about something*. They decide whether to pursue a conversation or to end it; they decide whether to intervene by providing an answer or asking a question; and so on. The nine dimensions are the things that teachers take decisions about; taking decisions is the way in which these dimensions are used. We will refer to this again later, after we have expanded further on the dimensions themselves.

Teachers we have worked with have found these categories, the nine dimensions, a useful, formal way of thinking about classroom work. They are useful when they are thought of, not as a particular lesson being 'direct instruction' or 'structured conversation', but as being the many things that teachers are taking decisions about in every lesson.

In the form in which they have been presented here the nine dimensions are only a set of *labels* for aspects of classroom work: we will all have different versions of what they really mean. We needed to establish a clearer definition for each dimension. Although it would have been possible to do this with a paragraph about each one we adopted a different approach: we described each dimension as a number of levels (seven or eight) ranging from relatively simple levels of performance to more complex expressions of competence. Figure 11.2 shows this for direct instruction.

The ways in which the nine dimensions are used in a deliberate approach in learning to teach is described elsewhere (Dunne and Harvard, 1993). What is important here is how they relate to the wider concern of what constitutes being a teacher. To begin with, our purpose in characterizing them in this way, as a number of dimensions each with a number of levels, was to ensure that the manner in which they are used, with students describing, explaining and justifying their classroom work in relation to them, involved decision-making in relation to publicly known standards. But these standards are written in such a way that their significance is only gradually appreciated as they are themselves examined in relation to practice. Our purpose in doing this is to capture in each limited aspect of classroom work and its analysis those very competences that we see as central to the work of the teacher. The central aspect that we have indicated is in our terms the *core competence* in teaching, and we distinguish this from the generic competences, as we shall explain later. This core competence is in fact *argument*, and it is this that we see as predominantly the aspect of the students' work that facilitates transfer. The nature of argument is clearly specified for the students and appears in every aspect of their work. Figure 11.3 shows the criteria for each of the four components of argument.

Figure 11.2 *Direct instruction.*

Dimension 1: Direct instruction
1. Attract children's initial interest; maintain appropriate sequence using supplied material for demonstrations and descriptions.
2. For demonstrations and descriptions, organize suitable seating arrangements, introduce material well, use appropriate visual aids, sustain children's interest.
3. Check clarity of explanation by appropriate questions; convey enthusiasm with appropriate verbal and non-verbal behaviour.
4. Choose appropriate examples, analogies and metaphors; explain as well as describe and demonstrate.
5. Choose concepts with both subject matter and children's interests in mind; ensure children's engagement and participation; use a range of examples and aids to meet diversity of children's attainments; summarize key issues.
6. Pace explanation in light of children's responses with regard to interest and comprehension; show grasp of possible content options and justify particular choices.
7. Make explanations efficient and concise; choose examples for their power in the subject.

The various techniques that we have developed during this work are designed to ensure that students utilize argument in close analysis of classroom practice. We pay considerable attention to this because we know that classrooms are the most precarious situations for the development of argument, having the understandable tendency to encourage defensiveness. But we do not allow this emphasis on analysis of practice in relation to performance criteria to proceed in the absence of a wider analysis. It is for this reason that we plan that any analysis of classroom work, whether or not it is related to actual practice, again emphasizes how the teacher's work is essentially uncertain and deliberative. For this purpose, of requiring an appropriate range for analysis, we show how any example of teaching (the observable aspects of what teachers and children can be seen to say and do) is only one part of the teacher's professional work: that the prior and interactive development of any example of teaching is in fact the focus of a complex instructional design.

This involves some consideration of two further aspects: (a) instructional design and

Figure 11.3 *The criteria for argument.*

DESCRIPTION:
1. Provide an account which contains sufficient points to represent the work accurately
2. Provide an account framed in own words and using verbatim quotations for specific illustration
3. Reorganize the sequence to improve coherence and make connections with supportive items from other pieces of work

EXPLANATION:
1. Identify and cite appropriate points for explanation
2. Orientate the reader to an appropriate basis for the explanation and explain succinctly
3. Support the explanation by applying it to other relevant items

JUSTIFICATION:
1. Make relevant claims for the significance of selected items
2. Relate claims to established concepts and empirical data
3. Challenge established concepts or empirical data

REFORMULATION:
1. Specify similar examples
2. Identify similarities and differences across several examples
3. Examine purposes and principles

(b) the generic competences of management, communication and subject matter knowledge.

INSTRUCTIONAL DESIGN

A teacher's classroom performance is one aspect of professional work and it is this that we have summarized as the nine dimensions of teaching. We emphasized how a central element in teaching is the decision-making that is constantly necessary to respond to and capitalize on changing circumstances. This involves making decisions about which classroom skills to employ and in what way to use them. But teaching involves decision-making that goes beyond the selection of the appropriate performance skills.

When in the classroom, teachers provide a classroom performance. While this is going on, usually as a result of it, children do things like listening, writing, speaking and so on. It is all these observable aspects of what the teacher and children do that we summarize as an *example* of teaching and it is this that is central to the work of the teacher. Although it is central, it is still only a small part of what the teacher is actually doing. The many other aspects are invisible to the observer but are crucially important. It is these other aspects that we will now describe together with how they together constitute the teacher's *instructional design*. It will be seen that this summarizes the very complex process in which teachers are involved when they provide an example of teaching. We begin by showing in diagrammatic form (Figure 11.4) how an example of teaching is related to the teacher's instructional design.

It can be seen from Figure 11.4 that we are suggesting that any example of teaching – the central, observable part of classroom life – is based on six aspects. These six aspects are just a part of the story. It is quite possible to be an established expert in each of these yet still not be effective as a teacher. The most important part of the

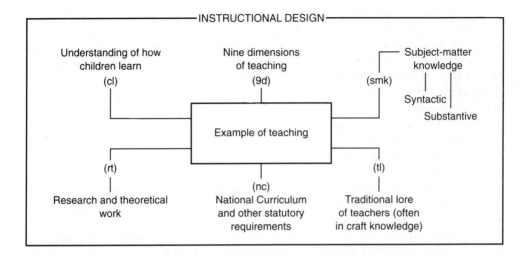

Figure 11.4 *An instructional design format.*

story lies in the lines that join these six aspects to the 'example of teaching'. These arrows imply not only that each aspect contributes to the overall design but also that complex and delicate judgements have to be made about what weight has to be given to each. It is these judgements and the consequent decision-making about the six aspects that can be described as the *pedagogical knowledge* of teaching.

The pedagogical knowledge that is the basis of producing an instructional design requires deliberation and judgement in selecting from each of the six areas and it requires knowledge of the six areas. But not just any knowledge: following our assertion of a basic tenet, above, it must be state of the art knowledge.

STATE OF THE ART KNOWLEDGE IN TEACHING

The six areas indicated in Figure 11.4 represent in outline the knowledge base for being a teacher; a detailed elaboration of these six aspects could be used to establish an appropriate base, and it would be possible for this to be specified at any level in the education system. A Government favouring central direction could specify the theoretical and other knowledge for teaching (although this would create a rather sterile system). A Government favouring devolvement could require this to be done by individual schools for their own staff, and the selection could be a matter for inspection as to the extent of its being 'state of the art'.

It is at this point that the crucial idea of 'state of the art' in teaching needs some discussion. What we are stressing is that there needs to be some formal criteria for individual teachers to develop, examine, value and advertise their knowledge base for the crucial reason that it is the extent to which knowledge is public that determines the extent to which it can be state of the art. We predicate this assertion on the belief that there is a great deal to be learnt from characterizing teaching as a science in the manner of Kuhn's (1962) examination, the main lesson for the present purpose being how developments in science are based on the conscious induction of novices into the practices, methods and vocabulary of the discipline. In teaching, there has been an absence of a generally accepted body of knowledge, and this means that new ideas, no matter how original or creative or right or bizarre or whimsical, are not amenable to deliberate and public examination against the currently established paradigm. It is the absence of widely understood and accepted methods and concepts that comprises a paradigm that makes collaborative critical deliberation impossible, and this is seriously debilitating for a profession no matter how imaginative are the individual members. We accept that the teacher's work is necessarily based on uncertain and fleeting information and that decision-making is consequently problematic. But we are concerned that this can be over-emphasized to the point that teaching has to be characterized as 'personal' and not amenable to shared development and analysis. In developing our view about the idea of 'competence' in teaching, we are seeking to demonstrate that there has to be a defined knowledge base generated in research and amenable to changes in detail through publicly known systems.

Our definition of 'state of the art' is not concerned with precisely what constitutes the knowledge base for teaching but with the manner in which and the point at which it is defined. We suggest that it is appropriate for each school (or group of schools) to define its curriculum and the principles on which it is based. It would then be incumbent on the school to specify the manner and the conditions under which the principles can be modified, the methods by which the teachers' knowledge is to be assessed and the style in which the practice is evaluated. In specifying what as a minimum is to be known and acted on by teachers in a school, and in specifying how this knowledge is to be assessed and its use is to be evaluated, a knowledge base is established that could be regarded as 'state of the art' for that school.

This discussion of the policy implications of state of the art knowledge in teaching is directly relevant to the question of personal competence: personal competence in teaching is not a useful concept in the absence of reference to the way in which knowledge in the profession is represented, developed and advertised. We can illustrate this with a small example. Arithmetic can be taught by first working at counting to quite high numbers and then gradually introducing addition and subtraction, followed by multiplication and division. Let us call this method A. On the other hand, it can be taught by concentrating on understanding the four rules (with the earliest emphasis on multiplication and division) and gradually applying this to relatively few numbers (method B). Each approach has a long tradition; each has its recorded successes; each has its theoretical arguments; each has its adherents. Reputations can be made on spectacular work with, say, method B: the personal skill of the teacher in securing the children's interest, developing skilled and autonomous use of materials and ideas by the children, evidenced by imaginative use of their arithmetic skills in problems generated by themselves, could become the focus of hordes of visitors from all over the world, paying homage to this paragon of professional virtue. Yet in the absence of continuity of this approach as the children progress through the school, all this may be wasted or even seriously counter-productive. The teacher using method B may actually be more knowledgeable than the other members of staff, knowing both methods and selecting the more effective. But this does not mean that method B is state of the art. But nor does it mean that method A, located in the established methods of teaching in England, is state of the art. What this illustrates is that the current system does not allow 'state of the art' meaningfully to be identified. If state of the art is defined, or at least accepted, in terms of individual expertise, then exponents of both method A and method B can be commended. We believe that this is roughly the situation that exists in teaching in England: that individual expertise is reified without consideration of how it refers to the overall need for continuity and coherence in planning work for children. But our definition of state of the art knowledge would require the kind of deliberative judgement and examination and advocacy that, based on a current paradigm, characterizes science. What we are suggesting is that 'state of the art' should be defined in the school. It may be suggested that this is in the nature of a school policy, but our suggestion goes beyond this. The definition of state of the art knowledge would further require some specification of first, the nature of the knowledge and skills required of teachers in relation to the state of art; and secondly the method by which new knowledge is incorporated into the system.

This characterization of state of the art knowledge carries substantial implications for the idea of personal competence: it establishes certain competences, beyond classroom performance, as central to the work of the teacher. In emphasizing the organic relationship between personal competence and the nature of the system (including, crucially, how to change the system), we are arguing for the generic competences of management, communication and subject matter knowledge to be given a high priority. We recognize their centrality in the work of teachers in any system, but we see the opportunity for their conscious application and increased visibility. This would then secure their place in the training of teachers.

In advocating this increased visibility of the generic competences of management, communication and subject matter knowledge in teaching, related to notions of 'state of the art', we are not suggesting that initial training becomes focused on, for instance, simulations of teamwork. On the contrary, it is in the establishment of these competences as a visible part of the teacher's work that we see the creation of the conditions for focusing on learning the craft of teaching in ways that develop these same skills in situations that are the established concerns of beginners (most notably, classroom performance). The important point here is that classroom performance can be developed within an approach that emphasizes the generic competences of management, communication and subject matter knowledge; it is these that comprise the transferable skills in teaching, but not because they are intrinsically or naturally transferable. They need always to be exercised in relation to the central competence of argument (see Figure 11.3) and need the conditions created by the fact of these competences being visible in the work of teachers: visible in aspects of work (focused on state of the art) different from those in which they are developed (predominantly, the classroom). The nature of these generic competences is discussed below.

THE GENERIC COMPETENCES OF MANAGEMENT AND COMMUNICATION

Our analysis of what it means to be a teacher convinces us that we should specify management, communication and subject matter knowledge as three generic competences. They are generic in that they are each characteristic of a group that has common structural features distinct from other groups. It is not in being distinctive that their interest lies; it is in their being applicable throughout a teacher's work. Our

---

Figure 11.5   *The criteria for means–end analysis.*

The context of means–end analysis
Level 1: accepts work as given and attempts to complete it
Level 2: evaluates set tasks in the light of specified needs
Level 3: identifies different types of needs
Level 4: adapts tasks in the light of an analysis of identified needs
Level 5: adapts to changing perceptions of needs

---

analyses indicate that it is these three categories that are consistently present in all aspects of the professional life of teachers. What we now need to define is the range of a teacher's work. We specify this as in two contexts: means–end analysis and planning. This means that we characterize being a teacher as needing, in every situation (the classroom; parents' meetings; planning meetings; and so on), to appraise the current situation (means–end analysis) and to look to the future (planning). And working in these contexts demands attention to the distinctive competences of management, communication and subject matter knowledge. In this characterization it means that we do not need to specify the vast number of individual components of management competence, communicative competence and competence in subject matter knowledge. What we need is criteria that describe progression in means–end analysis and planning, which themselves draw on the generic competences of management, communication and subject matter knowledge. These are shown in Figures 11.5 and 11.6.

THE DELIBERATE APPROACH IN LEARNING TO TEACH

Our work with students in initial training for teaching has involved extensive organizational features that make possible the creation of appropriate conditions and the wide use of certain techniques. It is not possible here to describe all aspects of this development but there are a number of crucial features that can be indicated.

The central competence of argument is specifically taught to students on entry: this is done in ways that are likely to be familiar to students coming from schools, that is, in the writing of essays, in summary of published articles, and relating this to

---

Figure 11.6 *The criteria for planning.*

The context of planning
Level 1: gets work done to deadlines
Level 2: sets time limits to complete work; organizes relevant resources
Level 3: works to a basic day-to-day plan; organizes diary and timetable effectively to meet set demands
Level 4: exhibits flexible use of time allocation to tasks; identifies and adapts to demands of different types of task
Level 5: organizes time on a long-term basis; makes time for self-set tasks; plans for extended activity and involvement

---

evidence of teaching on video and from their own experience of classrooms. The criteria for argument, increasingly understood, are required to be attended to in all further aspects of work, including the crucial conference work that the organization of the course facilitates. Conferences sometimes involve individual students and sometimes small groups, but in every case the emphasis is on evidence and the description, explanation, justification and reformulation that constitute argument. This central competence, argument, is specifically taught and deliberately used as the focus for aspects of the students' work.

The generic competences of management, communication and subject matter knowledge are identified by the students in the various parts of the work that they do; the apparent absence of these in some work provides the opportunity for examination of how they can become relevant and applicable. This examination involves attention to the contexts of means–end analysis and planning, that is, in increasingly sophisticated ways, they determine what is needed in a given situation and what to do to achieve it. This deliberate examination is promoted in conferences and the students' thinking is evidenced in the written argument that follows each conference. The process is taught and further guided and exercised by close attention to the instructional design format (Figure 11.4), this being constructed to focus attention on the way in which teachers, in the productive exercise of their work, are constantly making decisions on the basis of uncertain information. The students' work on this is more concentrated and more deliberate than could conceivably be possible in any real teaching situation, but the idea of course is not that this is exercised in real time but is exercised in exaggerated and formal ways together with a formalized and public language. It is this that underpins our approach to transfer.

PARTNERSHIP

One of the key features in recent requirements for student-teachers to spend a greater part of their training on a school site is the establishment of partnerships between schools and universities (DFE, 1992, 1993). Although this is an unremarkable requirement in many ways, it does seem that there is a tendency to concentrate on methods of interpreting in practical terms 'the true spirit of partnership'. In other words, the concept of partnership is being treated as unproblematic and energy is being diverted to creating systems for putting something into place that has not been dispassionately examined. We are not at all sure what others mean by 'partnership', but are concerned at some of its manifestations.

To begin with, there is a curious imbalance in the way in which transition to partnership is being managed. Enthusiastic about the contribution that school-teachers might make to course planning for initial training, universities and colleges are tending to elevate the notion of equality in partnership so that courses are planned from the assertions of representatives from the various groups involved. This means that given the (assumed unproblematic) notion of democracy that prevails in these contexts, courses are being put together in unprincipled ways. But this course, jointly created, becomes the one that the university offers to schools for their consideration; and schools can use the market-place to look for a better offer. What is lacking is a model of student learning and its careful translation into a competency model. This takes time, yet the pressure is on to instal these competency-based approaches rapidly.

A model of student learning would need to go beyond the specification of required behaviours. Our concern is not that the complex decision-making in teaching cannot be expressed in these ways; we think it can (although it usually is not). Our concern is that the need to involve school-teachers in more detailed ways in the preparation of students for teaching is concentrating minds on organizational matters, with the consequence that the specification of what students should do in order to learn is being treated in trivial ways. A model of student learning would specify what it is that changes when students successfully learn how to teach; which conditions and techniques contribute to this change; who is best placed to work with student-teachers for the various parts of their learning; to what extent and for which purposes an apprenticeship model is appropriate; the relationship of apprenticeship to a contemplative approach to teaching; the nature of the knowledge base for teaching. There is a real danger that what is already known about this will be excluded from the system. Worse, that the facilities for continuing work on it will be eradicated.

We have suggested above that an examination of the nature of competence carries with it the need to define in some way the 'state of the art' in teaching. The notion of 'state of the art' that we advocate is one that is based on individual schools (or small groups of schools) so that school-based staff are visibly implicated in the work that generates the knowledge base and the systems necessary for its examination. It is some such ingredient that needs to be in place, or put in place, for the idea of partnership to become meaningful. Partnership between schools and universities can then proceed in relation to the initial training of student-teachers: student-teachers would then focus not just on personal teaching skills, but on the examination of a well-defined system in order to develop and draw on generic competences. The idea of learning to teach then shifts from the development of personal capabilities to work that notably includes the essence of state of the art practice, specifically, dispassionate examination of how best to contribute to a system in which long-term aims are of paramount importance. We assert that it is a public definition of 'state of the art' that is fundamental to the provision of an appropriate training for student-teachers, for it is this that is central to a culture that encourages and facilitates close examination of teaching.

REFERENCES

Ball, C. and Eggins, H. (eds) (1989) *Higher Education in the 1990's: New Dimensions.* SHRE/OUP.

Blagg, N., Ballinger, M. and Lewis, R. (1993) *Development of Transferable Skills in Learners: Report no. 18.* Sheffield: Employment Department.

Debling, G. (1990) 'The new competence-based vocational qualifications in Great Britain placed in a European context.' *Competence and Assessment*, 2, Employment Department Training Agency.

DFE (1992) *Circular 9/92. Initial Teacher Training (secondary phase).* London: DFE.

DFE (1993) *Circular 14/93. The Initial Training of Primary School Teachers: New Criteria for Courses.* London: DFE.

Dunne, R. and Harvard, G. (1993) 'A model of teaching and its implications for mentoring' In D. McIntyre, H. Hagger and M. Wilkin (eds) *Mentoring: Perspectives on School-Based Teacher Education.* London: Kogan Page.

Elliott, J. (ed.) (1993) *Reconstructing Teacher Education*. London: Falmer Press.

Eraut, M. (1993) *Assessing Competence in the Professions: Report no. 14*. Sheffield: Employment Department.

Kuhn, T.S. (1962) *The Structure of Scientific Revolutions*. Chicago: University of Chicago Press.

Reynolds, M.C. (ed.) (1989) *Knowledge Base for the Beginning Teacher*. New York: Pergamon Press.

Ryle, G. (1949) *The Concept of Mind*. Harmondsworth: Penguin.

Slee, P. (1989) 'A consensus framework for higher education.' In C. Ball and H. Eggins (eds) *Higher Education in the 1990s: New Dimensions*. Milton Keynes: SHRE/OUP.

Chapter 12

Competence, Professionalism and Vocational Education and Training

Phil Hodkinson and Mary Issitt

CERTAINTIES AND CONTRADICTIONS

Competence is an apparently straightforward concept and at the level of common sense appears to offer a way of simplifying the mechanisms by which standards of performance at work can be assessed. At a superficial level it appears like a port in the storm of post-modernity, offering the promise of certainty in the development of standards for practice for the caring and education professions in the confusing world of the late twentieth century. However, the concept has been stretched and extended (Issitt and Woodward, 1992; Matthews, 1992) to cover a whole range of increasingly complex meanings and actions. In spite of the claims of its supporters that the NVQ competence approach provides an objective structure and framework, it is a concept around which few would claim neutrality. Nevertheless, the NCVQ is creating an increasingly complicated edifice of competence that is meant to rationalize and simplify the process of assessment of vocational qualifications, and provide easy access to, and portability of, qualifications (Jessup, 1991).

The polarized nature of the debate around competence is not surprising, given the ways in which the NVQ system has evolved. Hodkinson, in Chapter 5, has already alluded to the top-down, managerial rationale which underpins the system. In many occupational areas the approach is being forced on reluctant and sceptical users, both professionals and, as Field demonstrates in Chapter 3, employers. These tensions are present in areas other than those directly covered in this book. In a study of patterns of youth training in part of England, Hodkinson *et al.* (1993) also found that the majority of small employers interviewed did not view training as fitting the NVQ model. Some wanted mainly 'off the job' theory, while others wanted training that was restricted to their own idiosyncratic needs.

Yet within NCVQ and the Standards branch of the Employment Department, where the NVQ system originated and is being developed, there is a strong sense of idealism and purpose, which brooks no opposition to the fundamental principles. Members of these organizations are highly receptive to criticism which will enable the detail of the system to be refined, often resulting in increasing complexity. But there is little feeling in their literature (see, for example, the regular series of *Competence and Assessment* publications from the Standards branch) of an acceptance that their principles, as opposed to the detail, might require critical examination. It is, therefore, difficult for critics of their approaches to engage in constructive debate rather than opposition.

At the time of writing (early 1994) there is a sense that the opposition is growing and becoming increasingly vocal, and this book may be seen as part of that growth. To simplify, opposition comes from two very different ideological positions. One is represented by many of the contributions in this book, while the other is exemplified by Smithers (1993). In a highly charged and emotive television documentary, he compared developments in vocational education and training in Britain with those in other European countries, and concluded that the NCVQ-led development of NVQs and GNVQs threatens a 'disaster of epic proportions'. He attacked NCVQ for undervaluing knowledge and understanding, and for setting up a system where, he claimed, teachers have no syllabus to guide their teaching, assessment is complex and problematic and trainers are being paid according to the success of their trainees, when they themselves are measuring that success as assessors. The programme, and to a lesser extent the book which accompanied it, have been attacked for bias (see, for example, NCVQ, 1994). One of the main counter-claims of NCVQ, and indeed of some of the people and organizations Smithers used in the programme to support his case, is that Smithers had made his mind up about what he was going to find before the supposed 'investigation' began.

To judge the balance of argument on both sides, readers must study the two publications and the programme for themselves. It is our opinion that Smithers' critique was indeed coloured by his ideological position on education. As an eminent academic, he has firm and unwavering beliefs which are at odds with equally firm NCVQ ideologies. He is certain that effective teaching is normally didactic, with pupils (trainees) sitting in rows, with the lesson focused on the teacher, and has been consistently suspicious of any form of student-centred learning. For example, he describes the following practice, seen in Europe, as a model to be emulated here.

> High quality teaching and direct instruction: freed from the constant necessity to design courses and draw up teaching materials, continental teachers [of vocational courses] are able to concentrate on teaching; whole class teaching, unfashionable in Britain, was observed in every country visited and carried out to very high standards.
>
> (Smithers, 1993, p. 13)

He further believes in the need for separate tracks for vocational and academic students post-16, seeing young people as falling into distinctly different types, needing distinctly different forms of education. All this places him firmly in what Skilbeck (1976), drawing on Williams (1965) among others, calls 'classical humanism'.

The trouble with this slanging match between Smithers and NCVQ is that both hold ideological positions that give both an equally strong, but mutually opposed, certainty about what is right. In a Kuhnian sense (Kuhn, 1970) they inhabit different paradigms and there can be little constructive dialogue between them. It is noticeable that, in their response to Smithers, NCVQ (1994) do not respond to his criticisms of their fundamental principles, but content themselves with countering the detail and perceived bias in his methods and use of the opinions of others. Green, in Chapter 2, gives a much more comprehensive and rigorous analysis of European practice than Smithers. He agrees with many of Smithers' criticisms of British vocational education and training, without taking up the same ideological stance.

This polarized debate and the growing weight of opposition to NVQs risk one of two equally undesirable outcomes in the future. The first is that the NCVQ hegemony is further advanced and that a mechanistic and managerial model of competence is forced upon reluctant professionals. The second is that politicians and policy-makers, impatient for a quick fix, jettison the whole competence approach, just as it is becoming more sophisticated, and embark on some new, simplistic approach in its place. There is a worrying history of these sorts of abrupt policy switch in the field of vocational education and training in Britain, as recent histories of the Manpower Services Commission demonstrate (Ainley and Corney, 1990; Coffield, 1990; Evans, 1992). Here we are arguing for a more sophisticated position, where competence is explored in the wider framework of professional practice.

A central theme in this book is that competence is not and cannot be a fixed concept. All the contributors recognize that professionals are making complex judgements. These judgements need to be as clear and open as possible – but to pretend that they can be objective and value free is to delude those working in the professions and the users of their services. We need to recognize that in order to be competent we must constantly review and change our practice, and that practice is partly determined by the unequal society in which we live and which, as professionals, we sometimes need to challenge and seek to change.

Most contributors to this book, therefore, address competence from a different position from that of either Smithers or NCVQ. We are professionals engaged in educating other professionals, who see the relationships between theory and practice, and learning and teaching, as problematic rather than simply about performance or simply about 'whole class teaching'. In different ways, most contributors are articulating some form of reflective practice, although all would not use or accept that term. There is an arrogance in the positions of both NCVQ and Smithers, in their implicit assumptions that such professionals have little of substance to offer to the debate. The person-centred professions have been debating the notion of and identifying standards for practice throughout their history. Thus they do not engage with the NCVQ and its framework empty-handed or empty-headed – they already have a deeply grounded understanding of what competence is.

Ignoring this accumulated expertise risks fundamentally misunderstanding the nature of learning, of competence and of professionalism. It also builds in to NCVQ approaches the likelihood of failure. As Hodkinson suggested in Chapter 5, top-down imposed managerial change does not succeed even in its own terms. People are not like machines, to be redesigned or reprogrammed to work in new ways. As Hargreaves says of teachers,

> Teachers don't merely deliver the curriculum. They develop, define it and reinterpret it too. It is what teachers think, what teachers believe and what teachers do at the level of the classroom that ultimately shapes the kind of learning that young people get. ....
> The quality, range and flexibility of teachers' classroom work are closely tied up with their professional growth – with the way in which they develop as people and professionals.
> (Hargreaves, 1993, p. ix)

There is no reason to suppose that other caring professionals are any different.

TAKING COMPETENCE AND PROFESSIONALISM FORWARD

Contributors in this book have reflected upon a variety of ways in which competence is currently being applied within the caring professions, as well as developing a critique of what competence must mean for those who identify themselves as professionals. They have raised a number of important questions that need to be addressed by those professionals whose occupations will soon be subject to the functional mapping and standards definition through NCVQ procedures. A number of themes run through these contributions that are worth revisiting, and we begin with some common issues about how competence can and should be used effectively.

Holism

Within this book we have seen a number of imaginative approaches to the application of competence, but the resounding message which emerges is that it is a holistic concept, and any assessment framework which is developed needs to recognize this. We would suggest that two major dimensions to holism emerge which relate, on the one hand, to the person who is the 'reflective practitioner' and, on the other hand, to the education and training process. The first conceptualization of holism concerns the integration of knowledge and understanding, values and skills that reside within the person who is the practitioner. As Jones (Chapter 7) shows in her case study, the personal identity of the practitioner was as important to the client as the way she carried out her job. The dynamics of the relationship which is the vehicle for helping would also be difficult to unscramble in terms of a list of competences. If it is valuable, in some ways, to disaggregate professional performance as a tool to aid learning and assessment, it is also of vital importance to synthesize as well. To measure each competence attribute separately, be these elements, units, statements or something completely different, potentially atomizes and trivializes professional practice as described in this instance.

The second dimension of holism relates to the education and training process itself. At the beginning of this book we refer to the NCVQ model's emphasis on output. We see a major problem when discourse and action in relation to professional training centre around methods of assessing performance. We would reject the 'input/output' model as being an inappropriate application of an industrial model to working with people. As Stewart (1992) shows, and we ourselves argue in Chapter 1, the world of public service and private profit are based upon different values and premises. The input/output model has only served to confuse debates about quality in both training and practice. While it is important to judge professional workers by what they do, and we would not dispute the need for high standards of performance, that performance cannot be separated out from the education and training process. Competent performance 'on the job' may demand reflection and training 'off the job' in a completely different setting, in order to be energized and gain new insights on the job itself. This is particularly true for the development of good practice in relation to equal opportunities, where professionals in training need to reflect upon and understand their own and others' oppressive behaviours in the safety of a learning group before they try out their practice on service clients (Jordan *et al.*, 1993).

Expertise and state of the art

Many contributors are concerned that competence must be seen as more than a 'can do' threshold. For competence approaches to be valuable, they must aid personal professional growth and the development of real expertise. Harvard and Dunne (Chapter 11) use levels of performance within their competence scheme to facilitate just that. They also introduce the notion of state of the art, suggesting that training professionals need their practice exposed to and tested against the best practice known at the time of training. Jones (Chapter 7), in stressing the complexity of high-quality social work, makes a similar point. Yet NCVQ functional analysis of the role ignores expertise and the problematic fact that different professionals approach the same task in very different ways, with differing forms of success. Furthermore, a competence may not be transferable to another setting and professional judgement is required to deal with 'indeterminate zones' as each setting is, in some sense, unique (Schön, 1983, 1987).

Moreover, the level structure that runs through all NVQs is based on a hierarchical notion of responsibilities within work (see Figure 1.1), so that, for example, Level 3 is equated to a supervisory role. The NCVQ model, with the requirement to use units from other occupational areas, may exacerbate the trend to assign high organizational status to management competence rather than to skilled delivery of the professional task. Professions do not have to be structured like this. Hargreaves (1993) describes moves in one American city to move teaching into a career framework closer to the notion of expertise than to managerial hierarchies.

> Cincinnati Public Schools District's establishment of new career structures and professional review procedures, with the agreement and initiative of the teachers' federation, includes a four step career ladder of intern, resident, career teacher and lead teacher, promotion through which is based on a process of peer review.
>
> (Hargreaves, 1993, p. 257)

Performance is not everything

Another commonality from contributors is that, even where competence-based approaches do have some utility, they can only be part of the total picture, and this is true of assessment as well as teaching and learning. Being a professional is about much, much more than performance alone. Above all, contributors identify the need for professionals to be intellectually aware and reflectively critical, not just about their own practice but about the context in which they work, in the widest sense. This may be at odds with the 'new managerialism' which competence frameworks serve to confirm. From a black perspective, Ferns (1992, p. 29) argues that competence-based approaches to 'good practice' are inevitably more 'rigidly defined' and likely to confirm the oppressive status quo, blocking 'new approaches that challenge existing power structures. Consequently, innovatory approaches, such as those involving black perspectives are prone to be seen as inferior and incompetent.' There has to be room for negotiability around competence and to recognize that the approach may perpetuate rather than challenge oppressive stereotypes which become 'harder to challenge and ultimately more covert'. Ironically for the hegemony of NCVQ, such criticality must include a healthy scepticism for whatever qualification, training and assessment structure within which professionals are working. The experience of the development of community work standards has shown that it is hard to find technically correct language to express competence in the collective challenge of oppression.

As Issitt shows (Chapter 6), NCVQ has clear commitment to good practice in relation to equal opportunities and evidence is emerging of residential and day care workers feeling that their own practice and awareness on equal opportunities issues is being enhanced (George, 1994). Yet as understanding of difference becomes more sophisticated, the 'technically rational' systems-based response remains the same and the result is to develop even more complex standards that become increasingly prescriptive, individualized and inaccessible. This becomes paradoxical for a scheme that was designed to simplify and promote access to qualifications.

The importance of multiple meanings

We have already demonstrated that there is no single 'correct' version of professional performance and all the practitioner contributors in this book used different versions of a competence approach. It would, no doubt, be quite possible to critique these differing approaches, to identify strengths and weaknesses in each. However, it would be a mistake to suppose that the best features of such schemes could be combined into some definitive version which could, therefore, be legitimately imposed from above. There are two parts to this fallacy. The first is also true of mechanical design. You do not produce the definitive car by taking the gear box from one, the engine from another, and the brakes from yet a third. Even in the relatively simple world of machinery there is no 'correct car', nor even universal agreement about which is the best of a given selection which are aimed at the same segment of the market. Only the most extreme forms of totalitarianism would force all car users to buy one design, yet that is what NCVQ would do with competence.

Once we move away from machines to complex human interactions, the totalitarian response becomes even more ludicrous. What comes clearly through the chapters in this book is that it is not the actual design of the competence structure that is most important, but the ways in which any system is used, by teachers and learners, in the context within which it is located. Ownership is a key part of that. One of the reasons for the success of the FE Certificate scheme described by Maynard (Chapter 10) is that some of the college tutors using the scheme were central in its design. This does not mean, of course, that all structures are equally good or bad, and much of this book has been devoted to analysing potential strengths and weaknesses. However, just because some cars are better than others, it does not follow that it is possible or desirable to produce one definitive version. The same is true of competence structures. Such pluralism becomes more acceptable if competence is seen as a tool for achieving part of professional education, rather than some over-arching structure which must contain and define all of it.

Mentoring

Another commonality, highlighted particularly by Durkin (Chapter 8), Barnes (Chapter 9) and Maynard (Chapter 10) is the importance of mentoring. If a disaggregation into competence attributes is to aid learning and professional development, it is partly through an enhanced dialogue between trainee and mentor. Arguably, the quality of this mentoring support is much more important than the nature of the competence structures themselves. It is quite possible to conceive of effective mentoring without a competence framework, but very hard to see competence working without effective mentoring support.

Collaboration

Another common theme is the importance of collaborative practice. In the people-centred professions, we are emphatically not isolated individuals. Working with clients or pupils involves several people working together. In schools that is often several different teachers, although the involvement of other professionals, such as educational psychologists and careers officers, is important at particular times and there is increasing involvement of classroom assistants, technicians and even parents. In social work and youth and community work, the emphasis is much more on teams of professionals drawn from diverse professions and backgrounds. At one level, NVQ structures acknowledge this, for many occupational competence specifications include such factors as teamwork, communication and working with others. Yet there is a paradox. In a system designed on the principle that outcomes of performance are all that matter, the collaborative and collective outcomes of professionalism are unmeasured. As Issitt showed in Chapter 6, the NVQ conception is individualistic, with the built-in assumption that if each collaborator is competent, then their combined effect must also be competent. This flies in the face of all we know about group work and social interaction, where what one person does is deeply influenced by and in turn influences what others do. This is why industrial managers talk about synergy. When collaboration works well, it achieves more than the sum of the parts.

Harvard and Dunne (Chapter 8) raise another interesting aspect, for teamwork between different professionals and others, from different backgrounds, is also increasingly important in the education of professionals. This is clearly evidenced in Britain through the current drive for partnership between schools and universities in the provision of Initial Teacher Education.

Not enough is known about what collaborative competence structures, which go beyond measuring individual contributions to a team, would look like. These approaches are increasingly being promoted through inter-agency approaches to health and welfare problems. This is a real test for competence-based approaches. Can such systems avoid the individualization found in NVQs? If not, then their role in professional development must be carefully controlled and balanced by other approaches which acknowledge the competent team.

Just any form of collaboration is not enough, nor is collaboration automatically a good thing. Hargreaves (1993) distinguishes between collaboration and 'contrived collegiality'. The former occurs when professionals are allowed to develop their own working relationships, showing respect for each other and sharing ownership. The latter is when they are forced into teams against their will, because management structures dictate that that should happen. He suggests that while the former state is desirable for effective professional provision, the latter is normally counter-productive.

Hargreaves claims that collaboration can bring many professional benefits. These include: moral support, improved effectiveness, reduced overload and opportunities to learn, among others. However, collaboration also brings some dangers, which include complacency and conformism. Once more, as with competence, there are no simple solutions, just infinite complexity. For Hargreaves, effective collaboration and professionalism itself require appropriate structures and cultures to be in place. It follows that in making use of competence, or any other educational approach, attention to the detail of the system must not deflect us from attention to the structural and cultural contexts in which it takes place.

Grounded development

The NCVQ approach assumes that specifying and measuring assessment outcomes will force structural and cultural change in institutions as they strive for greater efficiency. In other words, that a technically devised system can be superimposed on the cultural and structural complexities of human life. The analysis presented by contributors here suggests the opposite and that the competence approach is retrospective, reflecting the status quo. Change will only be effective if it recognizes the complex realities within which it must work. This does not, of course, mean that things cannot or should not change, but that change begins from where we are now, not with a blank sheet of paper. The competence approaches described in this book were to a greater or lesser extent grounded in existing practice. They have been developed, and continually modified, from the ground up.

IMPLICATIONS FOR VOCATIONAL EDUCATION AND TRAINING

One of the cruder errors in the NCVQ approach is its assumption that, in spreading the system from its established base in Levels 2 and 3 in a limited range of occupations (Field, Chapter 3), the professions have much to learn from such practice, but not vice versa. Eraut (1989) suggested, in contrast, that NVQ approaches should be broadened, drawing lessons from experiences in teacher education. It seems clear to us that many of the principles of good quality education/training advocated in this book should not be restricted to the caring professions. With only minor variations, the principles of professionalism described in Chapter 5 can be applied with benefit to many other occupational areas, perhaps especially in the service sector, at Level 3 and above. What Hyland (Chapter 4) and Hodkinson (Chapter 5) say about learning, managerialism and innovation is arguably universal. From the analysis presented in this book, it is possible to draw out some over-arching principles for vocational education and training.

The dangers of managerialism

Much is made, in the post-Fordist literature, of the need to move away from Taylorism and dominant management control (Brown and Lauder, 1991, 1992). Kaisen involves all workers in shared responsibility for improving quality. For professional teachers, social workers and youth and community workers, even this possibly benign managerialism is worrying, as has already been made clear in the contributions to this book. However, in private industry, there is a worrying disjunction between the rhetoric of employee empowerment and involvement and NVQ approaches, for the latter, as Hodkinson shows in Chapter 5, are focused on increased management control in a broadly Taylorist sense. Take, for example, the following advertisement aimed at private old people's care homes:

> [named organization] will offer individual homes a training package to 'kick start' their own programme embracing the training of e.g. Verifiers, Lead Assessors, Assessors, NVQ II and III and Basic Hygiene.
>   An intensive course, tailored to each home's needs and to each home's pace, will enable each home to achieve certification at the level to which it aspires and also to apply for its own accreditation as a City & Guilds Centre offering NVQ qualifications in care. ... The home will no longer need to seek outside 'one off courses' but will be *self sufficient, employer led and in control of its own training and development and at no time challenge the authority of the management.*
>   (advert in the *Evening Sentinel*, 6 August 1993, our emphasis)

As Hyland (Chapter 4) suggests, this does not sound like a recipe for upskilling workers to enter a high skills equilibrium. Rather, it suggests control and deskilling, where workers do as they are told in ways Taylorism suggested. The danger for VET in Britain based on the NCVQ system is that such narrow, Taylorist approaches are most unlikely to work, even in their own terms.

Widening competence

The analyses of Green (Chapter 2) and Field (Chapter 3) also suggest that NVQ approaches are not likely to work in the ways which their advocates expect. Green presents a scholarly analysis of practice in Europe. He argues that vocational education in Britain needs to be much broader based than NVQs currently are. There are interesting parallels between his analysis and that of Hodkinson (Chapter 5), for both demonstrate, in very different ways, the fallacy of seeing workplace performance as the main determinant of educational needs. Similarly, Field suggests that the NVQ system is not really controlled by employers and does not really give them what they need. He argues, moreover, that changes in employment and the labour market may be more important than any qualification system, if the aim is to improve the quality of intermediate, technical level workers. Field's claim that NVQs are not for private employers, but are a Government initiative aimed at publicly funded trainees, also explains the current pressure to extend the system into those caring professions, including teaching, social work and youth and community work, which are predominantly within the public sector. In VET generally, as in the caring professions, either NVQ approaches to competence must be abandoned or radically changed so that they can be built upon.

MOVING FORWARD

In our view, it would be a mistake to abandon NVQs and start again. This would discard an enormous amount of high quality development work, alienate and devalue the contributions of many trainers and lecturers who have striven to make the best of the new system and risk a similar range of equally disastrous, if different, mistakes from yet another over-simplified, top-down invention.

Rather, the way forward must be to build from where we are now. We cannot return to some mythical golden age of apprenticeship-based skilled craft education, as Smithers (1993) seems to imply. Ainley (1993) demonstrates quite clearly that the old tripartite division of labour and education has gone for good. Furthermore, the enormous amount of literature on innovation and change almost uniformly stresses the importance of existing worker expertise, providing a sense of ownership and creating a situation where the majority can see personal gains from change outweighing losses. The link between quality, however it is defined, and worker empowerment seems self-evident, at least for the fortunate 'core' workers with full-time jobs.

The experiences of those contributors to this book, working with existing competence schemes, suggest an alternative way forward. We would contend that the issue for the effective use of competence, described above in relation to the caring professions, can also be applied with profit in a wide range of vocational areas. They provide pointers to the ways in which NVQ approaches need to be altered and widened, so that, in many occupations, a revised version of competence can be used as *part* of wider training, aimed at producing professional workers at all levels. High quality VET must focus on learning, not merely on assessment. Without some such changes, NVQs will fail to upskill the workforce or to empower workers. All this should not be left entirely in the hands of employers, NVQ and Government policy-makers. The challenge of competence, for caring professionals and for workers in other occupational areas, is to draw upon existing experience and spell out the parameters of a debate, in order to move forward to the development of a holistic, competent practice, that is owned by professional workers and consistent with open, democratic values that the best practice would espouse.

REFERENCES

Ainley, P. (1993) *Class and Skill: Changing Divisions of Knowledge and Labour*. London: Cassell.

Ainley, P. and Corney, M. (1990) *Training for the Future: the Rise and Fall of the Manpower Services Commission*. London: Cassell.

Brown, P. and Lauder, H. (1992) 'Education, economy and society: an introduction to a new agenda.' In P. Brown and H. Lauder (eds) *Education for Economic Survival*. London: Routledge.

Coffield, F. (1990) 'From the decade of the enterprise culture to the decade of the TECs.' *British Journal of Education and Work*, **4**(1), 59–78.

Eraut, M. (1989) 'Initial teacher training and the NCVQ model.' In J. W. Burke (ed.) *Competency Based Education and Training*. Lewes: Falmer.

Evans, B. (1992) *The Politics of The Training Market: from Manpower Services Commission to Training and Enterprise Councils*. London: Routledge.

Ferns, P. (1992) 'Implications of S/NVQs for black people.' In S. Burton, R. Dutt and S. Lyn-Cook (eds) *Black Perspectives in National Vocational Qualifications in Social Care*. London: National Institute for Social Work.

George, M. (1994) 'The First Rung.' *Community Care*, 17 February, 18–19.

Hargreaves, A. (1993) *Changing Teachers, Changing Times: Teachers' Work and Culture in the Postmodern Age*. London: Cassell.

Hodkinson. P., Sparkes, A.C. and Hodkinson, H. (1993) *Small Employer's Perceptions of Training Credits*. Training Credits in Action Project, Working Paper No. 4. Crewe: Crewe and Alsager Faculty, Manchester Metropolitan University.

Issitt, M. and Woodward, M. (1992) 'Competence and contradiction.' In P. Carter, T. Jeffs, and M.K. Smith (eds) *Changing Social Work and Welfare*. Buckingham: Open University Press.

Jessup, G. (1991) *Outcomes: NVQs and the Emerging Model of Education and Training*. London: Falmer.

Jordan, B., Karban, K., Mansoor, K., Masson, H. and O'Byrne, P. (1993) 'Teaching values: an experience of the Diploma in Social Work.' *Social Work Education*, 12(1), 7–18.

Kuhn, T.S. (1970) *The Structure of Scientific Revolutions*, 2nd edn. London: University of Chicago Press.

Matthews, A. (1993) *Does Gender Contribute to Perceptions of Job Competence?* London: NCVQ.

NCVQ (1994) *A statement by the National Council for Vocational Qualifications (NCVQ) on 'All Our Futures - Britain's Education Revolution', a Channel 4 Dispatches programme on 15th December 1993 and associated report by the Centre for Education and Employment Research, University of Manchester*. London: National Council for Vocational Qualifications.

Schön, D.A. (1983) *The Reflective Practitioner*. New York: Basic Books.

Schön, D.A. (1987) *Educating the Reflective Practitioner*. San Francisco: Josey Bass.

Skilbeck, M. (1976) 'Three educational ideologies.' In The Open University *E203 Curriculum Design and Development, Unit 3: Ideologies and Values*. Milton Keynes: Open University Press.

Smithers, A. (1993) *All Our Futures: Britain's Education Revolution*. London: Channel Four Television.

Stewart, J. (1992) 'Guidelines for public service management: some lessons not to be learnt from the private sector.' In P. Carter, T. Jeffs and M.K. Smith (eds) *Changing Social Work and Welfare*. Buckingham: Open University Press.

Williams, R. (1965) *The Long Revolution*. London: Pelican Books.

Name Index

Subject Index